At the Water's Edge

AT THE WATER'S EDGE

American Politics and the Vietnam War

Melvin Small

The American Ways Series

IVAN R. DEE   *Chicago*

www.ivanrdee.com

Library of Congress Cataloging-in-Publication Data:
Small, Melvin.
    At the water's edge : American politics and the Vietnam War / Melvin Small.
        p. cm. — (The American ways series)
    Includes bibliographical references and index.
    ISBN 1-56663-593-4 (cloth : alk. paper) — ISBN 1-56663-647-7 (pbk. : alk. paper)
        1. Vietnamese Conflict, 1961–1975—United States. 2. United States—Politics and government—1945–1989. I. Title. II. Series.

DS558.S55 2005
959.704'3373—dc22
                                                              2004056919

To my mother, Ann,
who at ninety is still engaged
in the political struggles of our times

Contents

Preface

ON THE LAST DAY of a recent conference on peacemaking during the Vietnam War, held at the Lyndon Baines Johnson Presidential Library, a participant noted that few presenters had paid attention to domestic politics in their analyses of U.S. diplomacy. Most had concentrated on negotiating tactics and strategies, military successes and failures, and the perceptions and philosophies of decision-makers. This was not surprising—the papers had been presented by diplomatic historians who spend their academic lives in the foreign-affairs sections of archives. There one rarely encounters a national security adviser or foreign minister advocating the adoption of one policy over another because of the November election. Politics and partisanship in the United States and other democratic countries are supposed to stop at the water's edge. Few American leaders have ever acknowledged in public or in their private papers that they were concerned about domestic politics when they constructed vital national security policies. It would be unseemly to do so.

But a careful reading of the American past—albeit often between the lines—suggests that presidents frequently consider the domestic political ramifications of national security policy in their decision-making. As I write this in the late summer of 2004, it is clear that President George W. Bush and his advisers have their eyes on the November election as they weigh their options in Iraq. Across the seas, American friends and foes alike also know that any foreign policy decisions they make during the run-up to the election could help determine its outcome. Moreover, their considerations do not involve only *foreign* policy. In the spring of 2004, rumors circulated that if the White House maintained cordial relations with its friends in Saudi Arabia, the oil sheiks would consider increasing output before the election to help drive down skyrocketing gasoline prices, improving Bush's reelection chances.

And so it goes, from the fierce partisanship of Federalists and Anti-Federalists in the debates over foreign policy during the French Revolution, to politicians playing to the Anglophobia of Irish Americans during the second half of the nineteenth century, to widely popular domestic anti-communism serving as a restraint on the inclinations of Presidents Dwight D. Eisenhower and John F. Kennedy to improve relations with their foes during the cold war, to Soviet leader Nikita Khrushchev "voting" for Kennedy in 1960 by not releasing captured American flyers until the Democrat was safely elected.

I have written about such topics in *Democracy and Diplomacy: The Impact of Domestic Politics on American Foreign Policy, 1775–1994* (1996). In addition, I have touched on domestic political issues related to the anti-war movement during the Vietnam War in *Johnson, Nixon, and the Doves* (1988), *Covering Dissent: The Media and the Antiwar Movement* (1994), and *Antiwarriors: The Vietnam War and the Battle for America's Hearts and Minds* (2002). But I have not concentrated directly on how domestic political issues affected decision-making and how the war affected domestic political issues. The more I studied the anti-war movement, the media, and the decision-makers, the more I was persuaded that the key to understanding American policy in the Vietnam War was American domestic politics.

This is not to say that American presidents and their advisers did not at all times take into consideration regional and global strategic policies as they structured their short- and long-term military and diplomatic approaches to the conflict in Vietnam. But they also had to consider the impact of their war policies on the home front and, conversely, the impact of domestic economic and political currents and timetables on the war. At times those

considerations played a major role in the determination of policies not only in Washington but in Hanoi, Beijing, and Moscow.

The rich literature on the Vietnam War continues to grow. In
addition to my own work, I have relied heavily on the memoirs
and monographs discussed in the Note on Sources. A good portion of Chapter 6 appeared in my article "The Election of 1968"
in the September 2004 issue of *Diplomatic History*.

I am most grateful to Michael Foley, Lloyd Gardner, Kenneth
Heineman, Chris Johnson, Jeffrey Kimball, Walter LaFeber,
Lynn Parsons, and Alan Raucher, who have read all or parts of
the manuscript, for their valuable suggestions for improvements.
John Braeman and Ivan Dee offered continuous support. Hilary
Meyer edited the manuscript in excellent fashion.

I am indebted once again to my wife and best friend, Sarajane
Miller-Small, who subjected the manuscript to the careful
scrutiny one would expect of a former Eugene McCarthy
precinct delegate.

M. S.

Royal Oak, Michigan
January 2005

At the Water's Edge

1

Saving South Vietnam, 1945–1963

FEW WARS in American history have had as profound and lasting an influence on domestic politics, culture, and economics as the Vietnam War. Of course, few wars in American history were as unpopular or as contentious as that war. And those that were, such as the War of 1812 and the Mexican-American War, took place in periods well before the telecommunications age that made any war potentially, in the words of the journalist Richard Arlen, "a living-room war."

The Vietnam War was a long war. The Pentagon dates U.S. participation from 1961, when the GIs "in country" were still mainly advisers to their South Vietnamese allies, to 1973, when the last American combat troops left the country. But it was an issue in American politics before 1961 and especially after 1973, when virtually every major American military or diplomatic crisis raised the specter of another Vietnam and all the anguish that word came to mean for those who lived through the era. Two of the major appraisals of the Vietnam War use the word "ordeal" in their title, two others use "tragedy," while still others refer to a "quagmire," the "suicide of an elite," an "unholy grail," the "war at home," "The Vietnam Wars," and a "wounded generation."

Most of those books concentrate on the failure of the United States to defeat the Communists in Southeast Asia. But all recognize the impact of U.S. involvement in Vietnam on the home front. More than most wars, the Vietnam War affected every

American institution, including the military, the executive and legislative branches of the federal government, the political parties, the media, religious organizations, the educational system, labor unions and corporations, and marriage and the family. Most important of all, beginning in the mid-1960s, the Vietnam experience led some Americans to lose a good deal of faith in their government, and many others to question what their leaders were telling them about foreign affairs.

There was a time in recent American history when presidents such as Dwight Eisenhower or John Kennedy appeared on television to announce a crisis and their constituents did not challenge their description of the problem. Not anymore. Senator J. William Fulbright (D-AR), one of the most erudite of American politicians, reported that "The biggest lesson I learned from Vietnam is not to trust government statements." In a related vein, low voter turnouts in elections and widespread cynicism about politicians have a good deal to do with the way the Vietnam experience affected Americans.

The fact that Vietnam was the nation's longest war suggests that its impact has to be at least as profound, lasting, and varied as the two world wars, both of which helped determine the contours of the domestic political terrain for several generations. But, unlike most American wars, political, social, and economic developments had a good deal to do with the diplomatic and military strategies adopted by the presidents and their advisers. Domestic political considerations, including the congressional and presidential election cycles, were never far from their minds as they fashioned military tactics and strategies and contemplated decisions about escalation, de-escalation, and negotiation. The seemingly endless limited war in a modern democratic society posed problems for American decision-makers confronted by few other political leaders in world history. The story of domestic politics and the Vietnam War is far more complicated than that for most other American and, indeed, international wars.

The history and analysis of decision-making during the Vietnam War is itself far more complicated than simply examining the impact of domestic politics. At each critical juncture, military and diplomatic concerns weighed heavily with presidents and their advisers. I will concentrate only on the domestic political variable, an important—but not always the most important— variable in the decision-making process.

The United States first became involved in Southeast Asia during World War II when, as leader of the victorious Allies, it had to make plans for the future of those countries and colonies that had been taken over by the Germans, Italians, and Japanese. In 1940, after the Germans defeated the French, Japan informally seized France's colony in Vietnam. During the war, Washington offered token military and political support to the Viet Minh, Ho Chi Minh's Communist-dominated coalition that was waging a guerrilla war for independence in Vietnam against the Japanese and the French.

More important, President Franklin D. Roosevelt seriously contemplated not supporting the return of the colony to France at war's end. Although most Americans knew nothing of the smaller conflict in Vietnam or Roosevelt's plans for that remote territory—an obscure issue compared to the war raging on the European continent and in China and in the Pacific—they generally opposed colonialism as practiced by their European allies. Their knee-jerk anti-imperialism had little effect on Roosevelt and Truman's ultimate decision not to support independence for Vietnam. A minor decision they never formally announced, it was barely noticed among far more important decisions in the tumultuous spring and summer of 1945.

Harry Truman's decisions from 1946 through 1953 to support the French effort to suppress the Viet Minh revolution barely turned up on most Americans' radar screens. Considering the many crises of the early cold war years that directly involved the

United States, including the Korean War that began in 1950, few American officials outside the Pentagon and the State Department expressed interest in the far-off war in Vietnam. There was a time, however, during the first part of 1954, when that war briefly became a serious issue in the United States.

The Viet Minh, who had been besieging a major French garrison at Dien Bien Phu in northern Vietnam, appeared on the verge of winning a dramatic military and, especially, psychological victory. When the French asked for assistance, the Eisenhower administration contemplated air strikes to relieve the garrison, with the chairman of the Joint Chiefs, Admiral Arthur W. Radford, even recommending the use of tactical atomic bombs if a conventional raid proved impractical. Radford's suggestion to use atomic weapons was dismissed by the president and his advisers because they knew that few Americans, let alone foreigners, would accept the use of such horrendous weapons for a cause that did not seem to impact national security.

As for a conventional raid, Eisenhower insisted on the advance approval of congressional leaders, among other conditions, before he would agree to intervene. He knew that the key leaders in both parties, including Senator Lyndon B. Johnson (D-TX), strongly opposed becoming involved in a war to save a French colony, even from communism. They had been distressed in January when they had not been consulted about the administration's dispatch of two hundred technicians to aid the French effort. Massachusetts Democratic senator John F. Kennedy warned that no amount of military aid to the colonial overlords could beat "an enemy of the people which has the support and covert appeal of the people." Eisenhower, who privately agreed with such sentiments, was pleased to be able to use congressional opposition as one of his reasons for refraining from intervention.

During much of his administration, the president found more support for his internationalist and noninterventionist policies from Democrats than from Republicans. The senator with the most expertise in Asia, Mike Mansfield (D-MT), had been a professor of Asian history. He worked closely and quietly, as was his wont, with Eisenhower and Secretary of State John Foster Dulles on their Vietnamese policies, serving as both a valued adviser and an intermediary with the Senate. He maintained a similar relationship with Presidents Kennedy and Johnson.

When Eisenhower's more hawkish vice president, Richard M. Nixon, hinted (in an off-the-record remark that became public) that the White House was considering intervention in Vietnam, the administration was greeted by a firestorm of opposition from bipartisan congressional leaders and the media. After extricating the country from an unpopular war in Korea the preceding year, the president knew that launching even a limited strike in what appeared to be a comparable war would be even more unpopular.

Instead the United States grudgingly attended the Geneva Conference in 1954, at which the French ended their war with the Viet Minh. The southern half of Vietnam was temporarily left in the hands of their former ally, Emperor Bao Dai, and the northern half in the hands of Ho Chi Minh. The Geneva Accords provided for national elections to be held within two years, at which time the Vietnamese would choose their new unified government. At this point the United States decided to draw the line at the 17th parallel and not permit the southern part of Vietnam to fall to communism. In 1953, Eisenhower had referred positively to the way France was "holding the line of freedom" against "Communist aggression." Now it would become the United States' task to support, in Eisenhower's words, the "falling domino" whose capture by world communism would lead to other losses to the West in the region and beyond.

This was not simply a case of balance-of-power politics. Implicit in the domino theory for Southeast Asia was the importance of that area's raw materials—rubber, rice, tin, oil, tungsten, and the like—to the U.S. economy and those of its European allies. American economic planners also believed they needed to

develop new markets in Southeast Asia to make up for the clo-
sure of the China market after the 1949 triumph of the Communist revolution. Since John Hay's Open Door Notes at the turn of
the century, American strategists had linked Asian policy to free
markets and the potential significance of that region for the
American economy. In the 1950s they were especially concerned
with safeguarding the region for the economic development of
Japan, which had become a major cold war ally in the Far East.

Eisenhower never made a formal announcement of his nation's acceptance of France's burden in South Vietnam. At no
time during the 1954–1955 transition period was there a specific
day when the French handed over their colony to the United
States. That is perhaps why so few Americans knew what their
president was getting them into. Those who did supported the
decision. John Kennedy referred in a 1956 speech to the American "finger in the dike" in South Vietnam that kept "the red tide
of communism" from drowning that nation.

Kennedy delivered that speech before the American Friends
of Vietnam (AFV), a lobby and support group for the new government of the Republic of Vietnam led by Ngo Dinh Diem. The
popularity of the idea of building a free, democratic Vietnam was
reflected in the membership of the AFV, which included senators
from the right such as William F. Knowland (R-CA) and from
the left such as Hubert H. Humphrey (D-MN), and even Mansfield, who later became a prominent critic of the American enterprise in Southeast Asia.

The AFV was based in East Lansing, Michigan, because one
of its key figures, Professor Wesley Fishel, was also head of
Michigan State University's aid program (MSUG) to South Vietnam. Beginning in 1955 the university provided teachers and
trainers of public and police administration for the Diem regime.
Some of the training involved controversial secret-police tactics,
and several members of the presumably academic MSUG program were operatives of America's Central Intelligence Agency

(CIA). A sensational exposé about the police training and the CIA appeared in 1966 in the radical magazine *Ramparts*, which featured a cover drawing of President Diem's sister-in-law as a Spartan cheerleader. The exposé led to considerable agitation at MSU and elsewhere for universities to halt their involvement in such programs and any others involving classified research.

But that was later, in 1966. Few Americans objected when the United States and President Diem decided against holding nationwide elections in Vietnam in 1956, as required by the Geneva Accords, because they feared that Ho would win. Most were not even aware of the decision. Diem held his own elections, as a sop to a United States that always wants its allies to at least appear democratic. He received more than 98 percent support in a rigged plebiscite held only in the South. American advisers had suggested that he report a more modest 60 percent support.

Vietnam first appeared as an election issue, albeit a minor one, in 1956. The hapless Democratic candidate, Adlai E. Stevenson, attacked Eisenhower from the right for permitting half of Vietnam to go Communist at the 1954 Geneva Conference. But the refrain, "Who lost Vietnam?" never resonated with the American public the way that "Who lost China?" had in the 1952 election. Despite the bipartisan consensus in support of containment from 1946 through 1967, the Democrats were perceived correctly as more willing to negotiate with the Communists and less committed to military solutions to international problems. It was impossible for Stevenson to make his soft-on-communism charge stick to Eisenhower.

When President Diem paid an official visit to the United States in 1957, he was hailed as the "savior" of his country, a "miracle man." In truth he was an authoritarian ruler, surrounded by corrupt advisers and generals, who often disregarded American advice about reforms that might win over the hearts and minds of his people. In 1959, Albert M. Colgrove, a journalist with the Scripps-Howard newspapers, published a series of articles about corruption and the lack of democracy in Vietnam. These led to other stories about Diem's shortcomings and ultimately to congressional hearings on the U.S. aid program. Here was the first example of a mainstream American journalist bringing home such bad but entirely accurate news of Vietnam to his readership. Despite clear evidence that Diem was failing to create a democratic society, a healthy economy, and a dependable military, the hearings ended with bipartisan support for continuing the South Vietnamese project. In fact, in 1959, Senator Gale McGhee (D-WY), who investigated the aid program, thought that it could become a "showcase" for the United States. This was the only time during the 1950s that the U.S. role in Vietnam appeared on the front pages for a sustained period of time.

Yet a Vietnam-like country, Sarkhan, was the center of *The Ugly American*, a 1958 best-selling novel. The authors, William Lederer, a naval officer, and Eugene Burdick, a political scientist, were not the usual novelists. They had an explicit agenda, hoping to influence the "foreign aid debates" in Congress with their portrayal of the effective counter-insurgency activities of tough American intelligence officers and diplomats against Communists in their fictional Southeast Asian country. Within a year, Lederer claimed that there were "twenty-one pieces of legislation being introduced into Congress which include the words 'The Ugly American.'" Senator Kennedy, who had carved out a niche for himself as an expert on Third World revolutions, sent a copy of the novel to each member of the Senate. The small guerrilla war depicted in *The Ugly American* soon appeared in real life in South Vietnam.

Diem's military forces, trained by Americans, had to contend with a Communist-led insurrection that began in 1958. In 1959 the North Vietnamese assumed control of the insurrection and, in 1960, helped to create the National Liberation Front, which the Americans and South Vietnamese called the Viet Cong, or

Vietnamese Communists. This was still a low-level affair in 1959 when President Eisenhower announced that "the loss of South Vietnam would . . . have grave consequences for the United States and for freedom."

Despite such a pronouncement, the issue of stopping communism in Vietnam did not appear in the 1960 election campaign. The relative lack of success of the Eisenhower administration in prosecuting the cold war was an issue, as the Democratic candidate, John F. Kennedy, assailed his Republican opponent, Vice President Nixon, for being part of an administration whose diplomacy was indecisive and weak. He pointed to the Soviet lead in satellite technology, its alleged lead in the development of intercontinental ballistic missiles, and especially the fall of Cuba to communism as proof that the nation needed a vigorous new leadership and increased defense spending. It was the Republicans' fault, he implied, that "For the first time in our history, an enemy stands at the throat of the United States," just ninety miles from the Florida coast. Kennedy was long on rhetoric and short on specifics when he promised to do a better job in the cold war. He was only returning the favor to the Republicans who rode to election victory in 1952 denouncing the appeasing party that had "lost" China to the Communists. During the campaign, Kennedy once asked his aides, "How would we have saved Cuba if we had the power? What the hell, they never told us how they would have saved China."

As with most presidential elections, foreign policy was not the main issue in the contest that saw Kennedy eke out an extremely narrow victory over Nixon. The weak economy and party loyalties figured more prominently than international affairs for many voters. But the young and untested Kennedy appeared knowledgeable and potentially pro-active in foreign policy, as seen in the first televised presidential debate in history, making it easier for many undecided Americans to trust the fate of their nation to him.

Kennedy made foreign policy a central theme in his inaugural address when he announced, "Let the word go forth . . . to friend and foe alike that the torch has been passed to a new generation of Americans [who] shall pay any price, bear any burden, meet any hardship, support any friend, oppose any foe to assure the survival and the success of liberty." He was reacting to a speech delivered by Soviet leader Nikita Khrushchev who apparently challenged the United States by declaring that the USSR would aid those fighting for national liberation against colonial powers. Kennedy did not realize that the Russians were not confronting the United States but had aimed their rhetorical assault at the Chinese Communists. Breaking their alliance with Moscow, they had positioned themselves as a people of color ready to champion the anti-Western movements of other people of color in Asia and Africa. Whomever the Russians were targeting, to Kennedy their new line meant that the cold war had shifted from a relatively stable Europe to Third World venues such as the Congo, Vietnam, and Laos.

When the president-elect visited the White House to discuss the most pressing foreign policy problems, Eisenhower informed him that the key crisis area in Asia was Laos, where the American-backed right-wing government was fighting a civil war against the Communist Pathet Lao. It was tiny, landlocked Laos, not its much larger neighbor Vietnam, where American military planners contemplated intervention. There were eight hundred American advisers in Vietnam at the time. While the Viet Cong was making headway against the Diem government, it did not appear to be in imminent danger of falling, which was not the case in Laos.

The Kennedy administration decided in 1961 not to assist the Laotian government through military intervention. Instead it backed a diplomatic settlement that brought to power a neutral regime which might save the country from communism. To some observers, this approach belied the tough line that Kennedy had promised Americans in his campaign and in his inaugural address. More important, in April 1961, Kennedy presided over one of the most humiliating defeats in American history—the failed attempt to overthrow Fidel Castro in the Bay of Pigs invasion. Several months later, Kennedy feared that he had appeared weak and been bullied by Khrushchev at their summit meeting in Vienna. And only two months after that, the United States watched the Russians alter the status quo in Berlin by erecting a wall separating the western part of the city from Communist East Berlin. Thus when the time came to consider options for Vietnam, Kennedy feared that he had to set limits or face more provocations from the Communists and, especially, electoral defeat for his party in 1962 and himself in 1964.

Kennedy looked like an appeaser. He remembered what had happened to the promising political career of his father, Joseph P. Kennedy, who had thrown in his lot in 1940 with an appeasement policy. Eisenhower had warned the president directly that the Republicans would hold him responsible "for any retreat in Southeast Asia." Congressman Melvin Laird (R-WI) was not alone when in 1962 he charged that the administration "has failed to act with sufficient vigor to frustrate the achievement of Communist objectives." Since the end of World War II the Republicans had been rhetorically more hawkish than the Democrats when it came to containing communism in Asia.

In the wake of the Bay of Pigs fiasco, Kennedy told an aide, "There are just so many concessions that one can make to the communists in one year and survive politically. . . . We just can't have another defeat in Vietnam." Looking back at the situation in 1963, he told another aide, "If I had tried to pull out completely from Vietnam, we would have another [Senator] Joe McCarthy [R-WI] red scare on our hands." Thus Kennedy ordered more military and economic aid to buttress the Saigon regime; from 1961 to 1963 he increased the number of American advisers in South Vietnam from Eisenhower's eight hundred to more

than sixteen thousand. Those advisers started to take a more active role in combat operations and began appearing in journalistic accounts as "advisers." In 1961 the United States, which had
experienced no combat fatalities in Vietnam the preceding year,
suffered eleven deaths. That number grew to thirty-one in 1962
and seventy-eight in 1963.

Congress was not involved with Kennedy's 1961 decision for
escalation. To be fair, few on Capitol Hill expressed much concern about what was going on in Vietnam. As early as June 1961
Senator Fulbright, the chair of the Foreign Relations Committee, worried in a speech about the misplaced emphasis on the
military and not the social and economic problems of South Vietnam. But Fulbright had been urging all through the fifties more,
not less, executive leadership in foreign policy, contending that
congressional interference had often been detrimental to U.S. national security interests. He would soon change his mind.

Another Democrat, Mike Mansfield, was also nervous about
American policy in Vietnam. The most important Asian foreign
policy expert in the Senate and an early admirer of President
Diem was becoming critical of his rule. Mansfield's knowledge
of the region carried such weight that when Vice President Lyndon Johnson traveled to Vietnam in May 1961, he brought with
him a member of the senator's staff to counterbalance the perspectives from the State and Defense Departments. Hearing accurate rumors of military leaders urging Kennedy to send
combat troops to Vietnam late in 1961, Mansfield privately urged
the president to reject such suggestions.

In another example of the way Kennedy made use of Democratic senators on the Vietnam issue, in October 1961 he asked
Missouri senator Stuart Symington, who visited Vietnam, to convey the following message to President Diem: If he was enter-
taining the idea of obtaining a mutual-defense treaty from the
United States, it would never receive Senate approval. The
power of the Senate to reject or amend treaties and of Congress

to restrict appropriations has often been used by presidents to explain to foreign leaders why they cannot always help them. Sometimes disingenuously they explain, "Don't blame me, I'm on your side, but I have to deal with the yahoos on Capitol Hill."

Whatever Mansfield, Symington, and other senators might have thought or said from 1961 through to the end of the war, they never once rejected an administration request for funding for the military in Vietnam, often in the form of special or supplemental appropriations. Congressional critics found themselves in the difficult position of having to approve increased military appropriations bills or appearing as if they were not supporting the GIs in Vietnam. But there were not many congressional critics of Kennedy's Vietnam policies during his tenure.

The same could not be said for the American media. In 1962 in particular, young American journalists David Halberstam of the *New York Times*, Neil Sheehan of United Press International, and Malcolm Browne of the Associated Press joined several of their senior colleagues to criticize the South Vietnamese government's ineptitude and corruption. They also pointed out that the army of the Republic of South Vietnam was failing to subdue the Viet Cong, despite official press briefings to the contrary.

Controversies still swirl around the role of the American media in affecting the outcome of the wars in Southeast Asia. Government officials perceived that stories filed by anti-war print and broadcast journalists weakened the U.S. military effort. This resulted in tighter restrictions on press coverage of later military interventions, including those in 1983 in Grenada and in 1991 in Kuwait. There was no official censorship in the "war" in Vietnam, as had been the case in several other U.S. wars, most notably World War II. The South Vietnamese and the U.S. Military Assistance Command, Vietnam (MACV) tried to restrict the movement of journalists and to control the flow of information to them. But they were not able to keep intrepid reporters and photographers from getting to the front to observe the battles firsthand. Much of the time, especially through 1968, journalists tended to support the American effort. Every now and then, however, as was the case in 1962, they took a different tack and raised important issues about the role of the media in a democracy fighting an undeclared war.

Few mainstream journalists who found fault with the South Vietnamese government opposed U.S. intervention in Vietnam. But they did not like the way things were going. Halberstam wrote that the administration's "cautious optimism . . . is not widely reflected among Americans stationed here," and that "there sometimes seems a tendency to describe results before they have been attained." The press, according to an embassy official, "believes that the situation in Vietnam is going to pieces and we have been unable to convince them otherwise." A *Newsweek* reporter concluded that "The basic problem is that the Vietnamese government does not command respect in the rural areas" because of "a sickening atmosphere of insecurity, suspicion, and government clumsiness." That government harassed such reporters, tapped their phones, and even "lost" or destroyed some of their dispatches sent over its cable system, especially when alerted to do so by Pentagon press officers. In one celebrated case, the South Vietnamese president expelled François Sully, a *Newsweek* correspondent, for criticizing the presidential family. Diem tried to do the same thing to the *New York Times'* Homer Bigart, but the American embassy intervened to save the distinguished war correspondent. Some in the American mission to Vietnam joined with South Vietnamese officials in asking Washington to pressure American media for the recall of critical journalists. For the most part, American newspapers, magazines, and television networks resisted. President Kennedy himself failed to convince *New York Times* publisher Arthur Sulzberger to send Halberstam on a long vacation. At the same time he reminded the Vietnamese that they should "not be too concerned by press reports." Washington "did not accept everything the correspondents wrote, even if it appeared in the *New York Times*."

Kennedy's motivations were more complicated than simple damage control. While concerned about the criticism of the Saigon government, he was also concerned that journalists were making too many headlines about American ties to the war. He hoped to sever them. He was especially disturbed by news reports that his "advisers" were doing a lot more than advising. Consequently he approved of directives that would tighten official control over journalists with what even friendly columnist Joseph Alsop labeled "news-control devices."

Kennedy had reason to be concerned about the immediate political impact of the critical perspectives adopted by reporters from elite publications. After the influential Mansfield met with Halberstam, Sheehan, and Peter Arnett in South Vietnam late in 1962, he informed the president that he was convinced the war was not going well. Mansfield also defended the journalists who had "the same objectivity, alertness, and appropriate skepticism of official handouts that are characteristic of American reporters everywhere."

As embarrassing as such reports were to South Vietnam, and to some degree MACV, in 1962 they interested only a small minority of Americans. The war in Vietnam remained a minor foreign policy issue in the United States. Moreover, respected establishment columnists such as Alsop, to whom MACV spoon-fed exclusive material, offered optimistic views of the U.S. effort in Vietnam. And some publishers and editors remained faithful to the cause, eliminating or altering negative reports from the field. Such was the case at *Time*, where its Saigon correspondent, Charles Mohr, was so irritated by that practice that he quit the magazine in 1963 to join the *New York Times*.

Although the media did not "lose" the war, after the fall of South Vietnam to communism, politicians and conservative political commentators attacked the anti-war and liberal biases of journalists who had allegedly undermined U.S. national security. The development of the still potent conservative political issue of the unpatriotic and even un-American media owes much to the purposeful misreading of their activities in Vietnam, which began in 1962 with a Democratic president's problems with critical correspondents. This was unfair to the hardworking and dedicated journalists. For the most part they had a much better handle on Vietnamese politics than did the "experts" in the White House.

The criticism of American involvement with a corrupt and repressive government in Saigon increased exponentially in the spring and summer 1963 during the "Buddhist crisis." It began on May 8 when Diem's military broke up a demonstration in Hue, the imperial capital, by firing into a crowd opposing a ban on the display of religious banners. This action led to more demonstrations and more government-sponsored violent retaliation as Buddhist agitation threatened to topple Diem or at least cripple his ability to prosecute the war against the Viet Cong. Unable to contend with the firepower of the ARVN, the media-savvy monks employed a sensational method of protest— self-immolation. On June 11, after his leaders had informed journalists about the particulars of the event, a monk sat down in a Saigon street, poured gasoline over himself, and set himself on fire. Like the rest of America, President Kennedy was completely taken aback by the crisis. "Who are these people?" he asked his aides. These people, the Buddhists, made up 90 percent of the population of Vietnam. They were not part of Saigon's predominantly Catholic establishment with whom American officials, like the French before them, customarily dealt.

On June 10, in a major address on the cold war at American University prepared before the self-immolation incident, Kennedy contended that the Soviet Union and the United States should "not interfere with the choice of others," that they should both "make the world safe for diversity." Diem's approach to diversity in his own society left much to be desired.

The pictures of the monk in flames shocked Americans and people around the world. During the summer of 1963 six other monks made the ultimate sacrifice for their cause. That cause was inadvertently aided when Diem's controversial and outspoken sister-in-law, Madame Nhu, dismissed the Buddhists' actions as "barbecues." Kennedy was becoming exasperated with Diem, who seemed incapable of winning the war against the Communists and establishing a stable and effective government. By this time the president was also becoming concerned about the impact of the chaos in Vietnam on the 1964 presidential campaign that was to begin within six months. Since much of his domestic political program, the New Frontier, remained to be enacted, his stewardship of foreign policy would play a significant role in the campaign. Republicans in Congress had already intensified their criticism of his Vietnam policies, calling for a more muscular approach to the Communist insurgency.

To head them off, in June Kennedy appointed a Republican, Henry Cabot Lodge, Jr., to be U.S. ambassador to South Vietnam. A former senator and his party's vice-presidential candidate in 1960, Lodge was, according to Frederick Nolting, the bitter foreign service officer whom he replaced, "a piece of Republican asbestos to keep the heat off Kennedy." It did not take long for Kennedy to become dissatisfied with Lodge. The ambassador often operated independently of Washington and did not provide the president with the objective reportage he felt he needed to construct Vietnam policy. But Kennedy muted his criticisms for political reasons and certainly could not relieve Lodge of his duties. The last thing he needed was to see Lodge back home, taking up the partisan Republican cudgels on foreign policy in the 1964 campaign.

Lodge, not the most diplomatic, knowledgeable, or energetic of ambassadors, was Kennedy's chief agent in Saigon from the end of August to November 1, 1963, during the negotiations with Diem over reform. The envoy tried to convince the South Vietnamese president to adopt policies stabilizing the situation in Saigon or, he hinted, face the loss of American support and possible deposition. Diem had gotten wind of the talks between American intelligence agents and South Vietnamese generals about the possibilities of a coup. He countered with veiled threats that he might just talk to the Communists about making peace, the first element of which would be the withdrawal of American troops from South Vietnam.

Facing his imminent reelection campaign, Kennedy was stuck between two potentially failing policies: withdrawal from Vietnam without defeating the Communists, or continuing support for the government of South Vietnam with its embarrassing chaos in Saigon. His adoption of either option could become a potent issue in 1964 for the Republicans. And at this crisis point, the president had to rely on a blundering Republican diplomatic agent whom he could not relieve because of politics. As a last resort, Kennedy reluctantly chose the deposition of Diem as a solution to both problems. A new government would end the talk of a Munich-type settlement with the Communists, would make peace with the Buddhists and other dissidents in Saigon, and would begin winning the hearts and minds of the people of South Vietnam. To increase the pressure on Diem, Kennedy quietly informed the Democratic leadership in the Senate that he would not oppose a Senate resolution that threatened to halt American aid to Saigon if the South Vietnamese president failed to clean up his act. On September 11 Senator Frank Church (D-ID) introduced such a measure, backed by twenty-three senators. But the pressure from Lodge, the Senate, the Vietnamese generals conspiring in the wings, and the president himself failed to convince Diem to change his policies. Thus on November 1 a group of prominent officers, knowing that they would have American support if they were successful, overthrew Diem.

Their assassination of the president and his brother, the chief of the secret police, disturbed President Kennedy, who had hoped the Diem family would merely be sent into exile. Ambassador Lodge did little to protect them.

The deposition of Diem led Kennedy to call for a complete re-examination of Vietnam policy, a reexamination that was cut short on November 22 by his assassination. There is no doubt that he had become exasperated by the war in Vietnam, by the steady military successes of the Viet Cong despite massive American aid to Saigon, and by the difficulty of nation building in South Vietnam. He had also become more and more pessimistic about his own military's ability to devise policies to defeat a nationalist insurgency like that of the Viet Cong without a massive commitment of ground-combat troops.

Whatever Kennedy's considerations, he was concerned about the upcoming election. With recent memories of Republican claims that his party was "soft on communism" at Yalta in 1945 and in China in 1949, he knew that it could be a fatal political blow to cede Vietnam to the Communists before November 1964. Several of his supporters claim that before he died he had made up his mind to withdraw. He allegedly told one of his aides that he would pull out of Vietnam after the election and that it would be "easy. Put a government in there that will ask us to leave." Mansfield reported that Kennedy told him on one occasion in 1963 that "I can't [pull out] until 1965—after I'm reelected"— and on another occasion, "We've just got to get out. We're in too deep." Secretary of Defense Robert S. McNamara also reported that Kennedy implied he would withdraw from Vietnam after the election. Most observers tend to downplay these three sources, especially considering no document or policy paper exists revealing such a plan. Whether or not Kennedy would have withdrawn, there is no doubt the election of 1964 figured prominently in his calculations, as it would have for any president in a comparable situation.

One study of such decisions finds that democratic states are less likely to enter wars before elections than after. In November 1963 that was certainly the case. Kennedy knew that in the absence of a major escalation on the Communist side, or their specific targeting of the American advisers and their installations, the vast majority of Americans would not accept a major military commitment to the unstable government in South Vietnam. The most politically prudent option was to maintain the commitment in Vietnam to placate the right and to avoid escalation to placate the left.

We will never know what Kennedy would have done in Vietnam in his second term. On November 22, 1963, Vice President Lyndon Johnson assumed the U.S. commitments in Southeast Asia. One of his first decisions was to retain Kennedy's key foreign policy advisers to demonstrate that there would be continuity between the administrations. The president may have changed, but the domestic political problems created by the war in Vietnam remained. Even more than Kennedy, Johnson would have to worry about the media, elections, and his domestic programs as he dealt with the military and political crises in Southeast Asia.

2

Winning an Election While
Losing a War, 1963–1964

UNLIKE KENNEDY, Lyndon Johnson preferred domestic
politics to foreign policy. And given his brilliant exploits in Congress as Senate majority leader and his progressive legislative
program that came to be called the Great Society, he hoped to
avoid major diplomatic conflicts that would make it difficult for
him to concentrate on his ambitious domestic agenda. As he contemplated escalation of the war in 1964, he mused about conservatives in his own party, "The war, oh, they'll like the war. . . .
They'll be against my [domestic] programs because of the war."
After he left the presidency, Johnson claimed he knew that "the
sound of the bugle put an immediate end to the hopes and
dreams of the best reformers: the Spanish American War
drowned the populist spirit; World War I ended Woodrow Wilson's New Freedom; World War II brought the New Deal to a
close. Once the war began, then all those Conservatives in Congress would use it as a weapon against the Great Society." One
could not have guns *and* butter.

At the same time Johnson also realized that were he forced to
choose guns and become "Dr. Win-the-War," like Roosevelt in
World War II, he might run the risk of arousing Americans to a
point where they would insist on all-out war, possibly leading to a
confrontation with North Vietnam's allies, China and the Soviet

Union. Secretary of State Dean Rusk warned that "a war psychology [was] too dangerous in a nuclear world."

Domestic politics affected Johnson's understanding of the war in Vietnam in another way. Beginning with his trip to Vietnam for President Kennedy in May 1961, he became convinced that the key to success in the South of the country was economic development and New Deal–style social programs. Until mid-1965 he continued to hope that a Mekong River Development Plan, like his country's own Tennessee Valley Authority, would obviate the need to send U.S. combat troops to Southeast Asia. Further, as his second national security adviser, Walt Rostow, pointed out, Johnson's "view of Asia was closely related to his view of the race problem and of social reform in the United States." When liberals began attacking his Vietnam policy, the president scolded them for being racists who were inconsistent when they fought for civil rights for black Americans but opposed those same rights for Asians overseas.

Johnson's immediate problem was that 1964 was an election year; a war in Vietnam that was going badly would be a major liability. As early as February, Senate Minority Leader Everett Dirksen (R-IL) began to criticize the administration for "uncertainty and confusion" in its policies in Southeast Asia. He was soon joined by influential representatives Melvin Laird and John Broomfield (R-MI). In the New Hampshire primary in March, the Republican hopeful, Arizona senator Barry Goldwater, supported "carrying the war to North Vietnam—ten years ago we should have bombed North Vietnam." He mused about what might have happened had the United States dropped a low-yield atomic bomb on the Communists during the siege of Dien Bien Phu.

Johnson's loyal secretary of defense, Robert S. McNamara, claimed that the president never decided foreign policy issues "on the basis of political expediency," and that he never told McNamara or the Joint Chiefs to "hold back" in Vietnam because of the election. The evidence suggests otherwise, as it does for every other president who claimed that domestic politics never influenced national security policy.

Domestic politics certainly influenced Johnson's decision to keep the ineffective loose cannon, Republican Henry Cabot Lodge, Jr., in the Saigon embassy. Early in March 1964 he instructed Dean Rusk to consider Lodge "Mr. God," and told McNamara, "as long as we've got [Lodge] there, then we're not in too bad a condition politically."

When the primary season began, two-thirds of those polled claimed they were not paying much attention to what was going on in Vietnam. Johnson's task, as he saw it, was to keep them uninterested, the same approach Kennedy had adopted in 1962. National Security Adviser McGeorge Bundy told a CIA official that we were "not going to do a goddamn thing [about Vietnam] while this goddam election is going on." Johnson moved National Security Council aide Michael Forrestal to Dean Rusk's office in April to "keep the lid on." He told him, "I don't want to have headlines about some accident in Vietnam. And if I do, Forrestal, it will be your fault." On one specific domestic matter, Johnson ordered that there be no consideration of any formal congressional resolution on the war until after the Civil Rights Bill made it through Congress. In late spring his aides had prepared such a resolution to provide authority for any future military escalations in Vietnam. Johnson believed the resolution would be necessary at some point to head off congressional opposition to unilateral escalation. As he commented, if he had been in Congress and the president had executed such an escalation, "by God, Lyndon Johnson would have torn his balls off."

But de-escalation was not a real option either. Johnson knew that if he signaled he was contemplating withdrawing from Vietnam, he would be hammered by the Republicans for being weak and soft on communism. "We do not want another China in Vietnam," he told a senator, referring to the Communist victory in 1949 that became a powerful issue for the Republicans. Leaving aside the potential repercussions in November 1964 from such a démarche, Johnson feared that he might be impeached were he to withdraw from Vietnam. At the least, he told one of his biographers, the loss of Vietnam would have led to "a mean and destructive debate that would shatter my presidency, kill my administration, and damage our democracy." Politics aside, there is no doubt that Johnson, along with McNamara, Rusk, and Bundy, believed that containing communism in Southeast Asia was a vital national security interest.

As things turned out, the Vietnam War did become a volatile issue in the election, but one that helped the Democrats. This was because the Republican candidate was the hawkish Goldwater. When Johnson took office in the fall of 1963, Goldwater was only one of several Republican contenders, including Nelson Rockefeller and Lodge, with Richard Nixon waiting in the wings. President Eisenhower, nervous about the rise of Goldwater in his party, had urged the moderate Lodge to come home from Saigon to run for the presidency. Lodge enjoyed his only success in New Hampshire when he ran ahead of Rockefeller, helping end the New York governor's candidacy. The former ambassador lost any chance for the nomination in the Oregon primary when his own role in the coup in Vietnam became an issue.

The defeat of the moderates Rockefeller and Lodge and the rapid rise to prominence of the more conservative Goldwater was a blessing for a president concerned about his failing foreign policy in Vietnam. Rockefeller, Lodge, or even Nixon would not have struck the majority of the population as irresponsible in their critiques of Johnson's policies and their prescriptions for victory in Vietnam. Goldwater blamed Johnson for the possible loss of all of Southeast Asia—"yesterday it was Korea. Tonight it is Vietnam"—and promised to unleash all the nation's military resources as president. On one occasion he suggested that he would "drop a low-yield atomic bomb on Chinese supply lines in

North Vietnam, or maybe shell 'em with the Seventh Fleet." On another occasion he suggested the "defoliation of the forest by low-yield atomic weapons."

In a few short years Richard Nixon would launch an attack on the alleged liberal media, the media that somehow provoked Goldwater into making such comments or took them out of context. Most journalists traveling with the Arizona senator liked him and understood his lack of tact and his tendency to make wild statements without thinking of the political ramifications. More often than not, they gave him every opportunity to retract what he had said before they included it in their copy for the day. Had the public known about some of his wilder shooting from the lip, they would have been even more concerned about his suitability for the presidency.

Johnson, who genuinely feared that a Goldwater victory "would endanger the United States and threaten world stability," promised a continuation of his low-key policy, with no major American participation in the war. He assured the nation that his policy was "To get the boys in Vietnam to do their own fighting with our advice and equipment." Although by the summer of 1964, half of those polled were unhappy with American policy in Vietnam, few Americans supported Goldwater's threat of all-out war. Johnson understood that his failing Vietnam policy could be a plus for him when compared to Goldwater's alternative, and thus he changed his campaign slogan from "Prosperity and Harmony" to "Prosperity, Harmony, and Peace."

Goldwater was clearly the more hawkish of the candidates. Naturally the Democrats helped burnish that image. As Johnson aide Bill Moyers advised, "We must make him ridiculous and a little scary . . . trigger happy, a bomb thrower, a radical." In one of the earliest negative television ads, the Johnson campaign ran a spot showing a little girl plucking petals from a daisy with her he-loves-me-he-loves-me-not allusion morphing into a countdown for a nuclear explosion. Because many observers considered the ad a low blow, Johnson ordered it pulled after one day. "Holy shit," he exclaimed. "What in the hell do you mean putting on that ad? . . . I guess it did what we goddamned set out to do, didn't it."

Despite its brief airplay, the offending ad had done its damage, especially when the television networks aired it again during their nightly news programs for illustrative purposes. Compared to the way negative advertising developed over the next thirty-five years, Johnson's ad now seems almost benign. Few Americans complained that a similar ad run by an anti-war group during the run-up to the 2003 war in Iraq was in bad taste.

The specter of a Goldwater presidency helps explain the Democratic congressional leadership's relative passivity when the president asked for a resolution to respond to the Communists' early August attacks on American vessels in the Gulf of Tonkin. The upcoming election itself, in which Johnson still appeared somewhat vulnerable to criticism of his weak or even appeasing policy in Vietnam, also helps explain why he felt compelled to send a strong message to Hanoi.

On August 2 three North Vietnamese patrol boats fired on the *USS Maddox*, an electronic surveillance vessel, off the coast of North Vietnam in the Gulf of Tonkin. Hanoi claimed the *Maddox* was within its territorial waters; the United States claimed it was in international waters when attacked. The vessel's primary function was to eavesdrop on North Vietnamese communications. Two days later, after he received word of a second attack in the Gulf of Tonkin, Johnson ordered a punitive air assault on North Vietnamese naval facilities and ports. But several hours after learning of the attack, the Pentagon received follow-up reports shedding doubt that the second attack had in fact occurred. Johnson even suggested a few days later that "those dumb stupid sailors were just shooting at flying fish." Most scholars now agree that the second attack did not take place and that nervous naval officers in the Gulf of Tonkin had misread the radar and other indicators of North Vietnamese aggression. At the time, however, few doubted that the attack had occurred and even fewer Americans opposed Johnson's retaliation against the Communists. They had fired on American vessels, which, McNamara explained, were on "routine patrol" in international waters.

Johnson did not retaliate against the Communists *because* of the election, but his aides advised him that the Republicans would hit him hard if he failed to respond with force. And he knew that his reaction would be popular and serve to answer critics who believed he had not been tough enough in Southeast Asia. McNamara thought that with his actions Johnson would appear "firm but moderate." Looking back several years later, one presidential aide even suggested that the *Maddox* had been sent into the gulf to provoke a Communist attack. This would permit the president to respond as he did, demonstrating that he could order tough military measures when necessary. There is no solid evidence to support that theory.

In July, 58 percent of those polled approved of the president's handling of the war; in August that figure rose to 72 percent. Eighty-five percent of those polled approved of the bombing of North Vietnam in the wake of the incident, with 48 percent calling for even more forceful action. During the same period, Johnson's lead over Goldwater grew from 64 to 36 percent to 71 to 29 percent. The president's overwhelming support reflected the general American predilection to rally round the flag during an international crisis.

The measured response to the attack or attacks in the Gulf of Tonkin established Johnson as a responsible defender of American interests in Southeast Asia and all but took the Vietnam issue out of the election campaign. He was pleased to announce Goldwater's support for his actions, with his rival proclaiming, "We cannot allow the American flag to be shot at anywhere on earth if we are to retain our respect and prestige," and he believed Johnson's response was "the only thing he can do under the circumstances." By signing on to the bombing raid on North Vietnam, Goldwater effectively removed the war from the political debate.

Johnson remained concerned about the impact of the war on his reelection, maintaining a special White House office to respond to Goldwater's expected attacks on his foreign policy. He even took the unusual tack of asking Rusk and McNamara to speak at the Democratic National Convention, which was to begin on August 24 in Atlantic City.

The Gulf of Tonkin incident offered an opportune time for Johnson to obtain support for his Vietnam policies through a congressional resolution that had been in the works since May. He had hoped to wait until passage of the Civil Rights Bill before introducing it, but now the North Vietnamese had forced his hand. Since he had already acted without authority, he felt it necessary to obtain congressional approval for the action and for future actions. He remembered that Harry Truman had been assailed by Republicans for Korean War policies that never received a formal resolution of support from Congress.

Immediately following the incident off the coast of North Vietnam, the Democratic leadership introduced the Gulf of Tonkin Resolution stating that "the Congress approves and supports the determination of the President as Commander in Chief, to take all necessary measures to repel any armed attack against the forces of the United States and to prevent further aggression." President Eisenhower had obtained similar resolutions to support his policies in the Middle East and Asia. Johnson claimed that the resolution, which was quickly approved by the House 416–0 and by the Senate 88–2, was "like granny's nightshirt, it covered just about everything." He also boasted privately that with the resolution, he "didn't just screw Ho Chi Minh, I cut his pecker off."

Senator Wayne Morse (D-OR), one of two senators who opposed the resolution, called for extensive hearings on the president's request. He quoted former senator Robert Taft (R-OH), who had pointed out in 1950 that "Article I, Section 8 of our Constitution does not permit the President to make war at his discretion." The most that Morse could obtain from Democratic leaders, who stressed the emergency nature of the situation, was one hour and forty minutes of private hearings and an eight-hour floor debate. For their part, House members passed the Gulf of Tonkin Resolution after forty minutes' debate.

In the Senate debate, Senator Charles Mathias (R-MD) correctly noted that the resolution reflected "a pattern or practice that had existed since the end of World War II." That pattern had led to what critics later called the "imperial presidency," which ran roughshod over congressional powers to declare war and approve treaties.

Several senators, nervous about the power they were giving the president, wondered whether this was indeed granny's nightshirt. On August 5 someone in the Pentagon leaked to Morse information that cast doubt on the administration's account of the attack. Under the secret OPLAN 34-A, the United States had been assisting Vietnamese commandos in land and amphibious sabotage missions on the coast and against islands just off the coast of North Vietnam. One such mission was taking place on August 2 when the *Maddox* was attacked. The North Vietnamese easily could have concluded that the vessel, whose main task was to gather electronic intelligence from North Vietnam, was involved in the South Vietnamese raid. The leak to Morse may have originated with McNamara, who feared that Republicans in Congress might call for even more forceful responses. If they knew the North Vietnamese had good reason to attack, he may have reasoned, the legislators would be more restrained. All of this was unknown to the public, and when Morse offered general comments about commando activity, his colleagues, and more important, the media, ignored him.

According to one White House aide, the resolution "was sold to the Democrats on the basis that it would help with the election . . . we mustn't let Goldwater get a free ride out of this." Senator

George McGovern (D-SD) later claimed that "It never occurred to me that we'd be staying in Vietnam once the election was over. I always thought that the Gulf of Tonkin Resolution was a political ploy to cut the ground from under Goldwater. And that's the way Bill Fulbright sold it to a lot of liberals in the Senate."

Senator Fulbright, the chair of the Foreign Relations Committee, shepherded the resolution through the Senate. He admitted he was "afraid of Goldwater," whom he considered a "Neanderthal" on foreign policy. He was horrified when the Arizona senator said on August 13 that he believed Congress had authorized the potential use of atomic weapons in Vietnam with the resolution, a comment that McNamara labeled "both unjustified and irresponsible."

Fulbright understood that the resolution offered the president broad powers to make war in Asia. Kentucky's Republican senator, John Sherman Cooper, asked him on the floor of the Senate, "If the president decided it was necessary to use such force as could lead us into war, will we give that authority by this resolution?" Fulbright responded, "That is the way I would interpret it." Trusting the president not to do anything dramatic without congressional consultation, Fulbright did tell Daniel Brewster (R-ME) that "there is nothing in the resolution . . . that contemplates" the sending of land armies to Asia, though the resolution "would not prevent it." Dean Rusk later assured Fulbright on this issue. A skeptical Mansfield voted for the resolution because he "took Fulbright's word at face value" that it was not a blank check and would merely result in a continuation of then-current military policy. When Senator Gaylord Nelson (D-WI) introduced language to limit the scope of the resolution, Fulbright saw that it was defeated as unnecessary.

Fulbright was one of the first senators to decry the Gulf of Tonkin Resolution and his support of it. Within a year he admitted that "my role in the adoption" of the resolution "is a source neither of pleasure or pride to me today." In addition, he later charged that he "was hoodwinked by the President of the United States, the Secretary of State, the Chief of Staff, and the Secretary of Defense who told us about certain alleged events that I do not believe occurred." Senator Church similarly "regretted . . . to the end of his life" that he voted for the resolution. In 1967 Senator Albert Gore (senior) (D-TN) considered the Gulf of Tonkin Resolution "one of the most tragic mistakes in American history," while one of the president's closest friends in the Senate, Richard Russell (D-GA), was "frank to say that I didn't expect the war to assume this magnitude at the time we passed the resolution." Beginning in 1967, senators began trying to rescind the resolution, which they accomplished in 1970, and to rein in presidents through a National Commitments Resolution that finally saw the light of day in the 1973 War Powers Resolution.

Senator Fulbright and most Democratic and several Republican senators were not the only ones who feared a Goldwater presidency. Secretary of the Treasury Henry Fowler was quite successful in recruiting normally Republican corporate leaders, apprehensive of Goldwater's apparent recklessness abroad and potentially destabilizing policies at home, to endorse Johnson. In addition, earlier in the year Johnson had approved the very Republican measure of the largest tax cut in history in order to stimulate the economy in time for the election. As for increasing the deficit, the president thought he could make up for the shortfall in revenues with reductions in defense spending, or at least better fiscal management of the Defense Department as promised by the former head of the Ford Motor Company, Secretary McNamara. McNamara was working on a plan, announced in December, for base closures, measures that are always unpopular with politicians from districts losing installations. They would have been even more unpopular had they known that the base closings would help pay for the increased costs of the Vietnam War. (Early in 1965 the newly elected senator from New York,

Robert F. Kennedy, first clashed with the administration over
base closings in his state.)

As the campaign began in August, Goldwater relaxed his criticism of the president's Vietnam policy, realizing that it was not
winning him many voters. He had made only a brief mention
of Vietnam during his acceptance speech at the convention—
"failures infest the jungles of Vietnam"—and also arranged with
the president to keep the volatile issues of Vietnam and civil
rights out of the campaign. But he did recommend in general
terms that "our strategy must be primarily offensive" to "liberate
the enslaved peoples of Asia," and that "war may be the price of
freedom." Moreover, while not discussing the details of his plans
for the war, he did accuse the president of "deceiving" Americans by not explaining to them why GIs were dying in Southeast
Asia. The number of U.S. combat battle deaths in 1964—147—
exceeded the total from the four preceding years combined.

As the campaign wound down and he became more desperate,
Goldwater accused Johnson of authorizing the use of atomic
weapons in the war and announced that he would send President
Eisenhower to South Vietnam if he won the election. The senator
also approved using Ronald Reagan's famous anti-Communist
stump speech in his campaign, a speech that emphasized the Soviet threat in Vietnam. Privately, Goldwater's position was not
much different from that of many politicos from both parties: either make an all-out effort to win in Vietnam or withdraw.

Johnson held to the middle ground between those who
wanted to withdraw and those who wanted to escalate. He and
his advisers knew, however, that some escalation shortly would
be needed because the South Vietnamese were losing the war.
McGeorge Bundy urged him to indicate as much lest "the record
suggest even remotely that we campaigned on peace in order to
start a war in November." Johnson refused during the campaign
to suggest that escalation might be needed, even though virtually
all his advisers agreed that the situation in Vietnam had become

desperate. In many ways Johnson was repeating the policy of his beloved role model and mentor, Franklin Roosevelt, who ran for reelection in 1940 promising peace but knowing that the United States might soon have to get involved in World War II. On scores of occasions during the campaign, Johnson proclaimed that "we seek no wider war." All the time, during the late summer and fall, he knew that his advisers were considering sending American boys and planes to Vietnam in much the same way that Franklin Roosevelt knew before the election of 1940 that his advisers were planning strategies for the likely entry of the United States into World War II. Between September 10 and 15, 1964, the Pentagon conducted war games called Sigma II, simulating the bombing of North Vietnam.

Two days before the election, the Viet Cong attacked a U.S. air base at Bien Hoa, killing five and wounding seventy-six Americans and destroying twenty-seven of thirty planes. Although it would be another four years before the concept of "October surprise" made its way into the political lexicon, a strong response to the Communist attack could have been used to rally last-minute support for the president. But a poll suggested that the public did not expect Johnson to react forcefully. He was worried that if he overreacted, voters might think he had manufactured a crisis to help with his election. It is possible that the Viet Cong knew it would be awkward for Johnson to respond forcefully on the eve of the election. Of course, decision-making was easy in this election since the polls predicted a landslide victory for the president. Unbeknownst to the public, on the day before election day he did request that the National Security Council begin planning tougher actions against the Communists. At the same time he worried about what escalation might mean for his Great Society and even thought it possible that Republicans and conservatives were advocating escalation in order to cripple his domestic reform program. Johnson was quite sincere in his hopes to win a war on poverty by improving the lot of the thirty-four million

Americans below the poverty line, thereby becoming the greatest economic and social reformer since Franklin Roosevelt.

He had that opportunity after the election when he won a whopping 61 percent of the popular vote, the highest percentage in modern history. Johnson did not have much time to enjoy his smashing victory. As he prepared to launch his domestic programs, he had to face the deteriorating situation in South Vietnam and the need to increase the U.S. commitment or surrender Southeast Asia to the Communists. He worried

> that if we let Communist aggression succeed in taking over South Vietnam, there would follow an endless national debate—a mean and destructive debate—that would shatter my Presidency. . . . I knew that Harry Truman and Dean Acheson had lost their effectiveness from the day that the Communists took over China. . . . And I knew these problems would be chickenshit compared with what might happen if we lost Vietnam.

He feared the left as well as the right. The president was convinced that if South Vietnam were lost, "there would be Robert Kennedy out in front leading the fight against me, telling everyone that I had betrayed John Kennedy's commitment to South Vietnam." Within his own party, many conservative Southern Democrats would oppose a withdrawal from Vietnam. As he looked over the divided and confused congressional opinion, where hawks outnumbered doves, and public opinion, where only 13 percent supported a withdrawal option, Johnson felt confident that moderate escalation of American strength would be supported. In addition, he had great confidence in the ability of the powerful United States to save South Vietnam from a takeover by a fourth-rate, impoverished, "piss ant" Third World nation.

Like many reformers who viewed America's mission abroad as an extension of its mission at home, Johnson believed he could extend the Great Society to Southeast Asia by bringing the wonders of democracy and capitalism to South Vietnam. He had been impressed with Barbara Ward's influential book *The Rich Nations and the Poor Nations*, in which she contended that the problems of the Third World could be resolved by the West through the application of its successful domestic reform models. Not much of a reader of scholarly monographs, the president was attracted to this one—"I read it like I do the Bible." For him, the Tennessee Valley Authority was the perfect model for a development plan for Vietnam's Mekong River Valley. And just as Franklin Roosevelt worked his magic on Congress to push through such measures, Johnson would work his own magic on Ho Chi Minh.

While most of his advisers were confident in the American mission in Southeast Asia, the under secretary of state, George Ball, warned the president against escalation. He looked back to the Korean War, when after a year of limited war with few gains in territory to show for the loss of life and treasure, more and more Americans began demanding an end to the conflict. Ball predicted that it would take even longer to subdue the Vietnamese Communists, and that as the months and years went by, the war could cripple his presidency. Johnson, Rusk, McNamara, and Bundy understood the argument and the analogy. They were more confident than Ball, however, that superior U.S. military technology would produce a satisfactory end to the war before the public tired of it. Moreover, their political calculus that it was better to escalate than withdraw was probably correct, given the administration's previous strong support for the commitment. The president was too good a politician not to realize in November 1964 that if the war continued through 1968, he would have difficulty getting reelected.

That was far off on election day in November 1964 when Johnson crushed Goldwater and the Democrats added to their hefty margins in Congress. This provided the president with an unparalleled opportunity to push through his domestic program, which he dubbed the Great Society in May 1964 at the University of Michigan. Goldwater lost because Americans perceived him as a right-wing radical on foreign and domestic policy (he implied that he favored privatizing Social Security and such popular government projects as the Tennessee Valley Authority), because the Democrats were still the majority party, and because Johnson was the incumbent. Too, many voters saw Johnson as picking up the mantle of the martyred John F. Kennedy.

Johnson knew that he if he wanted to push through his massive legislative program, 1965 and 1966 would be the optimum years. He was likely to lose a portion of his congressional majority after the 1966 by-elections. This factor was uppermost in his calculations as he made the decision in February 1965 to escalate quietly in Vietnam. He did not want his enemies to end the Great Society before it started on the grounds that the nation could not afford both guns and butter. Consequently he never went to the American people to outline what he believed to be the major national security threat in Southeast Asia. Without a declaration of war or its symbolic equivalent from the president and Congress, Americans did not rally around the flag in support of their president's foreign policies. They would find it even more difficult to support those policies as the stakes grew in terms of lives, treasure, and international standing.

Behind Johnson's decision were more than the needs of the Great Society. If he made too much of what he believed to be the vital importance of the war, the public might demand that the Pentagon employ all means to end the war quickly and cheaply to prevent further loss of American life. Johnson expressed concern that pressures from the public and Congress to use the powerful nuclear arm, which he kept tied behind America's back, could lead to World War III. He was convinced that the Soviet Union and China, already sending Hanoi significant amounts of military and economic aid, would not tolerate the United States destroying their ally. They were involved in their own bitter battle for hegemony in the Communist world; neither could afford to be labeled anything less than the defender of the faith in Vietnam.

While it would soon appear that he faced his major challenge from the anti-war left in the United States, Johnson was even more concerned about the fiercely anti-Communist right, which George Ball labeled the "Great Beast." That concern explains why the president refrained from arousing the public and why he met the demands of the escalators only halfway. He became that hybrid denizen of the Vietnam War aviary—a "dawk," between the hawks and the doves.

For many in the Johnson administration, the war in Vietnam was the prototypical cold war conflict of the future, a war of national liberation in which the United States supported the anti-Communists by nation building and by combating Communist guerrillas in a limited or low-intensity war. McNamara talked about the need to learn about fighting such wars in a way that did not "arouse the ire" of the American people. It would be difficult to maintain popular support for an increasingly costly limited war without doing so.

As Johnson contemplated his options in the weeks after the election, he had no way of knowing that the United States was about to enter the 1960s (1964–1974), a decade of unparalleled political and cultural turbulence, some of which was sparked by the Vietnam War but much of which developed independently. At the Democratic National Convention in Atlantic City in August 1964, the Mississippi Freedom Democratic Party, a group that opposed its lily-white state delegation, had demanded to be seated as the rightful representative of the party faithful in the Magnolia State. Lyndon Johnson took great pride in his Civil Rights Bill, passed in June, and the way his party was dismantling segregation and combating racism in American society. Yet here were ungrateful black reformers who walked out of the convention, refusing to accept his compromise seating plan.

When the president counseled patience, they demanded "free-dom now." In the months to come, the civil rights movement would be transformed in part into a black power movement, which became increasingly militant in its demands for an end to racist laws and practices. It started to move away from the goal of integration to one emphasizing political, economic, and cultural self-determination.

Although Johnson had beaten Goldwater handily, the Republican did win six southern states, accelerating the shift away from the Democrats in their longtime stronghold. As with his dawk policy in Vietnam, Johnson was whipsawed between southern conservatives who opposed his civil rights policies and his natural constituency among blacks, many of whom believed he was not doing enough to end racism. Beginning in August 1965 in the Watts area of Los Angeles, and lasting through 1968, the United States was rocked by a series of bloody urban riots or rebellions, mostly in northern cities such as Chicago, Detroit, and Newark. These events increased the popularity of "law-and-order" politicians who promised to crush black militants and weaken civil-rights programs. The riots in the cities and the war in Southeast Asia posed problems for Johnson comparable to those faced by his ally in Vietnam, who had to fight a jungle war against the Communists while dealing with coups and revolutions in the streets of Saigon.

Southerners shifting away from the Democratic Party primarily because of the racial issue had an interesting impact on Johnson's Vietnam policies. White southerners were generally among the most conservative Democrats who believed in a strong military and supported the war in Vietnam. As the party lost that part of its base, liberal northern Democrats from the industrial Midwest and the two coasts became more influential in the leadership and among the rank and file. Those Democrats wcre far more likely to oppose escalation in Vietnam than the southerners were.

Johnson paid far less attention to the events at the University of California, Berkeley, in the fall of 1964 than he did to the actions of the Mississippi Freedom Democratic Party at his convention. But they too prefigured a revolutionary situation, this time not on the streets of American cities but on college campuses. Reacting to a ban on political activities in specified areas on that campus, students challenged both the university administration and the local police with a paralyzing series of mass protests and sit-ins. Their leader, Mario Savio, announced that "There is a time when the operation of the machine becomes so odious . . . that you can't take part; and you've got to put your bodies upon the gears and upon the wheels, upon the levers, upon all the apparatus and you've got to make it stop."

Students around the United States soon followed suit in a wave of sometimes unruly protests against their universities' faculties and administrations that shook the higher educational system. At Berkeley and elsewhere, where students challenged the universities over *in loco parentis* issues and rigid curricula, campuses also became centers of agitation against the war and the draft and against racism on campus and in local communities.

The most severe turbulence generally took place at the most prestigious institutions. In congressional testimony, the longtime head of the Selective Service System, General Lewis Hershey, assured his listeners that he faced serious protests at only fifty or so of the several thousand universities. He then mentioned places such as Harvard, Berkeley, Columbia, Yale, Stanford, and other elite schools as among the relative handful of colleges posing difficulties for the Selective Service System. Those were the schools where upper-class leaders—the establishment—sent their children. Those students were the children of cabinet officers, members of Congress, editors, bankers, corporate executives, and other influential Americans. These leaders grew increasingly concerned about their sons and daughters who participated in anti-establishment and sometimes unlawful protests and who adopted lifestyles that would not prepare them for high-level positions in government or the corporate world, or business or law school.

Opponents of Johnson's policies in Vietnam also began to speak up publicly in the Senate. Senator Church, impressed with critical articles on the war from David Halberstam in *Esquire* and Professor Hans Morgenthau in the *New Leader*, met with each of them during the second half of 1964. He then organized a dinner on January 15, 1965, where Morgenthau presented his arguments to Fulbright, Senator Jacob Javits (R-NY), Johnson aide Harry McPherson, and influential journalists David Broder, Chalmers Roberts, Max Frankel, and Richard Strout. The main purpose for the dinner was to launch a national debate on the war in the media and in Congress, where Church hoped that Fulbright's Foreign Relations Committee would soon conduct hearings.

The previous month Church had granted an interview to the radical monthly *Ramparts*, parts of which were reported on January 15, 1965, in a front-page story in the *New York Times*. The Idaho Democrat contended that "The thing we must remember is that there is no way for us to win their [South Vietnamese] war for them. It is a guerilla war, at root an indigenous revolution against the existing government."

"The Sixties" had begun. As the storm clouds began to gather over his administration in the winter of 1964–1965, Lyndon Johnson was contemplating epochal decisions that would make the war in Vietnam an American war. Those decisions would also bring the war home.

3

Escalation, 1965

ON FEBRUARY 7, 1965, while National Security Adviser McGeorge Bundy was meeting with South Vietnamese leaders in Saigon, the Viet Cong attacked another air base, this time at Pleiku. They killed 9 and wounded 128 Americans and destroyed or damaged 20 aircraft used in the war in the South. A plan to bomb North Vietnam to bring Ho Chi Minh to the peace table, to slow the flow of supplies to the South, and to increase the morale of the South Vietnamese by making the northerners suffer as they were suffering had been drawn up several months earlier. Johnson had been waiting for an incident like the Pleiku attack to implement it. He knew he would not have long to wait, because after Bien Hoa the previous November, such incidents, according to Bundy, were "like streetcars" that would come along almost predictably.

The bombing of staging areas in North Vietnam north of the Demilitarized Zone (DMZ), which was called Operation Flaming Dart, led to retaliation by the Communists in the form of an attack at Qui Nhon, where 23 more Americans were killed. Ultimately Flaming Dart became Operation Rolling Thunder, the sustained bombing of North Vietnam that continued through 1968. The Johnson administration dropped 643,000 tons of bombs on North Vietnam. That seemed like a lot of bombs but not as much as were dropped on South Vietnam. Between 1965 and 1971 the Johnson and Nixon administrations dropped 6.3

million tons on all of Vietnam, two-thirds of which were aimed at Communist targets in South Vietnam. That figure was three times the tonnage of bombs dropped on Europe, Africa, and Asia during World War II. With the start of the bombing of North Vietnam, a country with which the United States was not constitutionally at war, the growing number of opponents of the war at home and abroad had a new and highly emotional issue around which to rally their forces.

Although the bombing decision had already been made, President Johnson made a show of consulting with congressional leaders, all of whom, except for Mike Mansfield, backed the new measure. Assistant Secretary of State William Bundy, commenting on the leaders' general support for Johnson, or at least their fear of challenging him, noted that this was "The only time I ever saw a member of Congress [Mansfield] who said 'Mr. President, I think you are wrong on basic policy' in any direct session" at which State Department officials or staff aides were present. For his dissent, Mansfield found himself gradually frozen out of Johnson's inner circle. Johnson did read his memos and was pleased that the influential Asian expert kept his dissent to himself. When Vice President Hubert Humphrey also expressed concern about the bombing, he too was frozen out. Johnson may have listened to the views of legislators, but he rarely came to them for advice before he had reached a decision and was disturbed when anyone challenged his position. Although Rusk, Ball, and McNamara all testified in the spring that the administration planned to consult with Congress on Vietnam policy, they continued to formulate the policy before "consulting."

Throughout the war, Johnson had more support from Republicans than Democrats. In the 1950s, it was Johnson who had led Senate Democrats to support Eisenhower's foreign policies against frequent opposition from anti-Communist or isolationist Senate Republicans. Now there was a role reversal, beginning on February 7, 1965, with Johnson's asking for and receiving Eisenhower's support. The former president called for even stronger measures against the Communists. On several other occasions over the next few years, Johnson asked the greatly respected Eisenhower for advice and for public expressions of support.

He was not the only prominent Republican to speak out in favor of Johnson's Vietnam policy. When Senator Church suggested that there were "limits to what we can do in helping any government surmount a communist uprising," Senator Dirksen referred to that comment as a call "to run up the white flag." On another occasion later in the war, Dirksen referred to the anti-war critic Senator Gaylord Nelson (D-WI), as "Comrade Nelson," and he described one anti-war protest as "enough to make any person loyal to this country weep." Dirksen soon began to appear more frequently at White House dinners than many Democrats. Johnson told him in February 1965, "I'm getting kicked around by my own party in the Senate and getting my support from your side of the aisle." Representatives Gerald R. Ford (R-MI) and Melvin Laird and Barry Goldwater were among other outspoken Republican hawks. Former presidential candidate Richard Nixon urged the president in July to pressure the Democrats to support administration policies.

Those who were dubious about the course that Johnson had set for the nation in Vietnam included, along with Church and Nelson, Republican senators George Aiken of Vermont, John Sherman Cooper of Kentucky, and Jacob Javits, and Democratic senators Joseph Clark of Pennsylvania, McGovern, and Fulbright, along with influential columnists James Reston and Walter Lippmann. In one famous meeting with the president and twenty-five other senators in which Church expressed his doubts about the wisdom of Rolling Thunder, Johnson replied, "Well Frank, next time you need a dam in Idaho, go ask Walter Lippmann for one." Johnson attacked him more obliquely when he referred to Church's hero, former Idaho senator William Borah, saying, "There once was a senator who thought he knew more about war and peace than the President . . . and predicted that there would be no war in Europe a brief two or three months before war broke out."

As for McGovern, who had a Ph.D. in American history, Johnson thundered, "Don't give me another goddam history lesson. I've got a drawerful of memos from Mansfield" (another history professor). One of Johnson's aides noted, "The boss gets wild about him [McGovern] sometimes." The senator soon entered White House purgatory when he was taken off the guest list, along with the even louder dissenter Ernest Gruening (D-AK), who, according to another aide, "drove Johnson crazy." Johnson also told McGovern not to worry about the bombing hitting civilians because "My boys don't hit a shithouse unless I tell them."

The most important public dissenter in the Senate would soon be Fulbright, the chair of the Foreign Relations Committee. At this point, however, Johnson's old friend kept his counsel mostly to himself, hoping he would have more influence with the president by expressing his doubts privately than on the floor of the Senate or in his committee. And even he had never voted against a military appropriation for the war during Johnson's presidency. Johnson told him in July, "If you want to get out of Vietnam, then you have the prerogative of taking the [Tonkin] resolution under which we are out there now. You can repeal it tomorrow."

The most important private dissenter was an even closer friend and mentor of Johnson's, Senator Richard Russell. Russell, who with Johnson had strongly opposed intervention at Dien Bien Phu in 1954, was loath to get involved militarily in the first place. Once in the war, he urged the president to do what it took to win or get out. Overall in the spring of 1965, Johnson's aides counted about ten senators and seventy representatives who were not pleased with his Vietnam policy.

From May 1965 through July 1968 the Senate considered eight major appropriations bills for South Vietnam. Most of the time only two or three dovish senators (frequently Morse, Nelson, and

Gruening) had the courage to oppose providing funds for American soldiers in Vietnam. In fact, of the 113 recorded votes on Vietnam issues to the end of the war in 1973, the presidents received congressional support in almost every one. It was difficult for senators to face the charge that they were responsible for the deaths of American boys by not providing them with the means to defend themselves. Johnson frequently challenged senators who opposed his policies in Vietnam to vote against the appropriations bills. It mattered little that senators such as Joseph Clark, after voting for military appropriations, had read into the *Congressional Record* that he did "not consider [his vote] an endorsement of the policy" in Vietnam. Through their approval of the blank check in the Gulf of Tonkin Resolution and their failure to vote against Vietnam-related legislation beginning with the escalation in February 1965, Congress tacitly authorized war in Vietnam. Because of the way they did it, they made it the president's war. Several congressional hearings about the war, particularly those held by Fulbright in February 1966 and by Senator John Stennis's (D-MS) Armed Services Committee in the summer of 1967, were important in the development of opinion and, to some degree, policy. But Congress's relative timidity throughout the Johnson administration frustrated anti-war activists. The Reverend William Sloane Coffin explained that "it was the passivity of Congress as much as anything else that pushed me and many like me toward civil disobedience."

By February 9, 1965, the White House had received fifteen-hundred telegrams concerning the bombing of North Vietnam. Those opposing outnumbered those supporting the action by a whopping 12 to 1 margin. (The margin after the Gulf of Tonkin bombing had been only 2 to 1 against the president.) By the end of February the Senate Foreign Relations Committee, a hotbed of Senate skeptics, had received five hundred letters, 80 percent of which opposed the escalation. Americans tend to send government officials complaining rather than affirming letters. Both

Johnson and the Congress were more impressed with the results of a Harris poll showing that 82 percent of the respondents supported the decision to bomb North Vietnam after the attack at Pleiku. Perhaps more would have been opposed had Johnson not downplayed sending the first American combat troops to Vietnam in March. Marine contingents were needed to protect the air bases in South Vietnam from more Viet Cong attacks. It was not until a press briefing in June that a story finally leaked about their pro-active combat missions.

Despite support for the bombing, Johnson did feel pressure from Congress to demonstrate a willingness to negotiate with North Vietnam. He was worried about the impact of congressional criticism on the media and public opinion. Using the occasion of a speech at Johns Hopkins University on April 7, 1965, the president offered his vision for a peaceful end to the war and the reconstruction of both Vietnams. He even offered previews of his comments to one of the key skeptics in the media, Walter Lippmann, and to Senators Church, McGovern, and McGhee. He told the senators, "Now I'm doing exactly what you fellers want me to do. I'm going to negotiate."

Johnson employed an American political paradigm in his approach to Hanoi. Considering Ho Chi Minh as only a slightly more exotic form of an American labor or congressional leader, he offered him a generous development plan in exchange for peace and permitting the people of South Vietnam to remain allied to the West. It seemed like a good deal to the president, one that made sense to a former master of the Senate. But Ho and his comrades employed a different paradigm. Recent scholarship has suggested that Johnson was not unsophisticated in the ways of world politics. He frequently demonstrated a flair for nuanced diplomacy when dealing with other problems, particularly in Europe. But he had difficulty employing traditional methods, which worked with the likes of Charles de Gaulle, when he confronted the battle-hardened, dedicated veterans of the Vietnamese Revolution.

In another attempt that spring to appease his critics, Johnson approved a one-week halt in the bombing in May. As with the carrot in the Johns Hopkins speech, he received nothing in return from Ho Chi Minh. With such complete rejection, and from Johnson's perspective humiliation, he would not offer Ho many more carrots.

In the spring of 1965, Vietnam was not the only foreign problem Johnson faced. In 1963 a military junta had overthrown the Dominican Republic's elected government led by Juan Bosch. In April that junta was itself overthrown and a civil war began, pitting forces loyal to the military against those supporting the return of Bosch. After receiving grossly exaggerated reports about the radical nature of the pro-Bosch faction, and fearing the installation of another Communist regime, Johnson dispatched fourteen thousand American troops on May 2 to end the fighting and install the military in power until elections could be held in 1966. That same day he called on Congress to approve a new military appropriation bill to cover added expenses in South Vietnam and now the Dominican Republic. He asked legislators to show with their vote that they backed their president's policies.

At first glance this relatively bloodless intervention, which led to the restoration of stability in the Dominican Republic, would seem to have little to do with the more important war in Vietnam. But it greatly concerned observers such as former Democratic standard bearer Adlai E. Stevenson, who commented, "When I consider what the administration did in the Dominican Republic, I begin to wonder if we know what we are doing in Vietnam." Senator Fulbright was even more worried about the way the Johnson administration was conducting foreign policy. The Dominican Republic intervention led him to begin breaking away from support of the president's policies in the Third World, particularly in Southeast Asia. Senator Eugene McCarthy (D-MN) was another member of the Foreign Relations Committee who broke with Johnson on this issue.

After hearings in his committee and considerable study, Fulbright denounced the Dominican Republic intervention in a speech on September 15, pointing to the administration's "lack of candor" and its trumped-up rationale for sending in the Marines. Without specifically mentioning the president, Fulbright asserted that "In their apprehension lest the Dominican Republic become another Cuba, some of our officials seem to have forgotten that virtually all reform movements attract some Communist support." This was the first time since the Roosevelt presidency that the chair of the Foreign Relations Committee had spoken out in public so strongly against administration policy. Fulbright had warned Johnson in July privately that "Vietnam is ruining our domestic and our foreign policy. I will not support it any longer."

Johnson was livid. He crossed Fulbright off the White House guest list, even for state dinners where he should have been invited, rarely if ever met with him in private during the remainder of his presidency, denied him a government jet for an official visit to New Zealand, and privately considered him a cowardly fellow, not a "stand-up kind of guy." Fulbright had already been nervous about the escalation in Vietnam. The intervention in the Dominican Republic and Johnson's reaction to his apostasy made it easier for Fulbright to become the most famous senatorial critic of American policy—a critic who, through his position as chair of the Foreign Relations Committee, had an impact on that policy. Johnson could not understand how one of the advocates of increasing presidential authority to meet the Communist menace could suddenly become one of the leaders of a faction wanting to strip the president of such powers. But it was not so sudden. Fulbright and others in Congress had been worrying for

quite some time about the unintended consequences of their earlier advocacy of releasing the president from his tether to Capitol
Hill in the dangerous new world of the cold war.

In the summer of 1965, while Fulbright was concentrating on the
Dominican Republic, Johnson and his aides were preparing to
make the second major escalatory decision of the year—that
Americans would assume the ground-combat role in Vietnam.
The bombing of North Vietnam had not brought the Communists any closer to a reasonable position for the opening of negotiations, and they continued to make gains against the South
Vietnamese army. Although American combat troops were now
going out on missions by themselves, there were not enough of
them to meet the increasing strength of the Viet Cong, which
was beginning to be supplemented in ever greater numbers by
North Vietnamese regulars.

On July 27 the president announced in a rather low-key manner that he was ordering fifty thousand more American troops to
Vietnam. He did not announce that the United States was assum-
ing the ground-combat role. This major escalation appeared in a
statement that also referred to Great Society programs and other
domestic issues. The military wanted him to announce that he
had already approved the sending of more than the original fifty
thousand troops at a later date. Johnson feared the appearance of
all-out war would jeopardize several key bits of open legislation
in Congress. He had yet to pass as much as one-third of his Great
Society program, including Medicare and the Voting Rights Act.

To address their needs, McNamara and the Joint Chiefs wanted
to call up the reserves, a decision needing congressional authoriza-
tion that would have produced a divisive debate. The defense secretary even thought it prudent to ask for a tax hike to help pay for
increased expenditures in Vietnam. Johnson predicted that if he
took that route, Congress would say, "You can't have guns and
butter, and we're going to have guns." Even Senators Mansfield

and Dirksen, who adopted opposing positions on the call-up, urged Johnson not to request any sort of additional supportive resolution comparable to the Gulf of Tonkin Resolution. They feared it would tear Congress and the country apart.

Calling up the reserves posed another type of political problem for the president. Although he could not predict it at the time, the longer the war went on, the more draftees would be needed to fight in Vietnam. Draftees, particularly those who were not enthusiastic about fighting in Vietnam, would prove to be far less reliable than reserves. But as the war went on, the reserves were becoming more and more a refuge from the draft for middle- and upper-middle-class college graduates. Sending them to the combat zone, as had been done in all previous American wars, meant creating an activist anti-war cadre among influential American parents. Their political activities and advocacies carried far more weight than those of the disproportionately blue-collar parents of draftees. The more unpopular and endless the war became, the more college students swarmed into the reserves, the less likely it was any president would take the political risk of calling them up. The reserves became a refuge for young men such as Dan Quayle, George W. Bush, and Tom Selleck.

In 1966, worried about the political implications of drafting increasingly large numbers of middle-class young men, McNamara came up with Project 100,000. This plan made draft-eligible 100,000 men whose low scores on the then-current intelligence tests would have precluded them from the military. Heavyweight boxing champ Muhammad Ali was one of those who qualified for the draft under the relaxed standard. Most of the 100,000 came from the lower class, often from minority groups, and most had not completed high school. McNamara saw this plan as solving two problems: it provided men for the military while improving their literacy and other skills. Ultimately 340,000 men joined the military under a program that enjoyed only modest success in preparing them for civilian employment.

The Johnson and later the Nixon administration's draft policies had an impact on another disadvantaged group. Because of
the exemption enjoyed by undergraduate and especially graduate students (until 1968), men were staying in college longer, creating new high-level employment opportunities for women.
Those opportunities appeared at the time of increased agitation
for women's rights and the birth of the modern Women's Liberation Movement. They opened white-collar and professional positions to women that might not have been available had there
been more men in the civilian workforce. Because men were
staying in school longer, married women were compelled to fill
their places in the job market to support their spouses. Many of
the leaders of the Women's Liberation Movement gained valuable experience in organizational tactics and strategies through
their earlier activities in the anti-war movement.

Johnson may not have called for a full-scale debate on his decisions in July 1965 but he did shore up his political bases before he
announced them. On July 8 he called together the President's
Special Advisory Group on Foreign Policy, a high-level, bipartisan group of former military and political leaders who soon became known as the Wise Men (the group included no women).
Among those who comprised this group were World War II
hero General Omar Bradley, former Secretary of State Dean
Acheson, former Secretary of Defense Robert Lovett, former
Kennedy administration Defense official Roswell Gilpatrick,
and former CIA Director John McCone. They listened to pre-
sentations from the president and his aides, offered advice, and
reported what their friends and business acquaintances were
thinking about Vietnam. The Wise Men enthusiastically endorsed escalation in July, as they did in several other meetings
with the president until March 1968.

Johnson also consulted with Congress but only with the leadership and at the last minute. On July 27, the day he made the

subdued announcement about the call-up, he asked legislators for their advice and consent. Again Mike Mansfield offered strong objections to the new military initiative with Senator Bourke Hickenlooper (R-IA) not entirely convinced. Mansfield called attention to growing public opposition to the war and the likelihood that civil rights leaders would soon join an anti-war movement. Of meetings like this which he attended, Speaker of the House Carl Albert later recalled, "We were always after the fact in giving advice." Few of his colleagues paid much attention to the curmudgeon Wayne Morse, who was not invited to the meeting and who had recently begun fulminating about impeaching Johnson. To buy some time for his policies, Johnson reluctantly agreed to Mansfield's request to lead a fact-finding mission to Vietnam. The Montana senator came back from Vietnam more pessimistic about the project in Southeast Asia than he had been before the trip.

Dovish-leaning legislators knew that the president still had a good deal of support for his Vietnam policies. A poll in September revealed that 75 percent of respondents wanted Johnson to hold the line or escalate. Of course, those respondents did not know about the importance of the first call-up of "only" 50,000 troops, nor did they expect that the call-ups would continue until 1968 when 550,000 American GIs would be in Vietnam. But the handful of critics feared as much, with Fulbright saying privately, "My God, I feel so alone. No one seems to give a damn. . . . I am walking among the blind and deaf."

Like the February bombing decision, the ground-combat troop decision in July appeared to be a short-term solution to the Vietnam problem. The administration believed that the addition of fifty thousand American GIs plus the continued bombing would be enough to convince Ho Chi Minh to enter into negotiations for a reasonable settlement of the conflict. Johnson led members of the Cabinet and Congress, as well as the media and the public, to believe that the war would soon be over and would have little further impact on American political life and the economy. In this tack he was supported by McNamara who, using the sort of cost-benefit analysis he had developed at Ford, assumed that with Washington raising the stakes, Ho Chi Minh would have to make the rational decision to end his revolution in the South.

While privately Johnson may have feared that he was taking the nation into a drawn-out war, he also made the best of a bad situation by convincing himself that the troop announcement would do the trick. Critics have claimed that Johnson deceived his own economic advisers along with the rest of the nation. He did not inform them that the war could be long and costly, and he did everything possible to keep it off the front burners and out of Congress where budget hawks were becoming nervous. In the fall of 1965 he told them that the defense budget for the next year would decline. The president may have deceived himself into believing such optimistic predictions. To do otherwise would be to admit that his policies in Vietnam were not working. Why would he knowingly take actions to wreck the economy? In the fall of 1965 some in Congress may have welcomed the deception. An extended discussion of the escalation would have necessitated budget cuts or tax increases, making it difficult for a Democrat to run in 1966. Wilbur Mills (D-AR), the powerful chair of the House Ways and Means Committee, opposed a tax hike before the elections. He supported a hike only after January 1967, with the next round of elections almost two years away.

At the time of his ground-combat decision, Johnson presided over a very healthy economy. Between 1960 and 1965 the Gross National Product (GNP) grew by one-third and corporate profits rose 88 percent. In 1964, 64 percent of white citizens polled expressed satisfaction with their family income. The 1964 tax and budget cuts had stimulated the economy; unemployment fell in one year from 6 to 4.7 percent, and continued to fall close to the 4 percent full-employment figure. The escalation in Vietnam, which demanded increased draft calls, also contributed to falling unemployment. Inflation was being held in check through informal wage-and-price guidelines strongly recommended by the administration. Wage increases averaged 3.2 percent in 1964 but began creeping up to 3.8 percent in 1965, and reached 4.4 percent by 1966. The same pattern could be seen in the rise of the consumer price index. It stood at 1.3 percent in 1964, rose to 1.7 percent in 1965, and ballooned to 2.9 percent in 1966.

Johnson's economic advisers, who began to fear an inflationary spiral as early as the spring of 1965, urged a cut in domestic spending as well as tax increases to stabilize the economy. They would have been even more concerned had they known that the increasingly expensive Vietnam War was not about to end in the near future. As Arthur Okun, a member of the Council of Economic Advisers and its chair in 1968, noted, "Vietnam plays the Danish prince in the *Hamlet* of recent economic history." His colleague, Walter Heller, another chair, complained that with its unforeseen $25 billion in expenditures, "The Vietnam escalation knocked things into a cocked hat." The war added about 3 percent in GNP at a time of full employment, with a good deal of inflationary pressure on the automotive, mechanical, textile, clothing, and rubber industries. As early as January 1966, the *Wall Street Journal* began to wonder whether "the U.S. is inflicting more injury on the Communists or itself."

The Federal Reserve raised the discount rate from 4 to 4.5 percent in December 1965, hoping to cool off the economy. As for his voluntary wage-and-price controls that were beginning to be ignored, Johnson appealed to business and labor to think of their boys fighting in Vietnam when they contemplated raising prices or demanding wage hikes.

In the short run, particularly 1965–1967, the economy appeared healthy. The combination of the 1964 tax cut and spending for the war led to virtually full employment and rising but still manageable inflation. Additionally, Johnson's anti-poverty program seemed to be working. In 1964, 20 percent of American

families fell below the poverty line. That number fell to 17 percent in 1965 and 13 percent in 1968, despite the fact that Johnson
was spending only about 1 percent of the federal budget on the
Office of Economic Opportunity (OEO). And even after domestic spending declined—especially in December 1966 when the
president cut his anti-poverty programs by 42 percent—the economic situation of many poor Americans continued to improve.
The head of the OEO, R. Sargent Shriver, knew that the economy, not his agency, was responsible for much of the temporary
success of the War on Poverty. When he heard that Johnson had
told his budget director in December 1966, "That son of a bitch
Shriver isn't going to get anything out of me" for OEO, a depressed Shriver offered to resign.

Johnson's threats to Shriver were partly in response to indicators of a weakening economy at home and abroad. Between 1961
and 1965 the United States ran a trade surplus with foreign
countries of $5.4 billion. By 1972 the trade deficit was $6.4 billion.
Part of this gap related to foreign outlays for military purchases
that increased, especially in Asia, from 1964 through 1969 by 70
percent. At the same time imports to the United States doubled
from 1960 through 1969 with the balance-of-payments deficit
running from $3.3 billion in 1964 to $9.4 billion in 1968. The war
contributed as much as 75 percent of those deficits. Concerned
about the inflated dollar and the balance-of-payments deficit,
Europeans in 1965 began a small run on American gold stocks,
trading in $1.7 billion for gold. American gold stocks had already
declined from $23 billion in 1957 to $16 billion in 1962. This
problem became more severe as the war went on, with French
president Charles de Gaulle in particular worried about Europeans holding so many inflated dollars.

With the military escalation of 1965, the war soon became
a major concern for those running the economy. But it would
take time to feel the inflationary impact of Johnson's budgetary

maneuvers. That was not the case with liberal and radical Americans who, in the wake of the February bombing, launched the largest and most powerful anti-war movement in American history. The not-so-surgical bombing of North Vietnam, a country that was not bombing the United States or even South Vietnam, took away the moral high ground from an administration that claimed it was fighting a democratic war to protect freedom in Southeast Asia. In late March, beginning at the University of Michigan, college students and their professors held a series of teach-ins to explore, mostly in opposition, the war in Vietnam and the way it was being prosecuted. In April the Students for a Democratic Society, the leading New Left campus group, organized a Washington demonstration that drew 25,000 participants to listen to speeches decrying the escalation. In October the First International Days of Protest, held in several American and foreign cities, attracted more than 100,000, while the next month a rally organized by the Committee for a Sane Nuclear Policy (SANE) drew as many as 35,000 to Washington.

At the time of the SANE rally, the vast majority of Americans supported administration policy in Vietnam, but a growing, politically significant minority was beginning to make its voice heard in the media and in the streets. Much of the leadership of the anti-war movement was composed of radical young people whose agendas for reform in the United States went well beyond ending the war in Vietnam. Most of those who turned out for their events, however, were liberals who were primarily concerned with the war. Some thought the war was immoral, others thought it was not in America's best national security interests, while still others were concerned about the draft and the possibility that they or their loved ones would end up in the jungles of Vietnam.

Whatever their motivations, the liberals in particular were of concern to the president. From the early 1950s through to the mid-1960s, American presidents could count on wide support among both conservatives and liberals for most of their cold war policies. That consensus was beginning to fall apart with liberals, who generally were found in the Democratic Party, deserting the president in increasing numbers over the war. These were the same liberals who should have been thrilled by Great Society programs and the president's commitment to civil rights. The liberals' concerns were evidenced in the developing critique of the president's Vietnam policy among members of the Americans for Democratic Action (ADA), the most important left-liberal group associated with the Democratic Party. At the end of 1965 this was only a small problem for the president. But from that point on, every week or so, another prominent senator, representative, liberal columnist, or respected political figure would announce his or her opposition to the course of the war.

The administration was also beginning to lose the nation's intellectual elite. Most prominent American writers, poets, and actors have always tended to be liberal politically and were consequently supportive of Johnson's domestic politics. Now many of them began to speak out publicly against his Vietnam policy. Witness the anti-war activities surrounding the White House's Festival of the Arts on June 14, 1965, where Johnson hoped to demonstrate that, like the Kennedys, he too had culture.

On June 2 the distinguished poet Robert Lowell's refusal to attend the conference because of the war became a front-page story in the *New York Times*. Lowell was immediately and publicly supported by other luminaries in the literary community, and the Festival of the Arts suddenly became a cause célèbre. Who would attend, and what would they do there? Johnson railed at the "sonsofbitches" who created the uproar, while his aide Jack Valenti remembered that "None of us realized . . . the tawdry lengths that some people would go to in impoliteness and incivility." The president came close to canceling the event that was marked by John Hershey reading an excerpt from his book *Hiroshima*—event hostess Ladybird Johnson failed to convince him to choose a different text. The critic Dwight

Macdonald spent his time at the festival circulating an anti-war petition. When he got to then-Democratic stalwart Charlton Heston, the actor told him what he could do with his petition and "ate his ass out."

The Democratic Party, far more than the Republican Party, could ill afford to alienate the influential literary elite upon whom it counted for support. The conflict over the Festival of the Arts reflected the growing opposition to U.S. foreign policy in the artistic community.

At the same time, and not yet noticed by the White House, the war began to produce more and more young recruits for radical and even revolutionary political organizations on college cam-puses. Organizations such as SDS, which claimed 100,000 members by the end of the decade, began adopting more radical strategies than those envisioned in the 1962 Port Huron state-ment, its founding document. The growing cadre belonging to Marxist and other anti-capitalist groups never accounted for more than a small percentage of all college students, peaking on active campuses at about 5 percent. Moreover, conservative groups grew apace, with the Young Americans for Freedom (YAF) signing up more members during the decade than SDS did.

But the number of students becoming radicalized because of the war was not the issue. Radical student organizations were found disproportionately at the most prestigious universities. "*All* of us . . . had sons or daughters who were involved in this," re-ported a State Department official. "I mean, everybody did. I had a son who was poised to go to Canada. . . . All of us were torn in our own family lives." Those in high positions in government as well as those in high positions in the American business commu-nity had children, grandchildren, nieces, and nephews who were becoming alienated from American society because of the war.

The hippie movement compounded the problem. To many middle-class Americans, the hippies were an even greater threat than the radicals. They rejected authority, disrespected the flag, smoked dope and used LSD, talked obscenely, wore long hair and torn jeans or sometimes no clothes, listened to incomprehensible music, and did not seem to care about getting a job. By 1966 or so, many young people who were not genuine hippies, including the political radicals, began adopting hippie music, clothing, culture, and irreverence, some of them accepting Dr. Timothy Leary's call to "Tune in, turn on, and drop out." (Leary himself had dropped out of academics after being fired from Harvard for giving students LSD.) Even members of the military on leave wore wigs and torn jeans in order to look like "normal" young persons.

For members of the establishment concerned about their Ivy Leaguers' politics, this was the last straw. Erroneously conflating the hippies with the political activists who now looked like hippies, they felt that the future of the United States, or at least of the next generation that would run the country, was in great jeopardy. Perhaps, many argued, if the war ended, the radicals and hippies would begin preparing in law school and business school to assume their rightful places in the boardrooms of Wall Street and along the corridors of power in Washington.

As the war continued through the Johnson administration, the number of hippies and radicals and radical hippies grew, as did their visibility in the media. This had a major impact on American politics in general. Presidential candidates Richard Nixon, a conservative, and Alabama governor George Wallace, a southern populist, promised that if elected they would deal with such lawless, unpatriotic, and un-American individuals in more effective ways than liberal Democrats like Lyndon Johnson, whose permissive and relativistic policies, they argued, had given rise to this dangerous and bizarre subculture. We could return to the "Happy Days" of the 1950s.

Just as the political threat from liberals, radicals, and hippies was relatively minor in 1965, so too was the threat from the August disturbance in a black section of Los Angeles. There had been riots in northern cities before, but the Watts area, with its palm trees and single-family homes, did not look like Harlem or other ghettos. More important, the national government had adopted the cause of civil rights and desegregation, the lode-stones of black political activism. When the riots continued through the Johnson administration, ultimately touching more than one hundred cities, many Americans conflated the unprece-dented lawlessness in the ghettos with lawlessness on the cam-puses and at anti-war demonstrations.

It is never easy being a president in wartime. Until Lyndon John-son, no president except Abraham Lincoln had to confront the multiple challenges of managing a long and unpopular war while trying to deal with unprecedented political and cultural revolutions at home, both exacerbated by that war.

4

Democrats Fall Out, 1966

THE YEAR 1966 was a pivotal one for Lyndon Johnson. He could contain the political and economic fallout from the war if his 1965 escalations convinced Americans that an end to military involvement in Southeast Asia was near. It was a congressional by-election year in which, by tradition, the president's party was bound to lose votes, making it more difficult afterward to pass the remainder of his ambitious Great Society legislation. The unsuccessful prosecution of the war could be a campaign issue for the Republicans or even for dovish Democratic insurgents challenging his leadership. By the end of 1965, 60 percent of those polled viewed the war as the nation's most urgent problem.

On the other hand, the United States was not yet in a crisis mode. Johnson's approval ratings stood at 64 percent. The number of young people joining the ranks of hippies and radicals, and the proliferation of urban disturbances in northern cities, would not reach a critical mass until 1967. The economy, which offered early warning indicators that it was headed toward an inflationary spiral, worried only the economists. Johnson still had time to resolve his problems brought about by the war, but, unfortunately for him, there would be no quick fix.

Recognizing that the rather limited Rolling Thunder program and the threat to send more combat troops to Vietnam were having no apparent impact on North Vietnam's willingness to compromise on his terms, Johnson decided to enlarge the scope of the bombing. But before he took the action that he knew would arouse congressional doves and media critics, he reluctantly acquiesced to a bombing pause starting on Christmas Day, 1965, and lasting until the end of January. During that period he sent his diplomats on a peace blitz trying to find Communists and other intermediaries who could convince the North Vietnamese to be more forthcoming in their terms for opening peace talks. He was not optimistic; he expected an outcry when he resumed and expanded the bombing.

By January 1966 at least twenty-eight Democratic and several Republican senators had expressed concern about the war, with several worried about its impact on domestic programs and the economy. In his State of the Union address on January 12, an apparently confident president announced that the nation was "strong enough to pursue our goals in the world while still building a Great Society at home." But word had leaked that he had already informed those in charge of the War on Poverty not to expect increased appropriations in the near future.

Anti-war critics on Capitol Hill still constituted a minority. Most of the senior leadership of both parties, aside from Fulbright and Mansfield, supported Johnson, with the Republicans calling for more rather than less escalation. Those Republicans were not as enthusiastic about the president's domestic policies as were the generally liberal anti-war Democrats. Late in January fifteen senators, led by Vance Hartke (D-IN), asked the president not to end the bombing halt. Seventy-seven House members joined them in that appeal. At the same time Fulbright suggested publicly that Johnson's escalations were not in the spirit of the Gulf of Tonkin Resolution. And although he was not among the most outspoken doves, Johnson's nemesis, New York senator Robert F. Kennedy, also began drifting away from the administration at this point. Ominously for the president in the winter of 1966, polls revealed that Democrats preferred Kennedy to him in 1968.

It was not just the commitment in Vietnam itself. It was the way the president ignored Congress. He continued to invite the leadership and even critics to the White House on many occasions to offer suggestions, and he made a show of listening to them. But as he had in the past, he ended up lecturing them about the wisdom of his predetermined initiatives.

When the bombing halt did not lead to promising diplomatic initiatives, Johnson decided to expand the operation in another attempt to raise the stakes. His military advisers had warned him that the longer the halt went on, the more the North Vietnamese could send matériel and soldiers to the South to rebuild the infrastructure destroyed by earlier bombing. The president knew that the bombing renewal would anger the growing number of outspoken senators. He feared that "We will lose a good part of the Senate." On the other hand, leaving aside the military reasons for starting up Rolling Thunder again, he explained, "I don't want to back out—and look like I'm reacting to the Fulbrights." Throughout the war, Johnson, and Nixon for that matter, did not want the enemy to think that American national security policy could be affected by dissenters outside the Oval Office. At least that is a plausible reason of state for Johnson's remark. He was also a proud man who did not wish to appear incorrect in his escalatory policies.

Although Johnson did not react to Fulbright, the Arkansas senator did react to Johnson when the Senate Foreign Relations Committee in late January approved by a 16 to 3 vote his proposal to hold hearings on Vietnam policy as it considered a military appropriations bill. Fulbright intended his hearings to educate the public about the Vietnam War and to raise questions about the direction of American policy. His committee was disproportionately made up of critics of that policy. Television network executives decided that the hearings were important enough to cover them live. In a celebrated flap, after the first few sessions CBS returned to its regularly scheduled programs, which included reruns of "I Love Lucy."

The Vietnam War was a "living-room war," the first conflict seen by almost all Americans on television. Only a small percentage of the population had owned sets during the Korean War. In the sixties the big three commercial networks were in their heyday, with powerful nightly newscasts that only recently had expanded from fifteen minutes to a half-hour. Although the war would have more total coverage on television today, the three networks would likely have abdicated the airing of hearings and other war-related stories to the cable news networks, with their relatively small viewership. But when presidents held news conferences in the sixties and seventies, for example, the three networks always covered them live. Beginning in the eighties, they began to leave that nonprofit enterprise to cable. Thus the Vietnam War was the first and perhaps the last living-room war in the sense that viewers could not escape its coverage on the 6:30 p.m. newscasts, albeit generally for only two minutes nightly.

Or perhaps they could. Media scholars have contended that the daily two-minute coverage of combat in Vietnam on the nightly news—or "shooting bloody," as news directors called it—was rather antiseptic and, more important, may have become so commonplace that viewers, sitting in front of their "TV dinners," were inured to the tragic dimension of the war. And when in 1968 the networks generally stopped their two minutes of shooting bloody to concentrate on peace talks, viewers may have forgotten about the combat side of the war.

This was not quite the living-room war of the Gulf War and after for another reason. During much of the Vietnam War the networks were unable to send live feeds directly from Southeast Asia. The news that Americans saw on television was often as much as twenty-four hours old because the film or videotape had to be flown to Japan for transmission to the United States. Given the substantial costs involved in satellite or cable transmission from Tokyo, the networks frequently chose to transport film by air directly from Saigon to New York, making their "news" even staler.

Whatever the impact of television's coverage of the war in Southeast Asia, its coverage of the political struggle at home did help to shape public opinion. The Fulbright hearings, as they came to be called, formed one of the most important televised events of the war. Lyndon Johnson, whose wife owned television stations, understood the power of the medium, and in this case even hastily called a summit meeting with South Vietnamese president Nguyen Cao Ky in an attempt to push the hearings from the headlines. Fortunately for the president, the networks did not make coverage of such hearings a regular part of their schedules during the remainder of his term.

Americans were indeed educated by the hearings, both by the spirited defense of administration policy presented by Secretaries Rusk and McNamara, and by the critique of that policy presented by George F. Kennan, father of the "containment" doctrine that became the philosophical underpinning of U.S. cold war policy, and retired war hero General James M. Gavin. Although the testimony was balanced between supporters and opponents of the president, the dovish leanings of the interrogators meant that much of the air time involved pointed questions about Johnson's policies. Viewers saw Senator Clark admit, "Personally, I am scared to death we are on our way to a nuclear World War III," and Fulbright explain how Americans looked to the Vietnamese opposition: "We are obviously intruders from their point of view. We represent the old Western imperialism in their eyes."

Neither Kennan nor Gavin challenged the initial commitment to South Vietnam, but they did express concern about the way the war had escalated. The fact that two loyal anti-Communist pillars of the American establishment found fault with the policy contributed to some citizens' confidence that it was legitimate to oppose American involvement in the war. The committee received twenty thousand letters and telegrams, mostly favoring an anti-war perspective, and Random House quickly published its proceedings in paperback.

Johnson was furious with Fulbright and the committee. He claimed, "It is easier to satisfy Ho Chi Minh than it is Fulbright," and ordered the FBI to investigate the senators' relationships with Communist diplomats and fellow travelers, asserting that both Fulbright and Morse were "definitely under the control of the Soviet embassy." The FBI investigation included monitoring the political activities of more than ninety of Morse's Oregon supporters to find their subversive links. During the Watergate investigations, Richard Nixon, whose misuse of the intelligence agencies for political purposes went far beyond that of Johnson's, nonetheless was correct in complaining about the absence of investigations of his predecessor's abuses of power.

In the spring of 1966 that was not the only conspiratorial activity afoot. At a lunch at New York's Quo Vadis restaurant, three prominent Kennedy Democrats, former Johnson speechwriter Richard Goodwin, former Johnson aide Professor Arthur Schlesinger, Jr., and former ambassador John Kenneth Galbraith, decided that the war had to end and vowed to do all they could to stop it. Only a year earlier, Schlesinger had defended the administration at a nationwide teach-in, and Goodwin had been the president's favorite speechwriter until he had been caught too many times leaking stories to the press. In 1966 all three published articles expressing concern about the direction of administration policy. In that same period, Schlesinger, the Kennedy family's favorite intellectual, began holding political strategy sessions with Robert Kennedy.

Johnson was aware of much of this activity, in part through the counter-espionage of his aide John Roche, who claimed to have learned secrets about the president's self-proclaimed "enemy" and what he labeled the "Kennedy government in exile" from a tipsy Kennedy loyalist, former Press Secretary Pierre Salinger. Johnson was also not happy about the amount of time Robert McNamara was spending at Bobby's Virginia estate, the alleged seat of a Kennedy government in exile. The defense secretary later claimed that the president never questioned his loyalty.

This activity of Kennedy stalwarts increased Johnson's paranoia about a growing cabal in the Democratic Party in 1968 determined to replace him with heir apparent Bobby Kennedy. It also made him more reluctant to accept their increasingly dovish approach to the war, an approach he attributed to domestic politics. After all, he believed he was only following the path laid out for him by John F. Kennedy. Johnson never forgot the way Bobby Kennedy tried to convince him to change his mind after he accepted the vice-presidential nomination at the 1960 convention. And he never forgave the snobby Ivy Leaguers in the Kennedy administration, including Bobby, who treated him with disdain and disrespect when he was vice president. In addition, Johnson was not amused by the bitter satirical play "MacBird," which in 1967 featured him as the evil murderer of Kennedy the king.

Despite the growing split among Democrats in the spring of 1966, 53 percent of the general public still approved of Johnson's policies in Vietnam, and 47 percent expressed disapproval. The latter did not represent a unified opposition since they were split between mostly Republican hawks and mostly Democratic doves. How long the middle would hold was debatable. As Johnson's press secretary, Bill Moyers, pointed out, few of his supporters were satisfied with the way the war was going. In June 1966 Americans again told pollsters that Vietnam was the nation's number one problem. Administration aides worried too about a developing credibility gap, related to increasingly antagonistic press relations.

That same month Mike Mansfield informed the president that while he still enjoyed support from a majority of Democrats in Congress, most hoped for a speedy end to the war, and most feared that its continuance was beginning to take its toll on the party. Even such a Johnson stalwart as Richard Russell was concerned, remarking privately, "I don't buy this so-called 'domino' theory." At the same time Richard Nixon had begun urging Americans to vote for Republicans in the congressional elections that fall because they backed the president's policy of hanging tough in Vietnam, unlike many Democrats. Everett Dirksen, for example, rejected the idea of negotiating with the Communists without first achieving a military victory, while Melvin Laird opposed a "Southeast Asia Yalta Agreement" that would sell out the South Vietnamese.

While supporting the president's policies and calling for even more escalation, Republicans were nonetheless critical of the president's failure to level with the American people, or, as Dirksen put it, "not being told the whole truth." Thus most could run in the elections as patriotic Americans who supported the military in Vietnam but not necessarily the way the president was prosecuting the war. With Democratic liberals deserting him on the war and Republicans staking out their own oppositional policy, Johnson's hopes for reelection were beginning to look more shaky. All presidents deny that they permit concerns about reelection or the prospects of their party to affect vital national security decisions. But they all do.

As the president surveyed the political landscape in the spring and summer of 1966, he entertained several options for dealing with the war during the campaign. When in May he referred to the doves as "nervous nellies," Democratic liberals feared he was trying to stifle dissent. Senator Fulbright's staff responded by wearing Nervous Nellie buttons. Unlike Richard Nixon, however, Johnson had a commitment to civil liberties that was strong enough to restrain him from publicly suggesting that his opponents were unpatriotic or cowardly, even though he expressed such thoughts privately. Late in 1967 he did say that "this dissent has [not] contributed to any victories we have had. . . . Please count to 10 before you say something that hurts instead of helps."

In 1966 Johnson generally remained circumspect in public. He rejected one adviser's campaign slogan, "A vote against Johnson is a vote for Hanoi," and decided not to use or even discuss the Vietnam War as a political issue during the 1966 campaign.

He was not worried only about Republican challenges in November. Elements in the predominantly Democratic peace groups decided to devote their energies that summer to nominating and electing anti-war Democrats to Congress. The National Conference for New Politics, organized earlier in the year, announced a fund-raising drive to collect $500,000 to pay for 1,000 campaign workers in two dozen contests. The doves came closest to their goal in a liberal district in the San Francisco Bay area where an anti-war Democrat received 45 percent of the vote against a liberal Democrat who backed the president on the war. The administration monitored that election closely and did everything it could to assist the incumbent. Overall at least 100 Democrats ran on peace platforms in 20 states during the election.

Despite their weak showing in the primaries, the one-district near win encouraged anti-Johnson factions in the party to continue their activities with an eye to the 1968 election. Among those encouraged were Curtis Gans and Allard Lowenstein, two young Democrat activists who began organizing doves to challenge Johnson's candidacy.

Congress was the target of many anti-war individuals and groups. According to one anti-war leader, while the president was insulated from public opinion by his aides, members of Congress "could be led on this issue. Often they . . . typified people having kind of a chocolate eclair for a backbone. I thought they could be had by pressure and public opinion." Presidents also considered congressional opinion to be one relatively accurate indicator of public opinion.

The White House was concerned as well about a referendum in Dearborn, Michigan, a predominantly blue-collar suburb of Detroit, where 41 percent of those voting called for an immediate ceasefire. (A majority of Dearbornites supported the same referendum when it was again proposed in November 1968.) The referendum had nothing to do with dissenting Democrats like Gans and Lowenstein. Orville Hubbard, the mayor of Dearborn, was a conservative Democrat whose main claim to fame was keeping blacks out of his suburb. He was also a former Marine who thought the war was not worth the lives of American boys, particularly since they came disproportionately from blue-collar families who made up much of the citizenry of Dearborn. He was serious enough about his views to demand a seat at the dais at an anti-war rally in Detroit. His demand, which he made as an elected official against the war, embarrassed most of the liberals in attendance who abhorred his notorious racial policies. In 1967 Hubbard added his name to an anti-war advertisement that was also signed by Dr. Martin Luther King, Jr. Politics sometimes does make strange bedfellows.

The Dearborn referendum had no practical effect on the Pentagon, but as the war continued other cities held similar referendums, giving the appearance that significant numbers of Americans disapproved of the continuation of the war. Johnson worried that the North Vietnamese would be encouraged by such referendums as well as by the victories of dovish candidates in local elections. Throughout both the Johnson and Nixon administrations, the presidents and their advisers feared that opposition to American military involvement, whether as evidenced in demonstrations, elections, or domestic politics, would encourage Hanoi to continue to fight until the doves forced their American leaders out of Vietnam.

During the 1966 campaign, dovish Republican senator George Aiken, with tongue in cheek, announced that the United States had fulfilled its commitment—it had stopped communism and won the war—and thus it could withdraw with its pride intact. When one of his aides, Leonard Marks, suggested to the president that it was not a bad idea—that he should just declare victory and bring the boys home—Johnson was furious. Later he told Marks that "in my gut I knew that you and George Aiken were right, and I couldn't do anything about it."

Instead Johnson called for a summit conference with South Vietnamese leaders in Manila. The conference would occur on the eve of the election in late October to publicize that the war was going well. Johnson told his advisers he wanted large crowds and favorable television coverage for this event, as well as for the rest of the 31,500-mile trip that took him to 7 countries in 17 days, the longest presidential trip in history.

Richard Nixon criticized the final communiqué from Manila because it called for "mutual withdrawal" from South Vietnam. He had carefully crafted his response with two wordsmiths, William Safire and Pat Buchanan, hoping it would attract attention. Safire was able to convince the *New York Times*'s Harrison Salisbury to run the critique in its entirety, and it appeared alongside a front-page news story on November 4. When the *Times* ran the two articles, the most important newspaper in the United States made it appear that Nixon was somehow the equal of the president, or at least the chief spokesperson for the Republican Party. Nixon received even more press when Johnson reacted angrily to his criticisms, calling him a "chronic campaigner" who "never realized what was going on even when he had an official office."

Johnson's anger may have been exaggerated. According to his aides, he wanted to elevate Nixon because in 1968 "the most vulnerable man in American politics" would be easy to beat. Nixon appeared vulnerable because of his image as a Neanderthal anti-Communist and an unprincipled politician. But he had always prided himself on his understanding of international relations and was in the process of fashioning a new image as a statesperson through foreign travel and observations on world events. He was pleased that Johnson had elevated him to leadership of his party.

Whatever Johnson's real motives, Nixon, whom the Republican National Committee chose to deliver the party's election-eve speech on November 5, 1966, was on his way to becoming the favorite for the 1968 Republican presidential nomination. His supporters later contended that the conflict with Johnson over the war on the eve of the 1966 election was the turning point in his nomination campaign. Later that month, Democratic senator Stuart Symington told Walt Rostow, "In 1968 Nixon will murder us. He will become the biggest dove of all times. There has never been a man in American public life that could turn so fast on a dime."

As expected in a by-election, the out-of-power Republicans made solid gains. They took 47 seats in the House to close the gap to 248–187, and 3 seats in the Senate where the Democrats emerged with a 64–36 advantage. The Democrats still commanded healthy majorities in both houses. The war did not figure directly in most of the elections, though Illinois Democratic senator Paul Douglas, a Johnson supporter, lost his seat to Republican Charles Percy, in part because dovish liberals deserted him. Mark Hatfield, a Republican dove, may have won his seat in Oregon because of his position on the war.

In December, Johnson's approval rating on his handling of the war fell to 43 percent. He also received a troubling letter from columnist Drew Pearson that offered the president a pessimistic perspective on his chances for reelection. And despite his large congressional majorities, the Great Society appeared to be winding down with Johnson devoting less of his time and fewer of Washington's resources to his pet programs. Democratic governors complained to him formally about his lack of attention to domestic politics as he searched for the end game in Vietnam.

Johnson was paying close attention to domestic politics but primarily those relating to fissures in the Democratic Party and his upcoming reelection campaign. In a memo to the president, McGeorge Bundy predicted that although Republicans would be unlikely to offer much of a policy alternative, debate about Vietnam would weaken the administration. More important, he warned that any settlement leading to a Communist takeover would result in a 1968 defeat.

Johnson faced the same problem that Kennedy had faced in 1962—and that Nixon would face in 1970. He had to construct Vietnam policy with one eye on the upcoming election. If he left Vietnam with a less than satisfactory peace that opened the door to a Communist takeover of the South, he would satisfy the doves but lay himself open to attacks from Republicans and hawks for "losing" a Free World bastion to the Communists. If he escalated more dramatically, even if it led to an improvement in the military situation, he would alienate the doves.

The dovish position had been strengthened immeasurably on Christmas Day 1966 when the *New York Times* published the first in a series of articles written by its distinguished foreign correspondent, Harrison Salisbury, reporting from Hanoi. Salisbury made international headlines when he affirmed North Vietnam's long-maintained position that U.S. bombing was killing civilians and destroying homes, schools, and hospitals. To this point the administration had claimed that North Vietnamese pronouncements about civilian casualties were propaganda—the bombing had been surgically applied only to military targets. Now Salisbury presented his own eyewitness evidence, including photographs, of the destruction of civilian targets. After initial denials, the Defense Department was compelled to admit that although it did not target civilians, some bombs might have gone astray and others might have hit military targets that the Communists had deliberately placed in civilian areas. One Defense Department official thought the administration "bungled" the issue and created "a national disaster."

The administration had its defenders. Taking their lead from Secretary of State Dean Rusk, who referred to Salisbury as "the man from the *Hanoi Times*," they accused him of being a traitor. The columnist's case was weakened when he revealed that some of his material came from official North Vietnamese sources. Nonetheless, after Salisbury's exposé, the administration could no longer maintain that its bombing destroyed only military infrastructures. It extracted a small measure of revenge when its supporters on the Pulitzer Prize committee succeeded in turning back the attempt to award Salisbury journalism's most coveted prize.

Other Americans traveled to Hanoi during the war, often bringing back U.S. prisoners of war and even peace plans, or, as Dean Rusk described them, returning to the United States "eight months pregnant with peace." Either because they were bamboozled or because they were sympathetic to the Communists, they also attested to the humane treatment of American POWs. Their use by the North Vietnamese may not have helped their cause in the United States, but it did influence opinion in European and neutral capitals, and it certainly served Hanoi's propaganda purposes among its own people.

It was bizarre to see American reporters, doves, and radicals in an enemy capital during wartime. One could not imagine an American journalist reporting from Tokyo or Berlin after Pearl Harbor. But Congress had not declared war against North Vietnam because the president chose not to ask for such a resolution. He feared that making the Vietnam War a "formal" war would endanger his Great Society at home and produce pressure from Americans to escalate more forcefully and apply rules of blockade to North Vietnam. Such actions might be challenged militarily by China and Russia. Because war had not been declared, the United States was not officially at war with anyone, let alone the North Vietnamese. Thus it was easier for anti-war elements to make their case in public without being considered dishonorable. It also made it easier for members of Congress, editors, columnists, and other public figures to call for an end to the war and to criticize the administration. And the absence of a war declaration made it virtually impossible to impose censorship, especially on the journalists in Vietnam who continued to report that things were not going well.

A considerable number of Americans, of course, saw little difference between a formally declared war and one that had not been declared. From their perspective, the hundreds of thousands of Americans who were in Vietnam risking their lives to defend democracy should have been supported in the same way as those millions who fought in World War II had been supported. Thus when people marched in the street against the war, and especially when journalists such as Harrison Salisbury seemed to aid the enemy through critical investigative journalism, many other Americans assailed the "enemy at home." Lips had been zipped during World War II—they should be zipped during the Vietnam War as well.

From the late sixties through the Nixon years, the allegedly unpatriotic media became a target for those who felt they were encouraging the enemy and discouraging their audience. Many politicians found the media—dominated, they claimed, by eastern liberals—to be a popular whipping boy. Both Presidents Johnson and Nixon believed the media were unfair to them and to their policies, with Nixon far more publicly antagonistic than Johnson. Both were concerned about the impact of a handful of editors and publishers, located in the East, who had an undue influence not only in setting the news agenda but in influencing public opinion. Both singled out the *New York Times* and the

Washington Post, *Time* and *Newsweek*, and the three television networks, ABC, CBS, and NBC, for special attention. Five of the seven had their headquarters in New York, the other two in Washington.

The television networks were somewhat different from the print media in that local affiliates exercised a good deal of editorial control. One channel in Detroit ran a fifteen-minute show every day featuring a conservative Wayne State University professor who refuted the alleged liberal distortions and biases on the 6:30 p.m. network newscast. When in 1967 Pete Seeger sang an anti-war song, "Waist Deep in the Big Muddy," in which he obliquely referred to Johnson as a "big fool," on the popular "Smothers Brothers Variety Show," several affiliates refused to carry the famed left-wing folk singer's performance.

It was not only the mass media that bothered the administration. Intellectual leaders and opinion makers in New York read and wrote in the strongly anti-war *New York Review of Books* and the *Village Voice*, among other relatively low-circulation weeklies. Later Joseph Califano, one of Johnson's aides, wrote that the president "misjudged the eventual power of the left in America, particularly in its influence on the formation of American public opinion."

The media's New York connection was a particularly inflammatory issue. Many Americans considered New York to be an exotic city dominated by ethnic minorities who had little relationship to or understanding of the rest of the country. When politicians attacked the eastern media they were also attacking the popular image of New York as a city dominated by Jewish people and culture. It did not help the national image of the seven major media institutions that all were either owned or headed by Jewish Americans, a failing that usually was left implicit by those who assailed their media.

It was also true that Jewish Americans were disproportionately liberal Democrats and that a disproportionate number of young Jewish Americans made up the leadership cadres of the New Left and the radical anti-war movement. Although Jews made up only 10 percent of the college student population, 23 percent of their number considered themselves to be part of the New Left. Twice as many Jewish students as others participated in political and civil rights campaigns, and four times as many as others protested U.S. foreign policy. In 1964 Johnson had received 93 percent of the Jewish vote, 11 percentage points higher than Kennedy in 1960.

Lyndon Johnson was bothered by the number of Jewish Americans who opposed his policies in Vietnam while he supported Israel in the Middle East. On several occasions he threatened to withdraw that support unless the Jewish community in the United States rallied around his war policies. He leaned on Israel to encourage its American friends to support him, suggesting that arms deliveries could be tied to Israel's ability to persuade Jewish Americans to refrain from joining the anti-war movement. Johnson was reacting to the fact that the Synagogue Council of America, which represented 3.5 million Jews, urged the president early in 1966 not to escalate during the bombing pause.

The administration's attacks on the media and others who allegedly behaved unpatriotically during wartime contributed to the growing polarization of American society. On the "unpatriotic" side stood blacks who were rioting in the streets; anti-war protesters who dishonored the flag at their frequent rowdy demonstrations; hippies and other members of the counter-culture who challenged mainstream American values; women's liberationists, Native Americans, Hispanic Americans, and gays who were demanding equal rights; and liberals, journalists, intellectuals, television network executives, and Hollywood studio moguls who, through their columns, news programs, and even movies, celebrated and defended the radicals, rioters, and dissenters—or so it seemed.

It was easy for Republicans especially to seize the flag and the values of the 1950s as they called for a return to "law and order." This polarization probably would have occurred without the Vietnam War, but the fact that a majority of Americans viewed the anti-war movement's spirited mass demonstrations as unpatriotic behavior accelerated the cultural divide in the United States. Poll after poll revealed that many Americans who privately opposed the war opposed the anti-war protesters even more.

Many of them joined Lyndon Johnson in contending that domestic and foreign Communist influences had power in the protest movement. In March 1966 the president noted in private, "Make no mistake about the Comm[unists]. Don't kid yourself for a moment. It is in the highest counsels of gov[ernment]—in our society. McCarthy's methods were wrong—but the threat is greater now than in his day." Johnson was too much of a Democrat and a civil libertarian to pursue this issue in public, but that did not stop him from encouraging the intelligence services to expand their illegal and extralegal surveillance and harassment of anti-war groups. As early as April 1965 Johnson asked FBI director J. Edgar Hoover to brief several congressional leaders about alleged Communist influence in the anti-war movement. The agency began wiretapping the Students for a Democratic Society in May of that year. In 1967 Johnson ordered the CIA to launch Operation Chaos, which by 1974 had developed files on more than 300,000 citizens—even though the CIA's charter forbade it to operate within the United States.

In his retirement Johnson went even further in his claims about the Communists' relationship to the anti-war movement. After Kennedy and King came out against the war, Johnson contended that "the Communists stepped in. They control the three major networks, you know, and the forty major outlets of communication. It's all in the FBI reports. They prove everything. Not just about the reporters but about the professors too." The problem was that the FBI reports that Johnson, and later Nixon, requested to demonstrate Communist influence in the anti-war movement turned up virtually no evidence of his inflammatory accusations. Nixon would soon escalate the secret and illegal war against alleged subversives and political enemies—with dire consequences for his presidency.

As 1966 drew to a close, the war in Vietnam increasingly dominated the domestic political landscape. With no end in sight, it had become the single most important issue confronting the nation. It had engulfed the presidency of a powerful and once-effective politician who hoped to win the war on poverty and provide economic justice and opportunity to minorities and the disadvantaged. But President Johnson could not successfully conduct his War on Poverty until he could bring the war in Southeast Asia to a speedy and politically acceptable conclusion in time for his 1968 reelection campaign.

5

The Opposition Grows, 1967

ALTHOUGH THE UNITED STATES won battle after battle on the ground in Vietnam in 1966 and proclaimed success in destroying enemy cadres, the light at the end of the tunnel remained dim, U.S. casualties continued to rise, and the president had to periodically dispatch reenforcements. By the end of 1966 there were almost 400,000 American troops "in country." In January 1967 the difficult situation was reflected in polls that revealed only 38 percent approval for Johnson's policies in Vietnam against 43 percent disapproval. The Senate reflected this distribution with one-third emerging as hawks, one-third as doves, and one-third as dawks. One of the president's political aides feared that, as the 1968 election approached, the Democratic Party would please few voters with its posture as "the war party on Monday, Wednesday and Friday, and the appeasement party on Tuesday, Thursday and Saturday."

Johnson's problems were compounded immeasurably by the entry of Bobby Kennedy into the national debate. He had expressed dovish sentiments in 1965 and 1966 supporting a "compromise government" in South Vietnam, but he had not been among the leading anti-war senators. In late November 1966 he did joke sardonically that with the bombing of North Vietnam, "We've solved their unemployment problem for them, putting them to work repairing bridges and roads." The problem for Johnson came in early February 1967 when Kennedy made statements at Oxford University and in an off-the-record press conference in Paris that hinted at the secret talks under way between W. Averell Harriman and the Communists. Johnson had informed Congress about these negotiations but had wanted them kept secret so as to avoid offending South Vietnam. At that same press conference, Kennedy announced, "I am not a strong advocate of the bombings . . . they do not accomplish any military purposes." He also met with a French diplomat who told him that Hanoi was willing to begin negotiations with the United States if Washington ended the bombing unconditionally. A story about that initiative also leaked to the *New York Times*, further infuriating Johnson.

Johnson met with Kennedy on February 6 and allegedly threatened, "I'll destroy you and every one of your dove friends in six months. You'll be dead politically in six months." When Kennedy finally informed him about a bombing halt leading to negotiations, Johnson replied, "There isn't a chance in hell that I will do that." One wonders whether Kennedy's association with the bombing halt made Johnson even more resistant to accepting it.

A promising initiative was then taking place in London involving British prime minister Harold Wilson and Soviet prime minister Alexei Kosygin. It was not coincidental that the administration's negotiating line on this initiative toughened considerably immediately after the Kennedy flap. Earlier Johnson did not wish to look as though he was appeasing Fulbright; now he did not wish to look as though he was appeasing Kennedy.

An added irritant was the publication of William Manchester's best-selling book about the Kennedy assassination, *Death of a President*. Johnson, who felt that Bobby Kennedy influenced the author's unflattering depiction of him, wanted the Kennedy family to stop the book's publication. The president's widow did bring suit against Manchester demanding that he make a number of changes in the book, many of them relating to his depiction of Johnson. Although Manchester agreed to make some of

the editorial changes requested, Johnson aide John Roche continued to believe that Kennedy had "a vested interest in the defeat
of the national ticket in 1968."

News of the acrimonious Johnson-Kennedy meeting, which
ended with Kennedy walking out, saying, "Look, I don't have to
take that from you," also leaked to the press. Kennedy told
friends that Johnson had been "abusive"; *Time* reported, most
likely erroneously, that Johnson had called Kennedy a "son of a
bitch" to his face. The rift between the two men and their two
factions of the Democratic Party now was too wide to be
breached. With a speech on March 2, Kennedy made his break
from the administration complete. Privately he explained, "I've
tried to stop the war in every way I can, but Johnson can't be
stopped." In his speech he did not call for immediate withdrawal
but laid out a moderate peace plan, the centerpiece of which was
a cessation of the bombing. Kennedy's approval ratings dropped
11 percent in the wake of the speech.

Johnson, for whom, according to aide Lawrence O'Brien,
"Congress was a twenty-four-hour-a-day obsession," called on
his friends to attack Kennedy's position. In a bipartisan one-two,
Washington's Democratic senator Henry Jackson and Republican Minority Leader Everett Dirksen critiqued the position
adopted by the president's bitter rival. Congress rallied around
the president on a military appropriations bill in March with the
Senate approving it by a 77 to 3 vote and the House by 385 to 11.
Mansfield was able to attach an amendment proclaiming Congress's support for the military in Vietnam (and, some contended, implicitly for the president's policy) but also support for
the Geneva Conference system of 1954 and 1962. When a dovish
representative offered another amendment to the appropriations
bill prohibiting the use of funds for military operations in or over
North Vietnam, it was defeated by a 372 to 18 vote.

The appropriations vote legitimized the president's policy. In
January he had contemplated asking Congress for another Gulf

of Tonkin Resolution supporting his actions in Vietnam, but advisers warned there would be considerable opposition and a divisive debate. He settled for the overwhelming victory on the appropriations bill.

Victory in the war was no closer, however. McGeorge Bundy warned his former boss that even continued escalation would not end the war before the 1968 elections. He was convinced that Hanoi was willing to wait out the elections to see how they affected U.S. policy. According to the president, North Vietnam was not merely waiting until the elections were over; it was trying to influence U.S. war policy. Johnson believed that the North Vietnamese were playing to Congress and public opinion in their diplomatic and public relations activities in an attempt to build up dovish pressure before the 1968 election.

There was little Johnson's supporters in Congress could do about the other major liberal defection in the spring of 1967, when Dr. Martin Luther King, Jr., publicly joined the anti-war movement and immediately became one of its most important leaders. King, who had won the Nobel Peace Prize, had been mildly critical of the U.S. war effort in 1965 and 1966 but had kept his strongest feelings to himself. He was unwilling to antagonize the man who had done more for black America than any president since Abraham Lincoln. He did say in May 1965 that "The war in Vietnam must be stopped. There must be a negotiated settlement even with the Vietcong," but he rarely spoke as bluntly over the next two years. Nevertheless, as early as November 1965 the White House worried about a possible alliance between the anti-war and civil rights movements.

Other moderate-to-liberal black leaders also held their tongues, relishing their cordial and politically potent ties to the administration. At a White House conference on civil rights in June 1966, some in attendance considered voting on an anti-war resolution but found it difficult to do so in the home of the president who had done so much for their cause. That traditional leadership was threatened by the Black Power movement, which saw a link between an alleged racist war in Vietnam and racism in the United States. Two weeks after the White House conference, Stokely Carmichael, the charismatic leader of the Student Non-Violent Coordinating Committee (SNCC), announced, "We're asking Negroes not to go to Vietnam and fight but to stay in Greenwood [Mississippi] and fight here." Or more directly, as a young black man from the Watts district of Los Angeles had earlier proclaimed, "If I've got to die, I ain't dying in Vietnam, I'm going to die here."

The Black Panthers in particular, a headline-attracting new organization of militant black nationalists, saw their struggle as part of the worldwide struggle of people of color against white imperialism. Huey Newton, one of their leaders, contended that "as Vietnam should be able to determine its own destiny . . . we in the black colony in America want . . . power over our destiny." Eldridge Cleaver, their most famous author, wrote in *Soul on Ice*, "Blacks . . . all over America could now see the Viet Cong's point: both were on the receiving end of what the armed forces were dishing out."

The relationship between the war in Vietnam and racial conflict at home could no longer be avoided by King if he wanted to maintain credibility among his supporters. In late March 1967 in Chicago and in early April in New York, King delivered speeches in which he claimed that the United States was "committing atrocities equal to any perpetrated by the Viet Cong" and that his country was "the greatest purveyor of violence in the world." He was genuinely distressed by what he perceived to be the immorality of the U.S. position in Vietnam and was especially concerned about what the diversion of Great Society resources to the war meant for his people. He lamented that young black men were fighting "eight thousand miles away to guarantee liberties in Southeast Asia which they had not found in Southwest Georgia or East Harlem."

In recent months King had moved dramatically from a concentration on civil rights issues to economic issues. He linked the problem of race in American society to class, a linkage he had first highlighted in 1963 in his address at the March on Washington for Jobs and Freedom. Like other liberals, he worried about the decline in funding for existing Great Society programs and the apparent ending of new reform initiatives. During the upcoming fiscal year, the administration's budget revealed a 35 percent decline in social welfare spending. Guns had finally trumped butter at the time of the most serious urban disturbances in U.S. cities, disturbances King attributed in good part to the economic conditions in northern ghettos.

King had come to his decision when he did in part because of an exposé in *Ramparts* magazine about the U.S. use of napalm in Vietnam. *Ramparts*, the slick left-wing newsmonthly, periodically revealed embarrassing secrets about American policy in Vietnam. It was the magazine that broke the story about Michigan State University's training of the brutal South Vietnamese secret police and CIA funding of the National Student Association. There had always been small radical and Communist newspapers and magazines such as the *Daily Worker* and the *Guardian* in the United States, but none had the circulation and professional look of *Ramparts*. Along with the *Village Voice* and the *New York Review of Books*, *Ramparts* provided opponents of the war with a steady diet of articles critical of the administration. Few times in American history have left-wing publications made headlines in the mainstream media so frequently with their reportage and commentary.

Although King was being challenged by radical leaders of SNCC, the Black Panthers, and the Congress on Racial Equality (CORE) for the allegiances of young blacks, he still commanded a towering position in his community, and as black radicals became more violent in their rhetoric and actions, he had become even more respected in the once-hostile white community. After his assault against Johnson's policies, King became one of the co-chairs of a new organization, Negotiations Now!. On April 15 he led the largest anti-war protest to date, a march from New York's Central Park to the United Nations that drew more than 200,000 participants. On top of that signal success for the anti-war movement, some liberals in the Democratic Party began talking about running King for president or perhaps vice president on a ticket headed by Bobby Kennedy. Others hoped King might head up a third-party effort. Either way he might siphon off from one-half to one-third of traditionally Democratic black voters and throw the election to the Republicans.

Fortunately for Johnson, another key element in the Democratic coalition, organized labor, remained loyal despite rumblings of anti-war opposition from elements in the traditionally left-of-center unions such as the United Auto Workers, the International Longshoremen's Union, and the United Electrical Workers. Those rumblings included a November 1967 conference of the Labor Leadership Assembly for Peace that attracted 523 leaders from 38 states. The next month, however, the president was well received at the AFL-CIO annual convention where he knew that "many of labor's sons have left their homes to risk their lives in Vietnam. . . . I know that you regret every dollar spent on the war—dollars that should be spent on the works of peace. But you and I know that we must persevere."

Mainstream union leaders, especially the AFL-CIO's George Meany, were firm cold war anti-Communists who also knew that defense industries provided lucrative jobs for many of their members. In addition, the college-educated, middle- and upper-class leaders of the anti-war movement appeared to oppose traditional values they supported. They often talked in leftist jargon that irritated union leaders who had been through bloody battles with Communists, Trotskyists, and other radicals in the thirties and forties. Many rank-and-file union members, no matter their views on the war and no matter their views on union-management relations, had begun to line up on the side of the national cultural divide that supported law-and-order politicians who promised to bring peace to their neighborhoods. Most would still follow their leaders toward the Democratic camp in 1968, but the trickle of defections became a torrent in the 1972 election.

Although the GOP was generally hawkish, demanding more decisive action from the president, several prominent Republicans lent their energies to the Democratic-dominated dovish cause, including Senators Goodell, Percy, Hatfield, Javits, Aiken, Cooper, and Case, all of whom, save for Percy and Cooper, came from the Northeast or the West Coast where anti-war sentiment was strong. In those and other states, anti-war Republicans joined anti-war Democrats to pressure Democratic supporters of the president such as Indiana senator Birch Bayh, Oklahoma senator Fred Harris, Maine senator Edmund Muskie, and Michigan senator Phillip Hart, in whose states the failing Vietnam policy was working against incumbents. Some Democrats admitted that they began to criticize the president on the war in order to maintain credibility among their constituents. Senator Joseph Tydings (D-MD) confided to a Johnson aide, "Any reasonably good Republican could clobber me if the election were held today." Johnson loyalist Massachusetts congressman Tip O'Neill expressed his opposition to the war in a constituent newsletter in September 1967, an act that brought the wrath of the president upon him. O'Neill had been influenced by briefings with military and intelligence officials who were not sanguine about prospects for ending the war soon. With the middle slipping away from him as reflected in O'Neill's defection, Johnson and his supporters faced increasing bipartisan opposition from hawks and doves. To little avail, John Roche called for "tough-minded liberals" to take on the "nihilists, commies, and opportunists" whom he felt constituted the anti-war movement.

Although he worried about Republican doves, Johnson's greatest concern was his own party. In May, Senator Church drew together fifteen other senators to issue a joint statement, cleared in advance with the State Department, expressing their commitment to a negotiated settlement. The next month Senator Clairborne Pell (D-RI) traveled to Paris to talk to a North Vietnamese diplomat at that diplomat's initiative. Several months later, senators introduced a resolution, opposed by the president, to ask the UN Security Council for assistance in ending the war. The previous March, several members of the Foreign Relations Committee had met with UN Secretary General U Thant for three hours to discuss Vietnam. As senators flexed their muscles sensing the president's waning political strength, such independent initiatives were becoming more common.

Senators even began talking about resurrecting their power to declare war. Fulbright held hearings in August on his National Commitments resolution that would call for a congressional vote when the commander-in-chief sent American forces into a combat zone. In 1973 those hearings ultimately led to congressional adoption of the War Powers Resolution. But it would be some time before Fulbright and his supporters could muster much support for their effort. Members of the Foreign Relations Committee were disturbed when Under Secretary of State Nicholas Katzenbach explained that the "expression of declaring a war is one that has become outmoded in the international arena." Senator Eugene McCarthy remembered being insulted when Katzenbach claimed that the Gulf of Tonkin Resolution justified everything the administration was doing in Vietnam.

Of more immediate concern to Johnson were the hearings held the same month in the Senate Preparedness Subcommittee of the Armed Services Committee. Here McNamara and the Joint Chiefs clashed in their evaluations of progress in the war. Commenting on the conflicting views, the secretary noted, "The Constitution gives the responsibility of Commander in Chief to a civilian" who was not to "follow blindly the recommendations of his military advisers." Because of their conflict with McNamara, exposed before the Stennis Committee, the Joint Chiefs contemplated resigning en masse, going as far as to set a time for a press conference to announce their unprecedented act. At the last moment they decided not to engage in what could be seen as a mass mutiny. Aware of the bitter conflicts between his secretary and the chiefs, Johnson began thinking about the need to replace McNamara. He also worried about the secretary's uncharacteristically emotional behavior and his rationality. The first secretary of defense, James Forrestal, had suffered a nervous breakdown in 1949 and ultimately committed suicide, in good measure due to the pressures of his job.

McNamara had lost confidence in the ability of the United States to compel the Viet Cong and the North Vietnamese military to agree to acceptable peace terms. He had become depressed about his role in supporting the bombing and escalation in 1965 and hated it when people referred to "McNamara's War." He was beset from all sides; his friend Jacqueline Kennedy once beat him on the chest as she tearfully asked him to "do something to stop the slaughter." In a Seattle airport a man spat at him and called him a "murderer." Both Margy, his wife, and his dovish-activist son Craig developed ulcers during the period. And when Margy died in 1981 after a long illness, he blamed it in part on pressures related to the experience of the Vietnam War.

During the month of those two important Senate hearings, Johnson's aides began personally to poll Democrats in Congress. Of 137 legislators interviewed, 104 were negative toward the president, 22 were positive, and 25 were noncommittal. Still, that did not mean that all those who were negative were ready to support an insurgent campaign to seize the nomination from the president. Johnson was confident he could defeat any primary challenge. He knew he could win the nomination because he controlled the party, and the party controlled the nomination process. Although some state parties were bound by the results of primary elections, there were not enough of them to balance the states that held conventions and closed caucuses to make their choices for the national ticket. But after the public bloodletting of a primary campaign, the president feared he might be fatally wounded for the national contest.

Democratic insurgents understood the situation and hoped to win enough primaries with dovish challengers that the party would be forced to drop Johnson, or Johnson would be forced to alter his war policy. At the end of 1966 and into 1967, committees of Concerned Democrats and Dissenting Democrats in many states joined with the powerful Reform Democratic Movement in New York and California's Democratic Council to demand a change in either national leadership or national policy. In Michigan, the state's party chair, one of the founders of a Concerned Democrat group, resigned his position because of the war. On May 20, 1967, the Americans for Democratic Action announced that it would support anyone who promised to extricate the United States from the Vietnam quagmire in an honorable fashion.

Former National Student Association president and liberal activist Allard Lowenstein, who had set out after the 1966 elections to remake his party, was joined by ADA staffer Curtis Gans in the fall. Soon the two were at the center of an initiative to find someone to oppose Johnson during the 1968 primary season. Their first choice was Bobby Kennedy. On August 4, 1967, Lowenstein broached the issue to the New York senator but found him not enthusiastic about taking on Johnson. Less than two weeks later at a National Student Association convention in College Park, Maryland, Lowenstein announced the formation of a "Dump Johnson" movement. He explained, "We had to start with the students because we had no money."

Lowenstein met with Kennedy again on September 23 at his Hickory Hill estate to try to persuade him to run. Kennedy, who listened to liberal columnist Jack Newfield tell him to run and Arthur Schlesinger advise him against it, finally decided (at least for 1967) that he would not oppose the president. Even though a Harris poll showed him leading LBJ by a 51 to 39 percent margin, Kennedy figured victory would be a long shot at best, and the issue of the war would be submerged in the personal conflict between Johnson and the so-called Kennedy camp. No doubt he was concerned about looking like a traitor to party regulars, a supposition that might have made it difficult for the young politician to run for election in 1972 or later. He feared that "People would say that I was splitting the party out of ambition and envy." The fact that Kennedy ruled out running did not stop his aides from continuing to plan strategy for a possible candidacy. And the senator offered no objections to those sessions.

With Kennedy's apparently firm rejection, Lowenstein and Gans looked elsewhere. Among those who turned them down were the Canadian-born John Kenneth Galbraith, who was surprised to discover he was ineligible for the presidency; General James Gavin, who revealed that he was a Republican; Representative Don Edwards of California, and Senators McGovern and Church, both of whom faced 1968 reelection campaigns. On October 20, 1967, almost at the final moment to launch a primary campaign and as the insurgents were running out of options, Senator Eugene McCarthy of Minnesota expressed interest in challenging Johnson. On November 30, after speaking engagements in Los Angeles and Detroit where he was greeted by enthusiastic crowds, McCarthy announced his candidacy. That same day the Senate voted unanimously for a resolution calling for the UN Security Council to help the United States find a way out of the war.

Although Lowenstein and Gans spearheaded the insurgency, other important Democrats fell in behind McCarthy. As early as January 1967, remnants of the Adlai Stevenson wing of the party had even broached the issue of challenging the president with McCarthy. In November he spent a good deal of time consulting

with them before he accepted Lowenstein and Gans's offer. Mc-
Carthy was still smarting from his embarrassment in 1964 when
Johnson publicly dangled the vice presidency in front of him and
then withdrew it. He "vowed I would get that son of a bitch, and
I did."

The challenger was a little-known senator from the back
benches who felt strongly about the war. A poet and something
of an intellectual, McCarthy was an understated, uncharismatic,
and unenergetic campaigner who did not relish fund-raising or
meeting with supporters. He admitted, "I'm not much of a pro-
jection man." One of Johnson's aides was pleased with the senator's challenge—"Gene's entry into the race is the greatest thing
that could happen to Johnson; he's so weak he makes even Johnson look good."

McCarthy was essentially a one-issue candidate, but he did attack the president for "abusing the Senate." On the stump he
struck the anti-Johnson *Village Voice* as "dull and vague, without
either poetry or balls." He knew he was not as popular or as
charismatic a campaigner as Robert Kennedy, who was Mc-
Carthy's own choice to lead the insurgency.

McCarthy's selection by Lowenstein and Gans demonstrated
how desperate they were to field a candidate and how powerful
Johnson still appeared to those who might have been able to
mount a more plausible campaign. But they knew how the system
was stacked against them. McCarthy, who did not expect to win,
felt strongly enough about the war to sacrifice his political future
tilting at windmills. Yet for a while he even hesitated entering the
first-in-the-nation New Hampshire primary. According to fellow
dove George McGovern, Lowenstein and Gans "were looking for
someone to frighten Johnson into changing his policy. They never
thought of actually taking the nomination away from him."

Johnson was more concerned about the unpopularity of the
war than he was about the challenge from this obscure Minnesota senator. In October his presidential approval rating had

fallen to 38 percent; the corresponding figure for his handling of the war was just 27 percent. By the end of 1967 he was working harder than ever to identify a formula that would end the war before it had a significant impact on his own and his party's election prospects. He was reeling from the most dramatic anti-war demonstration of his administration, the Siege of the Pentagon on October 23, 1967, which, according to Attorney General Ramsey Clark, was "the moment the fever broke in the whole anti-war movement."

The siege was not the largest demonstration of the period, but it was one of the most photogenic. The day's events began at the Lincoln Memorial where 50,000 or more had gathered to listen to speeches and music in a by-then traditional anti-war demonstration. Roughly 35,000 of those in attendance accepted the call to march across the Potomac to the Pentagon to "confront the warmakers." The world was then treated to evocative images of mostly young, long-haired American anti-warriors literally coming face-to-face with equally young, short-haired warriors in uniform, armed with rifles, guarding the complex. The most photographed sequence involved a long-haired youth putting long-stemmed daisies into the gun barrels of the soldiers in the defense line. The incantations of some of the protesters did not cause the Pentagon to rise into the air to permit the evil inside to fall out, as siege leader Abbie Hoffman had promised. But the Siege of the Pentagon, with American citizens directly confronting their military, turned out to be a successful demonstration as measured by the administration's response.

In November Johnson ordered General William Westmoreland and Ambassador Ellsworth Bunker to return from Saigon. Together they would assure the restive population that their boys were doing well in Vietnam and an end was in sight. Their overoptimistic evaluations would be remembered a little more than two months later when television newscasts showed Viet Cong sappers inside the U.S. embassy compound in Saigon.

Aside from politics, Johnson had to be concerned about deteriorating economic conditions. With only a few months to go before primary season, the economy was in decline, in good measure because of the war and the way it was being financed. In 1966, despite the relatively healthy economy, Johnson's key economic advisers—Gardner Ackley from the Council of Economic Advisers, Charles Schultze from the Bureau of the Budget, and Secretary of the Treasury Henry Fowler—had called for a tax increase to pay for the war, as well as a cut in spending and the suspension of the investment tax credit. Congress suspended the tax credit that year. But, as usual in U.S. politics, short-term political concerns trumped responsible long-term economic policy. Republican candidate Richard Nixon pledged to let the law suspending the investment tax credit expire in 1969 once he was elected. Needless to say, this campaign promise cheered some in the business community who traditionally supported Republicans.

Wilbur Mills, chair of the House Appropriations Committee, still opposed a general tax increase. Instead he advised Johnson to omit from his 1966–1967 budget the supplemental costs of the war. The president asked Congress for only $10 billion for Vietnam even though he knew the cost would be somewhere between $16 and $18 billion. He was going to run a large deficit, with its increased inflationary pressures, because of that deception.

From 1967 to 1968, defense spending jumped from 7.9 percent of the gross domestic product to 10 percent. The direct cost of the war in 1965 was $5 billion; in 1968 it was $33 billion. Given these ever-increasing costs, sound economics demanded raising taxes or cutting domestic programs, or both. In the words of a White House economist, "Vietnam has taken our pin money." One interesting partial solution to the problem, tax reform to close some of the gaping loopholes, did not interest Congress. Time and again Johnson's Council of Economic Advisers warned the president of dire consequences if he did not raise taxes, cut spending, or both. In April 1967 the Senate's Joint Economic Committee held hearings in which many witnesses presented solid evidence of the war's impact on the economy.

During much of 1967 the economy did have its bright spots. In January, unemployment levels were at a thirteen-year low and wages were the highest they had been in American history. But the rise in interest rates and the 4.5 percent gain in the consumer price index over the previous eighteen months were worrisome. Those looming problems led to a debate between Republicans and Democrats over the guns-versus-butter issue. Liberal Democrats wanted more spending on social programs while most Republicans and some Southern Democrats, who supported more defense spending, would not back a tax increase without a cut in Great Society programs. Mills told the president that in order to obtain a tax increase, he would have to offer "major slashes in domestic spending."

Quite reluctantly in the fall of 1967, Johnson felt compelled to ask Congress to enact a 10 percent surtax and, as part of the deal, promised to make cuts in 1968 in nondefense spending amounting to around $6 billion. The Great Society, never generously funded in the first place, was beginning to wind down. From 1965 through 1970 the Office of Economic Opportunity received 1.5 percent of the federal budget. That meant that if all those living below the poverty level received a direct cash payment from OEO programs, it would have averaged $70 a year per person—hardly enough to win a war on poverty. Moreover, the rise in inflation, related in part to Johnson's war expenditures, hit the poorest the hardest in terms of their buying power for essential goods and services. So they faced a double threat—the rise in their living costs and a decline in government programs. Even with the surtax, the deficit grew from $3.8 billion in fiscal 1966 to $25.2 billion, or 3 percent of gross national product, in fiscal 1968. Inflation rose to 6.1 percent in 1969.

While most in the business community called for fewer taxes and less spending on social programs, a minority was distressed with what they perceived as the war's pernicious effect on the economy. In May 1967 a new organization, Business Executives Move for Peace (BEM), placed an ad in the *New York Times* opposing the war on the practical grounds that it was damaging the economy. "As businessmen we feel that when a policy hasn't proven productive after a reasonable trial, it's sheer nonsense not to try to change it." BEM claimed sixteen hundred members that spring.

In August, Marriner Eccles, a former chair of the Federal Reserve Board, called for immediate withdrawal from the war because of its impact on the economy and on national priorities. Economists as well as businesspeople were also concerned about the weakness of the dollar and the growing trade deficit, both of which related in part to the weakening of the economy and the cost of the war. In 1965 and again in 1966 the United States was forced to bail out the British pound because of the fear that the devalued dollar, the world's other reserve currency, would be next. As for trade, Japan, for example, sold Washington $7 billion worth of war materials between 1965 and 1972, contributing to a fourfold increase in its exports to the United States. If that was not bad enough, observers at home as well as abroad were astonished by the unprecedented urban rioting in the United States, mostly in northern cities. It began in 1965 in Los Angeles and peaked in terms of deaths in 1967 with disturbances in Detroit and Newark. FBI officials worried about the impact of black veterans, trained in guerrilla warfare, returning from Vietnam to their turbulent communities. The United States, it seemed, was unraveling economically, politically, and socially.

In the second half of 1967, Johnson could find some good news. First, a serious contender for the Republican nomination for president faded after he made a Vietnam-related gaffe on a local Detroit television talk show. George Romney, the moderate Republican governor from Michigan who was something of a dove, told an interviewer on August 31, "I just had the greatest brain-washing that anybody can get when you go over to Vietnam." He was referring to the briefings he received from the military during his visit to the combat theatre. Eugene McCarthy suggested that when it came to brainwashing the amiable but not especially swift Romney, "a light rinse would have been sufficient."

After the story hit the national media, Romney's support in the polls began to evaporate. Many Americans felt that anyone who could be brainwashed was not smart enough to be president. Others thought Romney was criticizing Bunker and Westmoreland unfairly. Thus the Vietnam War indirectly contributed to ending the presidential ambitions of a moderate Republican, with an impressive resumé in business and government, who looked like a candidate from central casting.

On October 16 the formation of a prestigious Johnson support group, the National Committee for Peace and Freedom in Vietnam, was announced. Headed by former senator Paul Douglas, its two honorary co-chairs were Presidents Truman and Eisenhower. The White House secretly assisted Douglas in forming the committee, which to most Americans appeared to represent a spontaneous outpouring of establishment support for the administration's Vietnam policy. John Roche, a former leader of the liberal ADA, now a Johnson aide, was the chief operator behind the scenes. He told the president, "I will leave no tracks." He later saw nothing wrong with his under-the-table assistance in the foundation of an organization that joined the battle for America's hearts and minds. In December, Johnson was buoyed by co-chair Eisenhower, who in one of his few public comments on the war, announced that he would strongly oppose any precipitous pullout from Vietnam.

As 1967 drew to a close, Johnson was still confident that he would be the 1968 Democratic standard-bearer. Though an end to the war was still not in sight, Pentagon battle-death data revealed

that the enemy was paying a tremendous price to maintain its un-
yielding diplomatic position. As General Westmoreland told the
president and the country in November, the United States was
winning battle after battle. Yes, the challenge from dovish Democrats and the Kennedy forces, allegedly behind the scene, angered
Johnson. He was troubled as well by the deteriorating economy,
the growth of the anti-war movement, and urban rebellion. But
as he began the last year of his term, he was still in control of his
party and expected to be running against an eminently beatable
Republican opponent.

6

Campaign '68

MORE THAN IN MOST ELECTIONS, foreign policy issues, particularly the war in Vietnam, were an ominous presence for voters and candidates alike in Campaign '68. According to Lewis Chester, Godfrey Hodgson, and Bruce Page, who chronicled the election, their "narrative without Vietnam would be like Hamlet without the murdered king." But, paradoxically, neither party was able to attract voters based on its position on the war, for both parties' candidates, Richard Nixon and Hubert Humphrey, promised peace with honor. Only during the Democrats' primary campaign did voters see a clear distinction between the candidates on the war, with Eugene McCarthy and Robert Kennedy promising to end it much faster than the president whose policies they attacked.

Aside from his relative obscurity and less than energetic campaigning style, McCarthy's main problem was that there were too few binding primaries to gather enough delegates for the convention. The majority belonged to the president, who controlled most of the levers of power within the party. McCarthy could only hope that his candidacy would energize anti-war sentiment in the Democratic Party and compel the president to alter his Vietnam policy.

Although Johnson looked like the certain nominee as the campaign season began, January 1968 was not one of his better months. He was *Time*'s "Man of the Year," but David Levine's cover-page cartoon featured him as King Lear, assaulted by "family" members. One such family member was Health, Education and Welfare Secretary John Gardner who, unable to support the president's reelection because of domestic budget cuts related to the war effort, resigned. In addition, more than 40 percent of the population told pollsters that they thought getting involved in Vietnam had been a mistake, Johnson's approval ratings hovered in the low thirties, American battle deaths and casualties had reached 20,000 and 150,000 respectively, and economic weakness, affected by the president's guns *and* butter policies, had compelled him to call for the unpopular 10 percent tax surcharge. With a run on gold in March, the chair of the Federal Reserve Board worried about the "worst financial crisis" since 1931. McCarthy's low-key Vietnam stump speech stressed the cost of the war to the country in terms of lives, its values, and the economy.

On January 21 a B-52 carrying four hydrogen bombs crashed off the coast of Greenland. That accident was all but forgotten two days later when North Korea captured an American intelligence vessel, the *Pueblo*, without a fight. Nixon, who claimed that Johnson had made "an incredible blunder" in the incident, referred to it throughout the campaign as an example of the administration's timid policies.

In early January, Robert Kennedy had begun rethinking the decision about his candidacy. He seemed ready to enter the campaign on January 19, in part because he was upset about the appointment as secretary of defense of Clark Clifford, whom he erroneously equated with Attila the Hun. But the *Pueblo* crisis caused him to back off to a point where on January 30 he could "not conceive of any circumstances in which I would run."

Circumstances changed almost at once with North Vietnam's Tet Offensive, news of which reached the United States just after Kennedy offered his seemingly categorical disavowal. In his State of the Union message on January 17, Johnson had hailed the "progress" being made in Vietnam with "the enemy . . . defeated in battle after battle." That optimism followed the November victory lap taken by General Westmoreland and Ambassador Bunker in speaking tours across the country. And now the Communists had launched a nationwide conventional offensive with Viet Cong sappers entering the U.S. embassy compound in Saigon, a shocking and bloody intrusion seen on television news. At that point polling only 10 percent of New Hampshire voters, McCarthy was quick to pick up on the political significance of the Tet Offensive. "Only a few months ago we were told that 65 percent of the population [of South Vietnam] was secure. Now we know that even the American embassy is not secure."

The Tet Offensive was to American politics what the shocking capture of Dien Bien Phu had been to French politics fourteen years earlier. The Communist offensive was eventually turned back by the middle of February, but not before Americans discovered that the enemy was far from beaten. Television viewers were astounded to see the Saigon chief of police execute with a shot to the temple an unarmed Viet Cong prisoner on a city street. They did not know that the South Vietnamese suspected the young man of attacking a building sheltering family members of government officials. Even had they known the probable circumstances of the incident, the gruesome footage would have made Americans wonder about the sort of people their government was backing. In the Pentagon the relative initial success of the attacks from a battered enemy led Secretary of Defense Clifford to begin an agonizing reappraisal of the Vietnam project.

Clifford discovered that his military chieftains had no plans for victory except more of the same, including an additional 206,000 troops to add to the more than 540,000 already there. He organized what he called a "cabal" of like-minded officials in the White House and the Pentagon to persuade the president to begin thinking about de-escalation. By 1968 the United States had already committed to Vietnam 40 percent of its combat-ready divisions, 50 percent of its tactical air power, and 30 percent of its naval power.

Suddenly McCarthy's chances in the March 12, first-in-the-nation New Hampshire primary improved, as hordes of students from more than one hundred colleges—"Clean for Gene"—flocked to the state to work on his campaign, along with celebrities such as Paul Newman and Dustin Hoffman. After cutting their beards and hair, putting on coats and ties and skirts and heels, as many as five thousand students traveled to New Hampshire on weekends to ring doorbells and dispense literature at malls and plants. McCarthy did not have to rely on his student army alone. In the most expensive primary campaign in history up to 1968, the Minnesota senator enjoyed a good deal of support from allegedly oxymoronic wealthy Democrats.

Johnson, who had taken the primary so lightly that he was merely a write-in candidate, dispatched loyalists like Governor John King to warn that "Ho Chi Minh and his Communist friends . . . will be scrutinizing the returns for a sign of a breaking of the American will." Meanwhile New Hampshire Senator Thomas McIntyre accused the Minnesota senator of supporting draft-dodgers and deserters. Three days before the primary, Johnson was hurt by the leaking of news that the generals were asking for another 206,000 troops. He also feared that "Every son-of-a-bitch in New Hampshire who's mad at his wife or the postman or anybody is going to vote for Gene McCarthy."

Johnson did win the primary by a vote of 27,243 to 23,820 among Democrats, but when Republican write-ins for both candidates were counted, the president's lead was cut to 230—a shockingly weak showing. This was more a "victory" for those who opposed the war in general than for the doves, since as many as 40 percent of McCarthy voters favored escalation rather than withdrawal. Nationally, in the wake of Tet, more than half of Americans polled felt the war in Vietnam was a mistake, with 70 percent favoring Vietnamization. When asked whether they were hawks or doves, the nation split almost evenly.

The Tet Offensive, Johnson's sudden vulnerability with his approval ratings on the war dipping to 26 percent, his rejection of the Kerner Commission findings on the racial crisis late in February, the certainty that McCarthy could not win the nomination, and a genuine concern about the nation led Robert Kennedy to throw his hat in the ring on March 16. He had already offered Johnson a unique option that he had discussed with Chicago mayor Richard Daley in February. On March 11, Kennedy sent Theodore Sorensen to the president with his terms for remaining on the sidelines. Sorensen suggested that if Secretary of State Dean Rusk resigned to signal a policy change (a nonstarter for Johnson), or if the president appointed an independent commission to review Vietnam policy, Kennedy would not compete for the nomination. Although McCarthy did not believe that his rival was serious, Kennedy explained, "I don't care what they do to me with it, I said I would walk the last mile for peace, and I am going to do it."

For a few days it appeared that Johnson was attracted to the Kennedy proposal, with Clifford meeting with Kennedy and Sorensen on March 14 to discuss potential members of a commission. But later that day the defense secretary called the senator to tell him that the president had scuttled the proposal. It is difficult to explain why Johnson delayed several days before he rejected the unusual arrangement. He so disliked Kennedy—"that grandstanding little runt"—that one could not imagine how he would accept his lead on Vietnam policy. Indeed, Kennedy's dovishness made Johnson's acceptance of any dovish démarche even more unlikely because he did not wish to appear to be adopting his enemy's ideas. Johnson also worried that if he withdrew from Vietnam, Kennedy, the former dove, would end up "out in front leading the fight against me, telling everyone that I had betrayed John Kennedy's commitment to Vietnam. That I had let a democracy fall into the hands of Communists. That I was a coward. An unmanly man. A man without a spine."

With Johnson's rejection, to Kennedy "it became unmistakably clear that as long as Lyndon B. Johnson was our President, our Vietnam policy would consist of only more war, more troops, more killing and more senseless destruction of a country we are supposedly there to save. That night I decided to run for President."

Although he never made the linkage, the president did summon a sort of independent commission to the White House to offer advice on the war when at the end of March he brought together again his "Wise Men." This bipartisan group of former officials and generals had last met in November and, as they had done previously, had endorsed administration strategy. Now almost all of the Wise Men rejected that strategy, in good measure because of the briefing papers presented by Clifford, who contended that no end was in sight to the disastrous war. Moreover they knew that the war was tearing the country apart and damaging the economy. They were also impressed by a House resolution of a week earlier, signed by 139 members, calling for a full review of American policy in Vietnam. On a personal level, many of them had young relatives or knew young people in the "best" universities, groomed to become another generation of Wise Men, who were "dropping out" as hippies and radicals and might not graduate from college, let alone law school or business school.

Their arguments and those of Clifford's cabal, in addition to the political challenge he faced from Kennedy, convinced Johnson to present his epochal March 31, 1968, speech in which he refused to give the military the 206,000 new troops it requested, lowered the bar for opening talks with North Vietnam, issued bombing restrictions, and then stunningly announced that he would not seek reelection. For whatever combination of reasons, including concerns about his health, Johnson was most likely sincere when he told Vice President Hubert Humphrey, who later entered the race on April 27, "I've got to become totally nonpolitical" to end the war. McCarthy explained Johnson's decision in other terms, contending that "I don't think they could stand up against five million college kids just shouting for peace—There was too much will-power there."

Had Johnson accepted the escalation route recommended by his military chieftains, he faced the difficult problem of increasing draft calls or the calling up of units of the National Guard and reserves—units that had become refuges from combat for middle-class young men. These men had parents who were, on the average, far more politically active and potent than the generally blue-collar parents of the then-current draftees. Such a call-up might also be understood as an increase in the centrality of the war to national security, leading to a dangerous public demand to begin fighting a total war. Moreover the anti-war movement on campuses had already gained hundreds of thousands of new recruits after Johnson ended graduate-student deferments the previous year.

Johnson could have made up some of the shortfall in the new troop request by using stateside regular forces. For example, Westmoreland wanted to send the 82nd Airborne to Vietnam. The president could not honor the request because, "Frankly, I am afraid to move the 82nd because of the possibility of civil disturbances here." The previous year he had announced new troop deployments for Vietnam the day before he had to send 4,700 troops to quell an urban insurrection in Detroit.

Also important was the gold crisis, which Dean Acheson thought so serious as to have "dampened expansionist ideas. This town is in an atmosphere of crisis." The war, which was costing more than $30 billion a year, continued to contribute to a balance-of-payments deficit and an ever-weakening dollar. Because of its own financial pressures, Great Britain had devalued the pound

the previous year. Reacting to the overvalued dollar, foreign
banks began a frenetic run on gold during a four-day period in
mid-March withdrawing $1 billion, including $372 million worth
of gold on March 14 alone, an action that led the London gold
markets to close on that day. Secretary of the Treasury Fowler
told Johnson that sending 206,000 more troops to Vietnam would
cost an additional $2.5 billion in 1968 and $10 billion in 1969,
adding $5 billion to the balance-of-payments deficit. (The $10 billion in 1969 is the equivalent of more than $50 billion in 2005 dol-
lars.) In order to maintain the economy, he would have to raise
taxes still further or drastically reduce domestic programs. He ultimately accepted such a deal in June when Congress tied his tax
surcharge to domestic spending cuts.

A new troop buildup would also affect European perceptions
that the economy and the dollar were going to weaken even further, leading them to buy still more gold. Looking back on the
crisis two months later, Federal Reserve Board chair William
McChesney Martin commented, "I have been trying for the past
two years to make the point on 'guns and butter' and the cost of
the Vietnam War, economically, without too much success, but I
think in due course the chickens will come home to roost."

Johnson's health was also a concern. He had contemplated announcing that he would not run during his State of the Union
message in January. The war had taken its toll on him; it was not
much fun anymore being president, constantly hounded by anti-
war crowds hurling obscenities at him.

As the red lights went out on the television cameras on March
31, 1968, Johnson must have felt a tremendous sense of relief.
Now perhaps the unruly crowds would stop harassing him and
his family. Years later Johnson's daughter, Lynda Johnson Robb,
remembered that during those difficult days the last thing she
heard outside her White House bedroom window before she
went to sleep and the first thing she heard when she awoke was
"Hey, hey, LBJ, how many kids did you kill today?"

On the other hand, there is tantalizing evidence that Johnson soon had second thoughts about his decision and might have been prepared to run again had events turned out differently that summer. However one explains Johnson's decision on March 31, the Vietnam War had taken its first presidential casualty. No doubt, considering the control Johnson's forces held over delegate selection, he could have won the nomination. But it would have been a pyrrhic victory, destroying the Democratic Party and handing the election to the Republicans.

The North Vietnamese accepted Johnson's offer in his March 31 speech and agreed to meet in Paris for preliminary talks to arrange formal talks. From May through November, as Americans and North Vietnamese jockeyed for position in Paris, their discussions were affected by the U.S. presidential campaign. The president was convinced that the Communists appeared more conciliatory in public to encourage the doves to pressure him into concessions as the election neared. But he held firm. His instructions to chief negotiator W. Averell Harriman included obtaining Communist promises to stop their attacks on cities in South Vietnam, to respect the demilitarized zone, and to accept South Vietnam's participation in the peace talks. Harriman, who confessed, "I simply can't stand Nixon," exceeded his guidelines during the summer in an attempt to achieve a breakthrough before the election.

Many observers felt that Johnson was not entirely serious about giving up the presidency. Were he able to achieve a breakthrough before the late August Chicago convention, a convention that might be deadlocked among several candidates, he might be drafted as a "peace" candidate acceptable to all factions. At the least, the White House made preparations for a last-minute presidential trip to Chicago. However serious Johnson may have been about not running, his March 31 decision, directly tied to the Vietnam War, altered the shape of the political battlefield for years to come.

Because it was too late for Humphrey to enter the primaries, Kennedy and McCarthy competed directly for the insurgent vote in Indiana, Oregon, and California. A bitter McCarthy, who had offered to be a one-term president if Kennedy stayed out of the race, rejected the New York senator's proposal to split the primaries between them. He later offered a different explanation, contending that he had wanted to win three or four primaries by himself, then hand over the nomination to Kennedy. "Bobby could have come in as the unifying force."

Even without entering the primaries, Humphrey could count on party support. In the nonbinding primary in Pennsylvania, for example, McCarthy won the popular election but only one-fifth of the delegates. McCarthy, who was distressed about Humphrey's position on the war, bore no special animus toward his former senatorial colleague from Minnesota. He was so much more distressed about Kennedy's precipitous entry into the campaign that he told his supporters that if he did not win, he would support Humphrey. He also questioned Kennedy's Vietnam policy. McCarthy attacked the *Kennedy*-Johnson policy, observing, "Any man who played a prominent role in developing the policies of the early sixties, I think, can be called upon to explain his role in the process . . . [of creating a] systematic misconception of America and its role in the world." Kennedy, he asserted, was not firm in demanding that Saigon be prepared to share power with the Viet Cong. It appeared to McCarthy that Kennedy had begun "to water down his stand on Vietnam."

The Kennedy and McCarthy candidacies, supported by virtually all dovish Democrats and their sympathizers, had an interesting overall impact on the anti-war movement. With so much time, energy, money, and labor invested in the primary campaigns, opponents of the war found little time for demonstrations and other forms of protest against the war.

In tough primaries in Oregon and California, Kennedy campaigned nonstop, trying to touch all interest groups, including Jewish Americans. On May 26 he made an appearance at a synagogue in Portland where he proclaimed, "We are committed to Israel's survival." News of this aired in California, where a Palestinian refugee, Sirhan Sirhan, allegedly came close to weeping when he heard those words. During the candidates' televised debate in California the next week, Kennedy's support for Israel was again mentioned.

Although Kennedy enjoyed a strong lead over McCarthy in national polls, he lost the Oregon primary, the first time a Kennedy had ever lost an election. That loss invigorated McCarthy's supporters, who had been depressed ever since the charismatic Kennedy had entered the race. Kennedy was more than a one-issue candidate, and his energetic and passionate style contrasted to that of the professorial McCarthy who did not seem to have his heart in the campaign or in developing a serious position on any issue except the war.

On June 4, election night in California, a victorious Kennedy told his aide, Richard Goodwin, who had come over from the McCarthy camp earlier, that if the Minnesota senator withdrew he would appoint him secretary of state. McCarthy did not offer insurgent Democrats the complete reform candidate they needed to threaten Johnson's grip on the party. Kennedy never had a chance to make the offer, which would have been rejected. Sirhan Sirhan assassinated him in the early morning hours of June 5, most likely because of his robust support for Israel, in another example of the significance of foreign policy issues in the 1968 election.

At this point, despite the fact that McCarthy and Kennedy had compiled an impressive series of primary wins, and despite the fact that more Democratic voters supported them than Humphrey, the vice president was virtually guaranteed the nomination because of the way delegates had been selected for the Chicago convention: thirty-five state delegations had been chosen in party conventions. All the same, Humphrey knew that he had to unite the party by distancing himself from administration policies in Vietnam, if only marginally. He was already confronting picketers at his rallies who wanted to "Dump the Hump" and hecklers who shouted profanities at the "fascist."

Humphrey met with Johnson on July 25 to ask his permission to deviate from the party line by advocating a total bombing halt of North Vietnam, but the president rejected his plea. Johnson confided to an adviser, "The GOP may be more of a help to us than the Democrats in the next few months." This was not just a matter of pride to the president. He was convinced that he had a chance to obtain a better deal from the Communists if the candidates did not offer terms softer than his. Richard Nixon had endeared himself to Johnson when he told him that to accept a bombing halt would "undercut our negotiating position." It would also undercut the crafty Republican's candidacy.

Humphrey was stuck. He was assailed from the left by antiwar Democrats because of his loyalty to Johnson. And the president knew that Humphrey was itching to break away from the administration with a position on the war that the president maintained would undercut chances for peace. Some suggested that Johnson, who like most Democrats was not especially fond of Nixon, would not have been devastated had Nixon won. At the least, Johnson considered him to be made of tougher stuff than Humphrey.

The bombing halt was the key issue in the extended public and private debate over the Democrats' Vietnam platform plank. Again Humphrey's forces wanted to meet the doves at least halfway, but the White House demanded that they hold fast to the president's negotiating position. The vice president needed the doves' support for the campaign. The contest over the plank was so bitter—after all, the doves had won all the primaries—

that he feared they would withhold their labor, money, and even votes. Johnson was adamant, according to Humphrey, warning that "he would denounce me. . . . I would have the blood of his sons-in-law [in Vietnam] on my hands." The vice president lamented, "I've eaten so much shit in the last two years, I've almost gotten to like the taste of it."

The administration won the platform fight by a vote of 1,567 to 1,048 after Johnson informed his agents that the military was convinced that North Vietnam would take advantage of a unilateral bombing halt to launch major attacks on American troops. Johnson argued, "We are not going to stop the bombing just to give them a chance to step up their bloodbath."

On August 20 the increasingly bitter pre-convention debate over Vietnam policy became a minor issue when 200,000 Eastern bloc troops marched into Czechoslovakia to crush the reform movement "Prague Spring." McCarthy looked a little less than presidential when he commented, "I don't see this as a major world crisis." He meant to say that there was little the United States could do about it. The invasion was an even greater blow to Johnson. On August 21 the president had been planning to announce a summit conference with the Russians to be held at the end of September to discuss disarmament. This might have appealed to dovish delegates gathering a few days later in Chicago. Appealing to them became impossible when the convention turned out to be the most turbulent and violent in American history.

Because of the Chicago police department's rough tactics in April, employed against those who rioted after the assassination of Martin Luther King, Jr., thousands of anti-war protesters decided to stay away from the convention. Yippies filled the void, planning to nominate a pig, Pigasus, for president, and threatening sabotage, including lacing the Chicago water system with LSD. Yippie leader Jerry Rubin admitted, "I wanted to create a situation in which the . . . Daley administration and the federal government . . . would self destruct." Instead it was the Democratic Party that self-destructed.

Anti-Johnson Democrats were furious about their brutal treatment at the convention, run with an iron fist by Mayor Daley. Ten thousand protesters in the streets clashed with 11,000 of Chicago's finest (1 death, 668 arrests, more than 800 injuries), with the "whole world watching" on television what a commission later labeled a "police riot." Yippies screamed "Fuck Pigs, oink, oink!" while the police shouted, "Kill the commies! Get the bastards!"

Some young people provoked the police, though they sometimes were egged on by undercover police acting as agents provocateurs; but the police clearly overreacted. The demonstrators were also provoked by the limits placed upon peaceful protest and freedom of movement by the mayor. And, of course, they were provoked by the unwillingness of the Democratic Party to adopt their anti-war positions. All witnesses claim there was no justification for the bloody police raid on McCarthy headquarters at the Conrad Hilton Hotel, a raid that helped convince McCarthy that he would not support the Democratic ticket, at least not immediately. The Minnesota senator, who described the scene as "incredible, like a Brueghel" painting, was angered too by Humphrey's failure to condemn the invasion of his headquarters.

Expecting disturbances at the convention, Johnson had vetoed the idea of holding it in Miami because there the chief law-enforcement official would have been a Republican governor. He better trusted Daley to keep order. And keep order he did. Inside the convention hall, packed with a huge claque of city employees, Daley's security forces restricted the movement of journalists, often in a very rough manner. *Newsweek* was not far off the mark when it entitled a story about the convention, "Beat the Press." When Connecticut senator Abraham Ribicoff began to speak to the convention about the carnage outside and the police state inside, lip-readers could see the mayor on television shouting "Fuck you, you Jew bastard."

Some of the protesters thought they had won the day. As one SDS leader proclaimed, "The message of the week was of an America ruled by force. This was a big victory." One would think he had a point, especially considering what television viewers were able to witness live, but he did not count on the ever-widening national divide between the forces of order and the alleged forces of disorder.

Even though Daley complained about biased media coverage, Americans told pollsters that they supported the Chicago police by almost a 2 to 1 margin. Two weeks after the convention, in a sample of fifty households in the blue-collar Democratic suburb of Warren, Michigan, two thought the police were too rough, twenty-six thought they used just enough force, and twenty-two said they were not tough enough. This reaction reflected well the majority of Americans who told pollsters repeatedly that they opposed demonstrations, hippies, social and political revolutionaries, and others who were apparently destroying the country. As one scholar observed, "No matter what the average American may feel about the war in Vietnam, there is one thing which he is likely to feel certain about. This is his opposition to strikes, demonstrations, and other forms of protests."

After a failed attempt by doves to nominate Senators George McGovern or Edward M. Kennedy, Humphrey won the Democratic nomination. But he and the party never recovered from the unprecedented brutal clashes at their convention. Inspired by divisions over the Vietnam War, they alienated much of left-liberal America and reinforced the Republican argument that the Democrats were the party of disorder. Humphrey later complained, "I was a victim of the convention as much as a man getting the Hong Kong flu. Chicago was a catastrophe."

McCarthy was convinced that the convention riots were the main reason for Humphrey's dismal showing in the polls during

the rest of August and most of September. The party was so horrified by what had happened that it later instituted sweeping reforms for the 1972 race. These led to the disfranchisement and
alienation of many party regulars, the nomination of its most
left-wing candidate, George McGovern (who had headed the
party's convention reform commission), and the landslide that
gave Richard Nixon his second term. McGovern assumed erroneously that he would be able to count on the allegiance of party
regulars while appealing to the liberals and left-liberals who believed *they* had been disfranchised in 1968.

As for Nixon's path to nomination, he easily won the New
Hampshire primary over George Romney. Romney self-
destructed over Vietnam once again when he had to correct a
comment he made about Viet Cong participation in a South
Vietnamese government. In his statements about the war,
Nixon, formerly more hawkish than the president, softened his
line without spelling out specifics. He did refer to Saigon as
"the cork in the bottle of Chinese expansion in Asia," while
promising that "new leadership" will "end the war and win the
peace in the Pacific." When asked for details, he responded that
he did not wish to undercut Johnson or reveal his policy to the
enemy before he became president. His soon to become leg-
endary "secret plan to end the war" did not exist, though he
may have developed a general strategy by the fall. He was asked
about the plan and at least once did reply, "Yes, I have a plan to
end the war." He also said, "I have no magic formula. . . . But I
do have some specific ideas on how to end the war. They are
primarily in the diplomatic area."
    Nixon was close to developing a more specific plan in March
when his aides began working on a nationwide radio address to
be taped on March 30 for airing the next day. He told his speechwriters that he had "come to the conclusion that there's no way
to win the war. But we can't say that of course. In fact, we have

to say the opposite, just to keep some degree of bargaining leverage." Instead, looking for "the least assailable middle ground,"
he would say that he planned to rely more on airpower and to
pressure the Russians and Chinese to pressure the North Vietnamese to be more accommodating. Nixon canceled his address
when he learned that Johnson was going to speak on the same
day, then announced that he would not criticize the president's
policy while peace talks were going on. He later assured Johnson he would support him as long as he did not soften his position, an assurance that made it even harder for the president to
meet the doves halfway. As Clark Clifford noted acerbically,
Nixon offered "his support in return for inflexibility in our negotiating position."

The Republicans were themselves split over the war but they
kept their quarrels private. At their Miami convention they hammered out a compromise platform plank that called for "de-
Americanization" of the war and proclaimed that the "era of
confrontation" was over and that the world was entering a "new
era of negotiation." But it would be negotiation from strength,
with a stronger hand at the helm of American foreign policy.
Nixon enjoyed a large lead in the polls after the disastrous Democratic Convention. Although his stump speeches concentrated
on domestic disorder, he did promise new, experienced leadership in foreign affairs to end the war honorably and to stand up
to the Communists. He also ran a series of sixty-second ads in
which he promised to end the war.

Taking an even harder line was the third-party candidate, Alabama's governor George Wallace, who promised to crush
demonstrators and rioters and pursue a tough foreign policy line.
Both Wallace and Nixon capitalized on Americans' growing distaste for unruly mass demonstrations and social unrest. Late in
1967 they had told pollsters that anti-war demonstrations were
"acts of disloyalty against the boys fighting in Vietnam," by a 68
to 22 percent margin. Their distaste for demonstrations increased

with the spectacle in April of the seizure and occupation of buildings at Columbia University by radical students. The students' concerns included their institutions' contracts with the Defense Department. "Law and order," the dominant theme of both the Nixon and Wallace campaigns, related in part to the increasingly unruly protests against the Vietnam War and American foreign policy.

At its peak, Wallace's candidacy attracted as much as 20 percent of the electorate. His supporters loved his colorful attacks on "overeducated ivory-tower folks with pointed heads" who wore "sissy britches." Wallace's appeal began to fade because of a foreign policy issue, when his running mate, General Curtis LeMay (a model for the crazed general in the satirical film *Dr. Strangelove*) told a press conference in October, "I don't believe the world would end if we exploded a nuclear weapon." After Wallace tried to make LeMay tone down the rhetoric, the blustery former head of the Strategic Air Command shocked everyone by reiterating that he "would use anything we could dream up . . . including nuclear weapons, if it was necessary," to end the war in Vietnam. Because of this political *faux pas*, Wallace and LeMay became the "Bombsey Twins" to their detractors. The Democrats suggested in television advertisements that the impetuous and loose-lipped Republican vice-presidential candidate, Spiro T. Agnew, would also be an irresponsible leader were he to advance to the presidency.

Nixon escaped a potentially more damaging embarrassment related to foreign affairs. A dissident Greek journalist told Lawrence O'Brien, the chair of Humphrey's campaign, that the authoritarian Greek government had contributed more than $1 million to the Nixon-Agnew campaign. O'Brien asked President Johnson to investigate, but he refused. He considered the journalist in question to be a troublemaker, was angry about the direction Humphrey's campaign was taking, and perhaps thought he could use the information later against Nixon were Nixon to become president and uncover nasty things about him.

The old Nixon began to appear late in the campaign through Agnew, who accused Humphrey of being "squishy soft" on communism. Nixon himself, in a radio address on October 24, pointed out that during the Eisenhower administration there was no Berlin Wall, Bay of Pigs, and *Pueblo*. Further, with echoes back to 1960, he talked about "a gravely serious security gap" in the nuclear arms race, with the Soviets moving into the lead while the United States endorsed the dangerous doctrine of parity. Turnabout was fair play. When John F. Kennedy charged that the Eisenhower-Nixon administration had let the United States fall behind the Soviets, he knew he was exaggerating. But Kennedy did not outright lie as did Nixon in his election-eve speech when he announced that he had information that the North Vietnamese were at that moment sending "thousands of tons of supplies" down the Ho Chi Minh Trail that American forces were too weak to inderdict.

Nixon took off the gloves because he feared an October surprise. The year 1968 marks the origin of that term, which refers to the ability of the president to orchestrate a crisis, sign a treaty, or end a war just in time to assist his or her party in the election. Nixon was already running a little scared after Hubert Humphrey's Salt Lake City speech on September 30, when the vice president broke with Johnson by announcing a softer policy on a complete cessation of the bombing of North Vietnam. This time Humphrey did not ask the president's permission; he informed him fifteen minutes before his speech that "I don't think this is going to impair your hand, and it doesn't go as far as some people would like, but it goes a bit further than you would like." It certainly did not go as far as McCarthy would have liked. The former candidate withheld his support from Humphrey until late October.

Nevertheless, almost immediately, heckling decreased at Humphrey's appearances, his poll numbers began to rise, and anti-war Democrats began to wander back to the party with their labor and campaign contributions. He needed them. His campaign was in such bad shape that the Soviet Union, through Ambassador Anatoly Dobrynin, had offered him under-the-table financial support, which of course Humphrey refused. The ambassador thought it was a terrible idea but had orders from Moscow.

The Soviets tried to help Humphrey win with something more important than campaign financing. Preferring his victory to that of his famously anti-Communist rival, in late September they influenced the North Vietnamese to soften their terms for opening serious peace talks. Even without Moscow's prodding, Ho Chi Minh knew he could get a better deal from the Democrats than from the Republicans, who were leading in the polls.

Meanwhile Nixon discovered through secret sources that the Paris peace talks were moving toward a successful resolution. Bryce Harlow, who later became his liaison with Congress, had a friend in the White House who offered him information about the talks. In addition, Harvard professor Henry Kissinger, who was Nelson Rockefeller's ambitious foreign policy adviser, tried to pick up information in Paris where he visited in the fall, presumably to do research for an article. His spying for Nixon was surprising, given the fact that in a letter advising Harriman that he was coming to Paris, Kissinger wrote, "I am through with Republican politics. The party is hopeless and unfit to govern."

Although he may not have known all the details, Nixon was aware that a breakthrough in the talks had occurred around October 11. On October 16 Johnson informed all three candidates of the situation. But both Hanoi and Saigon expressed reservations about the deal, which resulted in a delay of the announcement until October 31. On October 21 Nixon enjoyed an eighteen-point lead in the polls. Two days after the deal was announced, his lead stood at two points. One wonders what would have happened had the breakthrough been made public two weeks earlier.

Johnson had worried about how his peacemaking would affect the election, fearing that "many people will call it a cheap political trick." Clifford advised him not to "let the date of the election concern you." Nixon was convinced it *was* a cheap political trick. On October 25 he issued a press release in which he maintained, disingenuously, that while some people would think it was "a cynical last-minute attempt by President Johnson to salvage the candidacy of Mr. Humphrey," he did not. It was true that the breakthrough was helping the vice president, and that the Russians and North Vietnamese expected better relations with the Democrats than with the Republicans. That was a far cry from claiming that the president waited until the final moment to announce his October surprise because he wanted to defeat Nixon. On the other hand, South Vietnamese president Thieu also suspected that Johnson was "trying to pull off a near miracle which . . . will be needed to stave off defeat for Mr. Humphrey and the Democrats in November."

In any event, Johnson's perceived playing politics with national security served as justification for the Republicans' own unprecedented meddling in a national security matter for political purposes. The sensational case came close to treason. Anna Chennault, chair of the Women for Nixon-Agnew Committee, had for several months been in contact with Bui Diem, the South Vietnamese ambassador to the United States, as an official, if covert, link to the Nixon campaign. She also had ties to officials in South Vietnam. Her task was "to convey the 'Republican Position'" to Saigon to "hold fast and not participate in the peace talks." As early as October 23, Ambassador Diem had informed South Vietnamese president Thieu, that "many Republican friends have contacted me and encouraged us to stand firm," and on October 27 he reported that he "was regularly in touch with the Nixon entourage." South Vietnamese vice president Nguyen Cao Ky remembered that "out of the blue Nixon's supporters stepped into the picture. Approaches were made . . . to the effect,

Hold on! Don't accept the invitation to go to Paris. If Mr. Nixon is elected President he promises to increase support for the Vietnam War."

During late October, Ambassador Bunker met with Thieu ten times trying to convince him to accept the agreement for peace talks. On October 30, Thieu informed Washington that he planned to reject the deal publicly, a response that Clifford labeled "horseshit" and a "calculated planned program to delay, to get through November 5." The peace deal had pulled Humphrey so close to Nixon in the polls that a disconsolate Pat Buchanan admitted, "By Sunday night [before the election], I thought we were finished." After news of Thieu's rejection reached the voters, the boomlet for Humphrey evaporated. Nixon won a very close election—by fewer than 500,000 popular votes. Ky later noted, "By holding out we deprived the Democrats of their election victory."

As the North Vietnamese had hoped for a better deal from the Democrats, the South Vietnamese certainly had every reason to expect a better deal from the Republicans. They probably would have rejected Johnson's offer without any encouragement from the Nixon camp. That encouragement came close to treasonous behavior that, at the least, violated the Logan Act, which prohibited private citizens from engaging in official diplomatic activity. It looked worse when, several weeks after he was elected, Nixon told Saigon to accept the deal his aides had told them to reject earlier. Johnson had predicted that "Nixon will doublecross them after November 5."

Discovering the Republican plot on October 29, Johnson ordered a phone tap on Chennault's residence at the Watergate apartments in Washington. He did not need to order one on the South Vietnamese embassy as it was already a target for surveillance, as were government offices in Saigon (and as was Humphrey's campaign). Therein lay one of Johnson and Humphrey's main problems—because were they to go public with the story, they might have had to reveal their intelligence activities against South Vietnam—an ally. In addition, the FBI could not produce the smoking gun proving that Chennault was getting her marching orders directly from officials in the Nixon campaign, or even from Nixon himself. But Johnson certainly had enough evidence to go public and perhaps to derail Nixon's election chances. On October 31 he did make a private phone call to the candidates, in which he informed them of rumors that "old China hands" were interfering with his diplomacy, but that he knew that "none of you candidates are aware of it or responsible for it." Suspecting that the president was on to his plotting, a panicky Nixon called him on November 3 to tell him that "There was absolutely no truth" in the rumors about Chennault, "as far as he knew." If Nixon did not know all the day-to-day details, he knew plenty about her operation.

Had Johnson or Humphrey, to whom the president offered the option, gone public with stories about how Republicans had quashed a peace plan, costing the lives of an untold number of American boys, the vice president would surely have won the election. According to Clifford, Johnson decided against that option for several reasons. He thought that Thieu might still accept the deal; he did not wish to weaken American support for Saigon or damage negotiations with Hanoi; and maybe he still had "ambivalence about Hubert Humphrey." In addition, Johnson feared that release of the information could, if Nixon were to win, lead to a national crisis or even perhaps to difficult times for him personally as an ex-president confronting a vindictive president.

In an interesting footnote to the affair, four years later Johnson almost went public with the story of Republican traitorous behavior on the eve of the 1968 election. In the fall of 1972, when Nixon was under pressure because of the Watergate break-in, he threatened to release information about Johnson's alleged illegal bugging of his 1968 campaign unless the former president called off Joseph Califano, who, representing the Democratic National

Committee, was pursuing a civil suit against the Republican Party. Nixon's chief of staff wanted "to use it on Johnson [to] get Califano . . . and if Johnson turns him off, it could turn them the other way." Johnson's trump card was his threat to reveal the Chennault-Thieu story to the public if Nixon released material about his illegal activities.

When Americans voted for Nixon or Humphrey for president on November 5, 1968, they voted for candidates who promised to end the war. With little to choose between them on the main issue facing the nation, they made their choices based upon party loyalties, the personalities of the candidates, and, most important, the unusually volatile domestic issues of the day. To suggest that the Vietnam War in particular and foreign policy in general were not the key issues in the 1968 election is to ignore the many ways they affected every aspect of the contest, from 1966 to election eve—when Johnson and Humphrey chose not to go public with the Chennault bombshell. Few elections in American history were so dominated by foreign policy, and few elections so strongly influenced foreign policy during a campaign.

7

The Politics of Polarization, 1969

AS RICHARD NIXON prepared to take office on January 20, 1969, the Vietnam War hovered over his presidency. The day before, ten thousand protesters had gathered in Washington for a "counter-inaugural." A small group in the crowd began shouting, "Stop the bullshit and take to the streets." Its leader was an agent provocateur from the D.C. police. Although they did not take to the streets on Inaugural Day itself, anti-war and anti-Nixon protesters lined the parade route, throwing sticks, stones, and even smoke bombs at the presidential limousine. They made it impossible for the new president to stand up and wave to the crowd, most of whom were supportive. The Secret Service arrested eighty-seven protesters for a variety of violations. Nixon's victory parade was ruined. Handfuls of peaceful protesters with placards had appeared at previous inaugurals, but the rowdy and disruptive activities at Nixon's were unprecedented.

Nixon's inaugural address, however, was conciliatory. "The greatest honor history can bestow is the title of peacemaker," explained the new president, who also proclaimed, "The simple things are the ones most needed today. . . . To lower our voices would be a simple thing. . . . We cannot learn from one another until we stop shouting at one another." Peace at home and abroad was his explicit agenda, the agenda of a candidate who had ridden to victory on the wave of the anti-hippie, anti-anti-war movement, anti-"sixties" sentiment abroad in the land. Whether he was serious on January 20, the president who had promised to "bring us together" would soon contribute to the polarization that was tearing the nation apart.

Nixon was not the only polarizer. With the war continuing and a presumed tough conservative in the White House, a small number of participants in the anti-war movement and of the New Left accelerated their violent assaults against the government. Symptomatic was the breakup of the Students for a Democratic Society in 1969 and the development of the tiny Weatherman faction that proudly proclaimed its intention to bring revolution to the United States. Bill Ayers, one Weatherman leader, called on Americans to "Kill all the rich people. Break up their cars and apartments. Bring the revolution home, kill your parents, that's where it's really at."

Between January 1, 1969, and April 15, 1970, there were several hundred bombings and more than eight thousand threats of bombings. During the academic year from 1969 to 1970, more than seven thousand young people were arrested on college campuses for violent activities, double the number of a year earlier. Nixon worried that leaders of American institutions were weak and "vulnerable to mob rule." This was certainly the case on many college campuses where administrators frequently gave in to the demands of protesters, even if they had broken the law and destroyed property.

Even more than most presidents, Nixon began planning for his reelection campaign very early in his first administration. Although his Committee to Reelect the President (CREEP) did not begin its work until March 1971, Nixon, the "chronic campaigner," started out with a surplus from his 1968 campaign of almost $1.7 million, which he used for his own political purposes. Like Kennedy and Johnson, he knew he would have difficulty being reelected if he made a peace that led, before 1972, to a Communist takeover of South Vietnam. Aside from his own

concerns, he foresaw that as a nation, "we would destroy our-
selves if we pulled out in a way that wasn't really honorable."
But unlike Kennedy and Johnson, he also knew that he could
not be reelected if the American involvement in Vietnam, which
had reached 540,000 troops by 1969, was not reduced considerably. It was difficult to reduce troops while still maintaining a
pro-Western government in Saigon, especially since Johnson's
concession to begin serious talks, which Nixon endorsed only after he was reelected, had halted the bombing of North Vietnam.

Aside from his reelection, Nixon had other concerns. He was
"convinced that how we end this war will determine the future
of the U.S. in the world," and that he could not "cut and run."
He needed a "peace with honor." Above all, he had to demonstrate to his adversaries beyond Hanoi that protesters in the
streets would not affect him as they had his predecessor. He had
contempt for those protesters, whose leaders he called "hard-core
militants of the New Left who hated the United States." Many of
their followers, he maintained, were not especially moralistic
about the war—they were draft-dodgers who just wanted "to
keep from getting their asses shot off."

Nixon believed that the American system was too open to
compete successfully with closed systems in the international
arena, especially when that openness allowed leftists freedom to
do their mischief on behalf of un-American causes. An effective
president, he believed, had to operate like an undemocratic
leader, ruthlessly and amorally in a global political system too
complicated for an uninformed and overly idealistic and moral
citizenry to understand.

One way to accomplish this was to practice secret diplomacy
that hid from the public, the media, and Congress activities they
would question or oppose. Although the trend had already begun with national security advisers McGeorge Bundy and Walt
Rostow under Kennedy and especially under Johnson, Nixon
took the major responsibility for foreign policy away from the

State Department. He delegated it to his National Security Council under Henry Kissinger. Kissinger, unlike Secretary of State William Rogers, did not have to appear before Congress to explain his policies when summoned. Just as important, he could contain diplomatic initiatives within the confines of a few offices in the basement of the White House. This was a major change in the balance-of-power arrangements in the American constitutional system, one that ultimately backfired on the president during the Watergate investigations.

The unparalleled secrecy in the Nixon White House led the Joint Chiefs of Staff to launch an intelligence operation of their own in the fall of 1970. It involved stealing documents from the National Security Council to discover what was going on in U.S. foreign policy. The chair of the Joint Chiefs ordered a naval yeoman who worked on the NSC to copy more than five thousand documents for them. The yeoman admitted that he "took so much darned stuff I can't remember what it was." When the espionage was uncovered in December 1971, the president insisted on keeping this "potential time bomb" a secret. He feared adverse reaction had the public discovered that his policies had compelled the chiefs to engage in such an unprecedented operation. Government departments always try to find out through leaks and informants what is going on in other departments. Wholesale theft is another matter. It could be justified, in part, by Nixon's determination to keep so many important national security secrets from his most senior and respected military officials. This astounding development was characteristic of an administration obsessed with secrecy.

Ironically, Nixon did not even trust his NSC to keep a secret. In the wake of a leak dealing with his intention to announce troop withdrawals in June 1969, he temporarily ordered the council to stop meeting.

In May 1961 Nixon commented after the failed Bay of Pigs attack, "The concept of a return to secrecy in peacetime demon-

strates a profound misunderstanding of the role of a free press as
opposed to that of a controlled press. The plea of secrecy could become a cloak for errors, misjudgments, and other failings of government." He was not in power when he made that statement.

As president, it was not just national security concerns that
drove his obsession. He was certain that newspeople, who he
thought had been persecuting him since his first rough congressional campaign in 1946, were his enemies. Convinced that at
most a third were objective, he believed the others would seek
any opportunity to undermine his policies because they "have no
intention whatever to be fair whenever they are able to get away
with unfair coverage." By the time he took office, four influential
major national publications—the *New York Times*, *Washington
Post*, *Time*, and *Newsweek*—had adopted critical approaches to
the war in Vietnam. In addition, like Lyndon Johnson, Nixon
and his media monitors believed that the three major television
networks, ABC, CBS, and NBC, were in the anti-war van. Most
presidents, even those who begin with good relations with the
press, end up in an adversarial relationship with editors and
journalists. Nixon's war against the media, driven in good measure by his felt need to keep Vietnam and other foreign policies
even closer to his vest than his predecessors, grew into a vendetta.

One way around the problem, aside from holding as few press
conferences as possible, was to use television as a bully pulpit to
address the American people directly, without the filter of prob-
ing journalists. More than Johnson, Nixon used television to
make prime-time speeches about his Vietnam policy. He was
aided by a compliant Federal Communications Commission,
which ruled that when the president announced a foreign policy
initiative, the "fairness doctrine"—which allowed for equal time
for the opposition—did not apply. In October 1972 the Supreme
Court ruled that the networks did not even have to permit the
Democratic Party to *buy* time to answer the president. The court
responded negatively to Joseph Califano's question, "Are the

public airways . . . to promote the sales of soap, brassieres, and deodorants but not to promote the exchange of ideas?"

Although it did well with its political use of the airwaves, the administration could not control the music dominating the playlists. Since the early sixties, most of the songs with political content had reflected an anti-war perspective. It began, not surprisingly, with the folk music of the early Bob Dylan, Joan Baez, Phil Ochs, and Peter, Paul, and Mary, whose lyrics critiqued U.S. foreign policy. This soon carried over to pop and rock when, beginning in 1965, Barry McGuire became an overnight sensation with his grim "Eve of Destruction." Simon and Garfunkle, the Rolling Stones, the Beatles, the Jefferson Airplane, and Crosby, Stills, Nash, and Young were among others who took issue, albeit sometimes obliquely, with U.S. policy in Vietnam. The plot of the wildly successful rock musical *Hair*, which opened in 1968, revolved around opposition to the draft and the war.

In August 1969 the Woodstock rock "Festival of Life"drew 400,000 to a farm in upstate New York, known as Woodstock "nation," where the mostly young concertgoers heard Arlo Guthrie, Baez, the Jefferson Airplane, and Jimi Hendrix among others, including Country Joe and the Fish whose bitter anthem, "I-Feel-Like-I'm-Going-to-Die Rag," joined "Give Peace a Chance" and "Where Have All the Flowers Gone" in the anti-war libretto. One adult hippie leader wrote to another, "Woodstock is the great example of how it is going to be in the future. We have the numbers. The loving and the peaceful are the majority. The violent and the authoritarian are the minority. We are winning. And soon."

Although a good deal of the music listened to by young people promoted counter-cultural or anti-war themes, the top hit of the summer of 1965 was Barry Sadler's patriotic "Ballad of the Green Beret." Merle Haggard's crossover country-music hit, "Okee from Muskogee," was another successful response to those who did not salute when the flag went by. Richard Nixon himself, more attuned to the big-band sound of Guy Lombardo and classical music, scored heavily with his constituency in December 1970 when he granted an audience to Elvis Presley. Presley wanted to help the president combat the nefarious influence on American youth of anti-establishment rock groups such as the Beatles. The now-famous meeting between "The King" and the president met with the approval of many adult music lovers. Young people, however, who were the footsoldiers of the anti-war movement—and who were potential draftees—received a solid diet of lyrics challenging the wisdom of their elders' foreign and domestic policies.

Like Johnson before him, Nixon's administration was dominated by the Vietnam War and its international and domestic ramifications. But unlike Johnson, Nixon fancied himself a foreign policy expert who realized that he had a better chance of controlling events in the international sphere than in the domestic sphere, including a Democratic Congress and the intractable problems of racism, inflation, and urban decay. During long periods in his first term, he concentrated almost exclusively on Vietnam; for example, in late April 1970 his chief of staff, H. R. Haldeman, reported that Nixon had "not much interest in domestic affairs as the whole focus is on the war." In fact, Nixon told his key domestic adviser, John Ehrlichman, to take over domestic affairs during the ensuing 1970 Cambodian crisis. On other occasions he told his aides he had no time to read their briefing papers on domestic politics because of his need to devote full attention to foreign affairs—in effect, don't bother me with civil rights, the environment, education, or economics unless the house is burning down. One unintended consequence of this lack of involvement in domestic affairs and Nixon's frequent delegation of authority to the relatively progressive Ehrlichman was that his administration's record in domestic legislation was surprisingly liberal.

The first Nixon administration produced (along with Congress) the most progressive environmental record since Theodore Roosevelt, an end to school segregation in the South, the Occupational Safety and Health Administration (OSHA), the eighteen-year-old vote, increased funding for the arts and humanities, and Title IX of the Education Act that guaranteed equal spending on athletics for male and female college students. One wonders how a conservative president not preoccupied with foreign affairs might have dealt with those policies. At the least, we do know that with the 1973 end to the Vietnam War, Nixon planned to cut back social welfare and other governmental programs. But the Watergate scandals crippled his ability to produce conservative initiatives on the home front.

Before the 1968 election, Nixon had told a Republican congressman, "If we're elected, we'll end this war in six months." Kissinger had used that same time frame. They were serious. As Nixon confided to an aide, "I'm not going to end up like LBJ, holed up in the White House afraid to show my face on the street. I'm going to stop that war. Fast."

The North Vietnamese and their allies preferred Humphrey to Nixon in 1968 because they feared that the inveterate anti-Communist would be tougher to deal with than his adversary. They had good reason to be fearful. Nixon's approach to a quick breakthrough in the peace talks involved both an olive branch to the Russians—in exchange for pressuring the North Vietnamese as part of his grand design of "linkage" politics—and a signal to the North Vietnamese that he could escalate the air war surreptitiously without arousing domestic or international anti-war opinion.

The former approach fell apart when the Russians rejected it. While Nixon waited for them to come around, he resumed intensive bombing of North Vietnam. A loophole existed in the previous fall's agreement permitting bombing in "protective reaction" against weapon sites preparing to launch missiles at reconnaissance planes. Most Americans did not know about this resumption of the bombing that they assumed had stopped with the January opening of Paris peace talks. They also were unaware of the bombing of Communist positions in Laos, which had begun under Johnson but intensified under Nixon.

More important for Nixon was his bombing of North Vietnamese–controlled areas in neutral Cambodia, which began in March 1969, and was known to even fewer Americans, including most officials in the Pentagon. At first, when the bombing began on March 18, the White House kept even the secretary of the air force in the dark. To keep the secret, Nixon ordered American pilots and their commanders to falsify bombing records so it appeared that bombs were being dropped in South Vietnam. He hoped to destroy North Vietnamese supplies and infrastructure along the Ho Chi Minh Trail network in Cambodia while demonstrating to Hanoi that he could freely escalate.

In May a *New York Times* reporter published a story about the secret bombing campaign. Although categorical White House denials quickly ended the flurry of interest in the issue, Nixon and Kissinger were furious about the leak. The FBI wiretapped thirteen members of the administration and four journalists trying to locate it. Of the first six National Security Council members whose wires were tapped, four were Jewish. This may have reflected the Jewish Henry Kissinger's need to demonstrate that he was loyal, considering that, according to John Ehrlichman, "Nixon would talk about Jewish traitors, and the Eastern Establishment-Jews at Harvard." Nixon's distasteful anti-Semitic comments were revealed during the Watergate investigations.

The phone taps, lasting as long as twenty-one months, continued even after some of the subjects had left the administration. The previous three presidents had ordered the wiretapping of only two government officials and several journalists from the Communist newspaper the *Daily Worker*. One of the officials who later found out about the illegal wiretapping sued the president and won his case, with Nixon having to pay five dollars in damages. It was the first time a president had been successfully sued for actions taken while in office.

The administration blamed the unsuccessful wiretapping on the ineptitude of the FBI and the increasing unwillingness of its chief, J. Edgar Hoover, to engage in illegal or extralegal activities on behalf of the president. This led Nixon to develop his own informal investigative office, which ultimately became known as the Plumbers—they plugged leaks. In June Hoover refused to wiretap journalist Joseph Kraft, a critic of the president's Vietnam policy. Nixon ordered White House aide John Caulfield to take care of the operation, the first of many he and others would undertake for the president. The activities of the Plumbers, as well as the secret bombing of Cambodia, figured prominently in the charges brought against the president during the Watergate investigations in 1973 and 1974. Vietnam War–related activities constituted the first major illegal operation of the Nixon presidency that later were bundled together with a variety of other high crimes and misdemeanors under the term "Watergate."

In the summer of 1969 more Vietnam-Watergate links began to appear. In an attempt to harass his enemies, Nixon began to use the Internal Revenue Service to investigate the finances of anti-war and other oppositional groups. In addition, faced with increasing violence on college campuses, the president significantly intensified the illegal and extralegal CIA, FBI, and military intelligence programs of surveilling and infiltrating student organizations that had begun during the Johnson administration. Nixon demanded information about what his enemies were planning and how he could influence or even control their actions. White House counsel John Dean felt that "a lot of the stuff that later resulted in Watergate was that mentality."

Military intelligence agents in particular were successful in working with university administrators to examine students' files. The superintendent of the Illinois State Police remarked, "I've never seen anything like the intensity of the current investigations in all my years of law enforcement," while anti-war leader Fred Halstead remembered the difference between the Nixon and Johnson administrations: "I mean, suddenly you were covered like a blanket. You could feel it."

Nixon claimed that such activities were not unusual for American presidents. National security interests demanded that the president defend the nation by ferreting out those who supported America's enemies. In justifying the surveillance of Democratic politicians, for example, Haldeman labeled them traitors—"The president's critics are in favor of putting a Communist government in South Vietnam."

Nixon was playing the sort of hardball politics that for him characterized the American political system. He could cite comparable cases of presidents' seamy activities. Franklin D. Roosevelt illegally used the FBI from 1939 to 1941 to keep track of his political enemies under the guise that they were giving aid and comfort to foreign enemies. But while some presidents abused the system some of the time in gray areas, none of his predecessors abused so many aspects of the system so much of the time.

Nixon decided early in his administration that it would be politically impossible to send more American troops to Vietnam and thus continued, under the rubric of "Vietnamization," what the Johnson administration had already begun. He would slowly bring American boys home while he built up the Vietnamese military to a point where it could defend itself. To that end, in June he announced an impending withdrawal of 25,000 troops. He began a process of periodically announcing withdrawals, implying to Americans that the war was winding down and buying time to achieve "peace with honor." Not only did he announce the withdrawal, he promised at a press conference that he would better the schedule for withdrawal proposed by former Defense

Secretary Clifford. One of his aides recalled that "We were under intense domestic pressure to give an appearance of a kind of
steady diminution of the American role."

The problem with this strategy, which related to American
domestic politics, was that the North Vietnamese—whose ances-
tors had fought the Chinese for a thousand years before expelling
them from their country—had little inducement to offer concessions. They could wait for the last American combat forces to
leave Vietnam to claim their victory. As Kissinger explained the
delicate strategy, the United States had to "withdraw fast enough
to ease public concerns but slowly enough to give Hanoi an incentive to negotiate. . . . The persistent domestic pressures . . .
turned this task into an ordeal."

Aside from periodic troop withdrawals, Nixon relieved those
domestic pressures in an even more important way. He had
promised during the campaign to replace the Selective Service
System with an all-volunteer force. In 1969 draftees made up 60
percent of the military. Nixon realized that drafting American
boys to fight in a long and increasingly unpopular war created
discipline problems in the army and political problems at home
among potential draftees and their families. By the time he assumed the presidency, 30 percent of the draftees who were sent
to Vietnam admitted to having used marijuana. They brought
the youth culture of the sixties to the combat theatre. But it was
not just drugs. The military had been rocked by increasing numbers of mutinies, refusals to follow orders, and even attempted
murders of officers by enlisted men. The official Pentagon tally
of such attempted murders, or "fraggings," had risen from 96 in
1969 to 209 in 1970. Those figures did not tell the whole story;
documented fraggings were only the tip of the iceberg.

By first reforming and then eliminating the draft, Nixon
could ease some of the pressure he would face when he had to
use the military again in operations that did not appear to be vital
to national security interests. Again, he was thinking about oper-

ating a foreign policy like his adversaries. They may have had a draft, but they did not have to worry about public opinion as they dispatched their troops to cold war hot spots.

In March 1969 Nixon appointed a carefully balanced fifteen-member commission to study the Selective Service System. Less than a year later it recommended unanimously the end of the draft. Before the draft ended in July 1973, Nixon established a lottery system in December 1969, whereby each year young men would know better their chances of being drafted. Call-ups would be based on a random rank-ordering of their birthdates. With the termination of the draft system that had been in place since 1940, Nixon explained, "Ending all dependence on the draft will be consistent with maintaining the force level and degree of readiness to meet our vital long-term security needs."

He also privately commented that "making that announcement during the campaign [August 1972] could have a very significant effect." This is not to say that Nixon ended the draft, with congressional approval, because of domestic politics. He had very good practical reasons of state to support such an initiative. Nonetheless, it is clear that such a reform benefited him politically.

Vietnamization, the lottery system, and the ending of the draft all contributed to a slow but steady decline in the anti-war movement and anti-war opinion in the United States. One reason for that decline was the realization, shared by almost all American political leaders and their supporters by 1970 or so, that the Vietnam War really *was* winding down. The only question became, was it winding down fast enough?

When the bombing of North Vietnam and Cambodia, and their playing of the Russian card, did not end the war in six months as Nixon and Kissinger had hoped, they were able to confront those who demanded a speedier finish with another issue. In 1968 parents, friends, and relatives of American prisoners of war (POWs) and those missing in action (MIAs) formed an organization, the National League of Families of American Prisoners and Missing in Southeast Asia, to pressure the government to find out about their loved ones. In the fall of 1969 the Nixon administration adopted their cause as its own, calling for a National Day of Prayer in November. This highly emotional issue involved millions of Americans wearing bracelets engraved with the names of POWs and MIAs. One of the leaders was data-processing tycoon H. Ross Perot, who tried on several occasions to fly to North Vietnam to bring gifts and mail to prisoners and to find out more about their plight. While Perot's antics troubled Nixon and Haldeman—he had a "monumental ego" and "a *total* lack of sophistication"—his cause was useful to them. From late 1969 through 1972, Nixon repeatedly claimed that he was unable to make peace largely because of the Communists' unwillingness to release or account for all POWs at war's end. This was not a major issue in the negotiations, but the North Vietnamese refusal to provide information gave Nixon a patriotic and emotional argument to explain his lack of progress in ending the war.

Nixon needed all the arguments he could muster to hold off the growing number of Americans who wanted the United States quickly to extricate itself from the wars in Southeast Asia. His situation was more difficult because he was the first president since 1853 to be elected without having his party control at least one house of Congress. The Democratic margin in the House was 243–192 from 1969 to 1971, 255–180 from 1971 to 1973, and 242–192 from 1973 to 1975. Senate Democratic margins for the same periods were 58–42, 54–44, and 56–42.

Dovish sentiment was stronger in the Democratic Party than among the Republicans. With Nixon's election, more congressional Democratic doves began to reveal themselves, no longer having to fear the wrath of President Johnson and a loss of patronage. They were soon joined by allies from labor unions, such as the United Auto Workers' Walter Reuther, who also no longer had to worry about offending their patron in the White House.

From 1969 through 1973, Democratic congressional leaders made it more and more difficult for Nixon to continue the war in a manner he may have preferred. During the secret peace negotiations between North Vietnam and the United States, Kissinger was frequently exasperated when Le Duc Tho quoted dovish senators to make his points. Tho resorted to that gambit to counter Kissinger's boasts about the widespread approval of the administration's Vietnam policies.

Early in his administration, however, one of those doves, Mike Mansfield, privately offered Nixon a most unusual option for a withdrawal from Vietnam with political cover. He promised that if the president called for a cease-fire and immediately began the withdrawal of all U.S. troops, he would back him, announcing that Nixon had made the "best possible end of a bad war," a war he had inherited from the Democrats. Mansfield felt so strongly about the war that he was, in effect, promising that the Democrats would not try to capitalize on the withdrawal in 1972 by charging Nixon with having lost Vietnam. This was virtually the first and last olive branch offered by the Democrats.

In February 1969 Senator Fulbright set up a special committee to study commitments abroad. The Arkansas senator charged the committee to pursue his national commitments resolution calling for congressional approval when American forces were sent into combat. Although Fulbright explicitly eliminated Vietnam from the purview of the so-called Symington subcommittee, it did investigate commitments in Laos. Senator Stuart Symington revealed that "We have been in Laos for years, and it is time the American people knew the facts." The administration worried that Senate investigators "have been scooping up secret data all over the world and leaking it to [the] press."

In addition, in May, forty House members opposed the military appropriations bill, the largest opposition to date. In December, Congress approved for the first time a resolution to limit U.S. military activities in Laos and Thailand. During Nixon's first term, of the eighty-six Vietnam War resolutions introduced in the Senate, almost three-quarters involved some sort of restriction on his options.

To keep anti-war senators at bay, Nixon, early in his administration, sponsored regular informal meetings between Kissinger and dovish senators such as Fulbright, Cooper, and Percy, to keep them informed about war progress. Although such meetings may have bought a little time in 1969, the senators soon became disillusioned with administration policies.

When Nixon failed to achieve an early breakthrough with Hanoi, on July 15, 1969, he issued a secret ultimatum to Ho Chi Minh: soften your peace terms by November 1 or else. "Or else" involved a variety of options considered by strategists in the White House under the rubric Operation Duckhook. Kissinger, who referred to "a savage punishing blow," could not believe "that a fourth-rate power like North Vietnam doesn't have a breaking point." To punctuate his threat, Nixon placed the Strategic Air Command on special alert in October, an alert capable of being picked up by Russian intelligence but kept secret from the American people. It was one thing to send a secret ultimatum to Hanoi. It was quite another to place the peacetime United States on nuclear alert for a good part of a month without informing the public about the potential international crisis.

Nixon knew that after November 1 it would be difficult to escalate. At the end of August, Kissinger advised that "we need a domestic plan to go with it [the escalation] . . . and reaction here." Haldeman thought that the successful mission to the moon that month enhanced development of "strong nationalism" which might help with domestic problems relating to the war.

As the deadline grew closer late in September, he reported that Nixon "turned the House hawks loose today, demanding we resume bombing, etc., as a counter on the right to all the pressures on the left to cop out." The House was always more friendly than the Senate to the Johnson and Nixon administrations. In December a four-hour debate over whether to leave the Capitol lights on and the flag flying in support of anti-war activities constituted the longest House debate on the war to that point.

As Nixon planned a variety of responses for the November 1 deadline, the anti-war movement—some of whose members had given the president time to end the war as he had promised—began to increase its activities. Leaders from the moderate wing of the movement devised the idea of an October 15 Moratorium. Instead of large rallies in one or two cities on a weekend, they called for a weekday moratorium from work or school for a few minutes, a few hours, or perhaps the entire day, in cities around the country. Local Moratorium committees would make their own plans that included marches, speeches, leafletting, prayer services, and other methods to send a simple message to the president—you are not withdrawing from the war as speedily as we expected. The national committee promised that if there were no change in the pace of withdrawal from Southeast Asia, it would sponsor moratoriums for two days in November, three days in December, and so on.

The Moratorium was the most successful anti-war demonstration of the entire Vietnam War era, and the most successful such demonstration in American history. Its activities attracted at least two million people in more than two hundred cities. It was successful because it was unique, peaceful, and highly telegenic—images in the media were generally positive. On October 15 all three television network newscasts devoted most of their programs to the Moratorium. It helped that organizers were able to arrange events that attracted a disproportionate number of middle-class adults who were nothing like the hippies and radicals that had dominated the coverage of previous rallies. *Time* concluded that "Nixon cannot escape the effects of the anti-war movement."

It could not have come at a worse time for him, two weeks before the ultimatum deadline for Hanoi. Even though he had vowed at a press conference three weeks before the Moratorium, "under no circumstances will I be affected whatever by it," he was indeed influenced by the quantity and quality of the demonstrators. When the November 1 ultimatum came and went with no movement from the Communists, Nixon did not call their bluff. He later explained that the Moratorium, by encouraging the enemy, "destroyed whatever small possibility may still have existed to end the war." No doubt it figured in his calculations, but the protesters were also a convenient scapegoat for the simple fact that the planners of Duckhook could not devise an acceptable escalation that would compel the North Vietnamese to make concessions.

Whatever the main rationale for his personally embarrassing failure to punish the Communists for their perceived insolence, Nixon was furious at the anti-war movement and especially at the media, which he felt presented the demonstrators in far too positive a light. In the wake of the Moratorium, he began planning a new campaign to combat his opponents and to attack the media for its anti-war and anti-Nixon biases.

During a three-week period after the Moratorium, he worked on an address to the nation that he later considered the most important speech of his presidency. In his November 3, 1969, "Silent Majority" speech, he called out to the "the great silent majority of my fellow Americans" who did not demonstrate and march, to support his policies of peace with honor in Vietnam. He rallied them to his side because "North Vietnam cannot defeat or humiliate the United States. Only Americans can do that." Americans sent fifty thousand telegrams and wrote thirty thousand letters to the president, 90 percent of which supported his policies. In addition, he received support from three hundred representatives and fifty-eight senators. He was pleased because the "White House Press corps is dying because of that television speech. . . . You can get across your point of view without having what you say strained through the press, and that drives the press up the wall." He was so pleased that he posed for photographs, which made most front pages, that showed huge piles of approving letters and telegrams on his desk.

Many of those supportive responses were not spontaneous. Early in his administration Nixon had organized a national letter-writing operation, through the Republican National Committee, to challenge the media and support the president whenever he spoke. Thus the word went out after the Silent Majority speech to inundate the White House and the media with letters expressing strong approval for the president. Not knowing about the secret operation, the media reported the favorable response, some of which was manufactured. This was crucial because opinion itself can be affected by the reporting of opinion trends. Americans on the fence on November 3, who had to be impressed with the overwhelming evidence that their fellow citizens approved of the president's policies in Vietnam, might have decided to climb aboard the popular presidential bandwagon. Nixon would claim that his tactic was merely an attempt to level the playing field controlled by the allegedly biased media.

But he went beyond the letter campaign. The reaction to the Moratorium intensified an assault on the media that had begun early in his administration. On October 17 one of his aides circulated a memo, "The Rifle and the Shotgun," contending that previous campaigns were not focused—what was needed was the rifle approach. He suggested threatening the television networks with anti-trust actions, sending the Internal Revenue Service after journalists, encouraging the FCC to monitor reportage, and increasing the circulation of pro-administration newspapers by giving them exclusives and private interviews. As the months went by, the White House adopted all of those recommendations and developed more. Nixon's aides gleefully went about their legal and extralegal chores, with Charles Colson once threatening hyperbolically, "I hate the [New York] *Times* as much as anyone else and would like to be in the first wave of Army shock troops going in during the second term to tear down their printing presses."

Scholarly analyses by scores of historians and journalists suggest that while Nixon himself may have been treated more negatively than other presidents by the elite media, other media generally supported most administration policies in Vietnam. More important, with a few notable exceptions like the Moratorium, journalists did not offer favorable images of the anti-war movement. Nixon's media monitors, ever on the lookout for slights reinforcing the president's strongly held convictions about the media, never pointed this out to the president, who felt justified in his unprecedented attack against American newspapers, newsweeklies, and the television networks.

He certainly felt justified in the hours after his Silent Majority speech, when the networks offered roundtable discussions of what the president had just reported to the nation. As was the case in all such commentary, panelists were carefully balanced between supporters and opponents of the president, but Nixon thought the decks had been stacked against him. He requested the chair of the FCC, one of his appointees, to ask the networks for transcripts of the roundtables as preparation for a possible investigation. In addition, his administration launched a war against so-called "instant analysis" by telejournalists. He believed they should withhold commentary on the president's speech until the next day—the American people did not need anyone to explain to them what the president had said. In fact the analyses were not instant. In almost all cases, presidential speeches are given to the media hours ahead of presentation, with an embargo proviso prohibiting them from publishing anything about it until the speech has been delivered. The networks were not immediately cowed by the president's threats, though CBS later agreed temporarily to stop its practice of instant analysis. Because television was federally licensed, it was more vulnerable to administration intimidation. Even some newspapers such as the *Washington Post*, which also owned television stations, soon found themselves challenged.

The FCC ploy was only the first shot from the rifle. Nixon unleashed his vice president, Spiro T. Agnew, to take on the media directly in a speech before a Republican group on November 13 in Des Moines. The timing of these attacks was important because the administration was attempting to influence the coverage of the second Moratorium and the Mobilization demonstrations, scheduled for November 13–15 in Washington. Agnew took on the "concentration of power" in the media, especially the three television networks and their "querulous criticism." More than 100,000 responses poured into the networks with supporters of Agnew outnumbering opponents 2 to 1. Almost as many responses were sent to the White House, where fewer than 5 percent opposed Agnew's critique of the media.

The administration contended that what it called the agenda setters—the three television networks, the two major newsweeklies, and the *Washington Post* and *New York Times*—were dominated by liberals who lived and worked in New York or Washington and who were unrepresentative of the rest of the country. As noted earlier, one unstated undercurrent in this critique was the fact that all of them were owned or directed by Jewish Americans. Nixon once expressed his hostility to the Jewish lobby and the mass media that were "essentially the same Jewish circles."

He was correct about his media enemies' control of the news agenda, especially the role the *New York Times* played each morning in helping set the programming for the evening telecasts. It was also clear that the *Times*, the *Post*, *Time*, and *Newsweek* had taken hostile editorial positions to the presidents' Vietnam policies.

In the short run, Agnew's speech worked. The networks did not cover the second series of monthly Moratorium demonstrations as intensively as the first. More important, the unprecedented assault on the media and their alleged liberal biases contributed to a long-term undermining of Americans' confidence in their daily newspapers and television newscasts.

Beginning in the Nixon era and continuing for the rest of the century and beyond, Americans repeatedly told pollsters they did not trust the media. This was a new development in American history. It owed much of its traction to Nixon's aggressive strategy to weaken the media's influence on American opinion, particularly opinion dealing with Vietnam policy.

In 1969 the president also supported passage of the Newspaper Preservation Act, which permitted joint operating agreements between newspapers in the same city. Nixon believed that most newspaper owners who favored the act were administration supporters. He also offered under-the-table assistance to Vanderbilt University's Television News Archive, which began taping and archiving the evening newscasts, among other news programs. This project has been a boon to historians, but Nixon was not thinking of them when he encouraged its development. He was convinced that if the networks knew someone was documenting their liberal biases for posterity, they would tone down their anti-administration reportage.

By the end of 1969 Nixon had begun to regain his footing after aggressively taking on his opponents in Vietnam and at home. But that polarizing assault on his domestic opponents in Congress and the media, and in the streets, represented only a quick political fix. Some of the questionable actions he endorsed at home and in Vietnam, some of the new enemies he made, and some of the old enemies he antagonized would not only make it even more difficult for him to achieve his peace with honor but would contribute to his ultimate downfall in the Watergate scandals.

8

A War at Home, 1969–1971

NIXON'S CALL for the Silent Majority to speak up, and Agnew's demand that the media alter their stories about the war and the anti-war movement, seemed to work. The November 13–14 Moratorium produced telegenic shots of marchers calling out the names of the war dead as they passed the White House. And the mass demonstration in Washington led by the Mobilization on November 15, 1969, with as many as 300,000 participants, was the largest anti-war rally in American history. But the media did not cover them as intensively or as favorably as the October 15 events. In its headline, *Newsweek* referred to a movement on a "treadmill" while other newspapers, magazines, and newscasts emphasized scattered incidents of violence. When the Moratorium, which had promised comparable events every month, failed to mount a successful protest in December, it appeared that Nixon had trumped his critics. From that point until the following spring, the anti-war movement was relatively inactive. It was not surprising that in April 1970 a sputtering Moratorium formally went out of business.

The continuing gradual withdrawal of American troops and accompanying decline in battle deaths contributed to a rise in support for the administration position. In June 1969 there were 539,000 troops in Vietnam, and the previous six months' battle-death figure was close to 8,400. At the end of 1969 troop levels had fallen to 475,000, and battle deaths for the previous half-year

had fallen to 3,900. By June 1970 the respective numbers were
415,000 and 3,000; by the end of that year, 335,000 and 1,300.
Nixon was making slow but steady progress in extricating the
United States from the war. It was not fast enough for the anti-
war movement and many Democratic politicians, but the pace
seemed to satisfy most Americans.

Vietnamization was important to the president as he entered an
election year. He hoped to break the general pattern of the presidential party losing congressional seats in mid-term elections.
While war pressures had temporarily subsided, economic pressures, created in part by the costs of the war, threatened Nixon's
prospects. The unemployment rate for 1969, which stood at a
quite healthy 3.9 percent, by the end of 1970 reached 5.3 percent.
In addition, inflation, which had been rising at the end of the
Johnson administration, continued its ascent from 4.7 percent in
1968 to 6.1 percent in 1969. Wages rose every year from 1966 to
1970, but prices climbed at a faster clip, so that in four of those
five years, real wages adjusted for inflation actually declined.

Although the objective condition of American workers did
not improve during the first two years of Nixon's presidency,
social issues, particularly those relating to violent, radical, unpatriotic, dope-smoking, free-loving, anti-war hippies, helped him
reorder priorities for many voters. Even though most of these
issues were unrelated to the Vietnam War, many Americans
viewed anti-war activists as foul-mouthed dope users and law-
breakers. Those were the rabble on whom sensation-seeking
media concentrated their skewed coverage of anti-war demonstrations and marches. If Nixon was to chip away at Democratic
majorities in Congress in 1970 and guarantee his reelection in
1972, he needed to appeal to millions of blue-collar workers
whose union officers traditionally supported Democrats and
who had helped since the New Deal to make that party the majority party.

Nixon was successful in convincing many Democrats to support his cultural agenda and ignore pocketbook issues. He was the architect of the realignment that later produced the Reagan Revolution in the 1980s and the dominance of conservatism in the 1990s into the new century. The domestic conflict over the Vietnam War and the way Nixon wrapped himself in the flag were fundamental to that realignment and the movement of the Democratic Party toward the center. This resulted, ironically, in Nixon's being the last liberal president. He was also the president who popularized the wearing of American flag lapel pins.

Nixon had not forgotten that on November 1, 1969, the North Vietnamese had called his bluff and he had not responded with the escalation threatened in his July ultimatum. In March 1970 neutral Cambodia moved into the United States camp after a right-wing coup deposed longtime neutralist leader Norodom Sihanouk. For years the Pentagon had advocated invading Cambodia to disrupt the Ho Chi Minh Trail network that passed through that country. In March of the previous year, Nixon had ordered the secret bombing of the trails in Cambodia. While this made it more difficult for the North Vietnamese to bring men and matériel to South Vietnam, the bombing was not completely successful. In addition, the headquarters for the Communist insurgency in South Vietnam, COSVN, was in Cambodia.

Nixon had occasionally mused about cleaning up the North Vietnamese in Cambodia but began serious planning for the invasion only in mid-April. Here domestic politics may have played a contributory role. On April 8 the U.S. Senate rejected his second consecutive nominee for the Supreme Court, G. Harrold Carswell. Earlier it had rejected another southerner, Clement F. Haynesworth, Jr. On April 13, in the context of the Cambodian initiative, the president told his national security adviser, "Those senators think they can push Nixon around on Haynesworth and Carswell. Well I'll show them who's tough."

Nixon did not order the invasion of Cambodia because of his failure to appoint a southerner to the Supreme Court, but it certainly put him in a fighting mood, seeking revenge against the senators by ordering a military escalation that he knew a majority would oppose.

The president also decided in April that he could not attend the spring graduations of his daughter Julie and his son-in-law David Eisenhower from Smith and Amherst Colleges because of the unruly reception he would receive from their classmates. He would show the young demonstrators he was in control with his bold escalation that he knew would spark massive demonstrations. The president almost looked forward to the confrontation with the movement. As Colson predicted, "We'll catch unshirted hell no matter what we do, so we'd better get on with it." Brought in at the end of planning because of his expected opposition to the invasion, Secretary of State William Rogers, in an uncharacteristically crude comment, feared that the invasion "will make the students puke."

On April 30 the president appeared on national television to announce the invasion of Cambodia, which he labeled an "incursion" to make it sound less like a permanent escalation. In the speech he referred to the neutrality of Cambodia, a country that had not been involved in the war. He did not tell the nation about the continual bombing of the Ho Chi Minh Trail network in that country that had begun in March 1969 when he first gave the orders for the operation. That omission, which finally came to light in 1973, became one of the bill of particulars against the president during the impeachment investigations.

As Rogers had predicted, the campuses erupted after Nixon's speech in one of the greatest crises ever faced by American institutions of higher learning. Nixon contributed to the outrage when in an off-the-cuff remark on May 1 he referred to "bums . . . blowing up the campuses." He later claimed he was not referring to the protests that day but to the April 24 firebombing of the Center for Advanced Study in the Behavioral Sciences at Stanford University. Most likely those who bombed the center, an apolitical think tank, confused it with the Stanford Research Institute, whose employees did engage in classified research for the government. The still-unsolved bombing resulted in the destruction of several scholars' offices, including that of the distinguished Indian sociologist N. S. Srinivas, whose research was destroyed. Nixon made available to him government resources to try to restore his notes. The fire almost consumed the only copy of Harvard philosopher John Rawls's nearly completed masterpiece, *A Theory of Justice*.

Few who heard Nixon's referral to "bums" knew that he was allegedly referring to the Center fire. By the time the furor over the Cambodian invasion had died down, 89 percent of all private universities and 76 percent of all public universities had experienced anti-war activities, many of which took violent forms. Strikes and closures occurred on at least 448 campuses. Several institutions were so shaken that administrators closed their colleges for the remainder of the spring semester, which meant canceling final exams and deferring the graduation of thousands of students until the fall.

The protests and violence intensified after May 4 when four young people were killed and nine others were injured after National Guard troops fired into crowds at Kent State University. Some in the crowds were protesting the Cambodian invasion, some were throwing stones toward the guardsmen, while quite a few of those fired upon were merely students going to class. The president seemed to have declared a lethal war against those who opposed his policies in Vietnam. The administration did not help itself when it publicly suggested that the students had brought on the killings because of their violent behavior. The president explained, "When dissent turns to violence it invites tragedy," while the vice president labeled the killings "predictable."

Nixon viewed the first two weeks in May 1970 as "among the darkest" during his tenure in office. The public agreed, telling pollsters that campus unrest was the nation's number one problem. Nixon appointed Vanderbilt University president Alexander Heard to advise him on the campus crises and soon after selected former Pennsylvania governor, William Scranton, to head the President's Commission on Campus Unrest. Although Nixon urged the Republican moderate not to "let higher education off with a pat on the ass," when the Scranton Commission delivered its balanced report at the end of September it concluded that "the indiscriminate firing of rifles into crowds of students and the deaths that followed were unnecessary, unwarranted, and inexcusable." Nixon was not impressed—he labeled the report "crap."

The fact that the killings occurred at Kent State University, then a relatively obscure public university in Ohio, demonstrated that unrest and protest were not confined to elite campuses such as Harvard and Berkeley. The governor of Ohio had ordered the National Guard to Kent State because of the burning of a Reserve Officer Training Corps building on that campus. Most university students were not radical activists, nor did they share their political perspectives, but the Kent State killings galvanized even apolitical students on campuses throughout the nation. (On May 15 two students were killed and eleven injured at Jackson State, a predominantly black university in Mississippi, in a much less publicized event.)

On top of the campus unrest, Nixon had to confront hostile reactions from within his own administration, from a majority of the Democratic-controlled Congress who assumed that Vietnamization meant an end to escalation, and from the anti-war movement. Within the administration, 3 members of the National Security Council resigned, 250 foreign service officers signed a protest note to the secretary of state, and Secretary of the Interior Walter J. Hickel and Commissioner of Education James

Allen publicly criticized the president. As for the foreign service officers, a furious Nixon instructed Secretary Rogers to "make sure all those sons of bitches are fired in the morning." Rogers ignored the order. But the president did ask for Allen's resignation several days later, and he fired Hickel in November, in good measure because of the way he had broken ranks in May. Thus Hickel's support for anti-war critics ultimately hurt the environmental movement, since he had become a surprisingly strong advocate of its programs.

Many congressional Democrats were as infuriated by the Cambodian invasion as were the college students rioting on campuses. Senate Majority Leader Mike Mansfield, a longtime discreet critic of Johnson and Nixon's war policies, was so distressed that on May 1 he spoke out against the invasion on the floor of the Senate. For the first time in a long and distinguished career, Mansfield publicly opposed a president's foreign policy. To the Montana senator and his allies, the escalation contributed nothing to the administration's claim that it was trying to end the war in Vietnam.

The White House had briefed several key congressional leaders in advance of the action, but only in the vaguest of ways. Senate Democrats used the occasion to intensify their attempts to repeal the Gulf of Tonkin Resolution, theoretically undercutting the president's mandate to send troops to Southeast Asia. Perhaps because he knew he was fighting a losing battle, Nixon chose not to contest the repeal that was approved in January 1971, contending that the commander-in-chief does not need such resolutions to protect U.S. national security.

On April 30, just before American troops went into Cambodia, Senators George McGovern and Mark Hatfield introduced an amendment to a military appropriations bill. It prohibited the use of funds for operations in Southeast Asia after December 31, 1970, and called for all troops to be withdrawn by June 30, 1971. On May 12, in the wake of the invasion, the two senators, along with several others, took a loan to buy time on NBC to promote their bill and discuss the crisis. Their plea for contributions of $70,000 to pay for the half-hour produced $480,000. But the "Amendment to End the War" was defeated in September by a vote of 55 to 39, with even some anti-war senators worried that it went too far in challenging the president's prerogatives.

More important, fifty-eight senators, including sixteen Republicans, voted for the more moderate Cooper-Church amendment cutting off funding after June 30 for troops involved in the Cambodian invasion. The previous December, Senators Cooper and Church had obtained passage, by a 78 to 11 vote, of their original amendment. It barred funds in a military appropriations bill from being used to support American combat forces in Laos and Thailand. Although they considered adding Cambodia at that time, they decided to omit it from the proscribed areas. This marked the first time that the Senate successfully tied passage of a military appropriations bill to restraints on a president's policies. It would not be the last.

Even before the incursion, senators had begun to discuss expanding their amendment to include Cambodia. After the invasion they settled for the June 30 pull-out date. In a concession to the White House, they included language suggesting the amendment was not meant to challenge the president's ability to protect U.S. military personnel abroad.

Although the House did not follow suit, Nixon did pull the troops out of Cambodia before the deadline, claiming mission accomplished, that he had never intended the incursion to be more than a temporary occupation. According to Haldeman, "Democrats are only going for political benefit of appearing to have forced P[resident] out of Cambodia when he's already going to get out anyway." Perhaps, but had American forces remained beyond June 30, the White House knew it would be in for a major battle on Capitol Hill. In January 1971 Nixon did sign a revised Cooper-Church amendment, which represented the first legislative restraint on a president in wartime.

Far more angry with the handful of dissident Republicans than with the Democrats, Nixon threatened to withhold support from their reelection campaigns and even to encourage primary opposition. Most of those senators were moderates from northern industrial areas, a part of the party that the president increasingly marginalized while courting southern Democrats who supported him on national security issues. Issues such as Vietnam contributed to the transformation of the two parties from broad umbrella organizations—where New York's Jacob Javits could comfortably be a Republican and Texas's John Connally could comfortably be a Democrat—into more classic conservative and liberal parties. Undoubtedly racial issues played a major role in the transformation, but one should not overlook the significance of the Vietnam War.

Another manifestation of party transformations involved the May 8, 1970, attack by two hundred "hard-hat" construction workers on a small group of anti-war protesters in New York City. They physically assaulted the protesters, chanting "All the way U.S.A." and "Love it or leave it." After knocking to the ground a young lawyer, several shouted "Kill the commie bastard" as they beat him with tools of their trades.

Charles Colson, the administration's liaison to labor, had developed close ties with Jay Lovestone, the foreign policy expert in the leadership of the AFL-CIO. This was part of the administration's operation to seduce labor and the union's attempt to maintain support for its foreign enterprises, including the anti-Communist trade movement it had helped to develop in South Vietnam. Colson urged the union to support the May 20 nationwide pro-administration rallies. On that day, at least 100,000 hard hats and their supporters marched in New York to express their approval of administration policy in Vietnam. There were hard-hat rallies as well in San Diego, Pittsburgh, and Buffalo, among other cities. Nixon was so gratified that he invited to the White House Peter Brennan, head of New York construction workers, and other union leaders for a colorful "photo-op" and for a "serious, in-depth briefing on the situation in Cambodia." Brennan gave Nixon a hard hat at the meeting, with cameras flashing, as a "symbol of our support for the fighting men and for your efforts in trying to bring the war to a proper conclusion." Michael Dono-van, a union leader whose son had died in Vietnam, brought tears to the president's eyes when he said, "Mr. President, if someone would have had the courage to go into Cambodia sooner, they might have captured the bullet that took my son's life." After the next presidential election, Nixon selected Brennan to be secretary of labor.

Although "labor" never came over completely or perma-nently to the Republican Party, many union members and blue-collar workers were more angry at flag-burning anti-war demonstrators and hippies than they were at the party that their leaders claimed supported economic policies favoring the rich. White blue-collar workers, more concerned about social issues than economic issues, were an essential part of the new winning coalition that Nixon was developing. They may have been the key to success in the 1970 victory in New York of Conservative Party candidate James Buckley over anti-war Republican Sena-tor Charles Goodell. The blue-collar vote was helpful as well in 1972. AFL-CIO head George Meany and several of his col-leagues in the leadership of the union were strident anti-Communists, convinced of the need for the United States to be in Vietnam. Meany crossed swords with the president over his economic policies, particularly wage-and-price controls that were introduced in 1971. He maintained his union's neutrality, however, in the 1972 election, after the Democrats nominated George McGovern, one of the leaders of the Senate doves. Nixon also did well with the Teamsters, in part by commuting the prison term of former leader Jimmy Hoffa, and with leaders of the maritime unions, to whom he promised more govern-ment support for merchant-ship building. The maritime unions

prospered because of the increased shipping to the combat theatre. Between 1965 and 1969, for example, their vessels carried
more than 14 million tons of petroleum to Vietnam. They had
become part of the military-industrial complex, dependent upon
the war for their well-being, like the 93,000 workers at the
Lockheed aircraft plants. Many of those workers were also attracted to the foreign policy and social messages of the Nixon
White House.

Outside the beltway, anti-war leaders hastily called on their angry followers to meet in Washington on the weekend of May
9–10 to protest the Cambodian invasion and the Kent State
killings. They were so angry that the administration feared attacks on or even "incursions" into federal buildings, including
the White House. Kissinger referred to Washington at this time
as a "besieged" city. The White House was barricaded with district buses, and elements of the 82nd Airborne, secreted in the
Executive Office Building, prepared to take defensive action
should the buses and the capital police fail to restrain the demonstrators. Colson later reported that, for a while, the White House
resembled the presidential palace in a Latin American country
preparing for a coup d'état.

More than 100,000 people attended what turned out to be a
peaceful demonstration. The fact that the virtually moribund
movement could bring 100,000 people to Washington in less than
a week demonstrated the skill of veteran organizers and the
commitment of the mostly young people who felt betrayed by the
administration. They would have agreed with Ron Ziegler,
Nixon's press secretary, who told colleagues in the embattled
White House, "We are at war."

In the early morning hours of May 9, an agitated Nixon suddenly left the White House to visit with the protesters camped
out near the Lincoln Memorial. He made the unusual brief trip to
the "enemy camp" without alerting his aides, sending a panicked

Secret Service into emergency mode. After all, buildings had been firebombed and other violent activities had only recently occurred on these students' campuses. But the emotionally agitated president felt it was important to talk to them and to explain that he understood their concerns.

As the young people rubbed their bleary eyes in disbelief, Nixon engaged them in conversation ranging from the war to foreign travel to college football. Unfortunately for him, the media's accounts, based on selective interviews with those who had talked with the president, emphasized his frivolous remarks about travel and football, not his attempts to engage them in conversation about their opposition to the war. Such reporting irritated but did not surprise the president, who never expected positive treatment from his "friends" in the press.

Those friends would have been even more critical had they known about the White House meeting Nixon arranged on June 5, 1970, with the heads of the FBI, the CIA, the NSA, and other officials. He sought to develop new and more effective practices and institutions to monitor potentially violent dissenters and other radicals allegedly working to overthrow the government. Out of this meeting came the Huston Plan, drawn up by Nixon aide Tom Huston. This would create a secret White House agency to direct stepped-up intelligence gathering about those who were out to destroy the nation. One of the main reasons for Nixon's advocacy of such an agency, according to Haldeman, was that the "Vietnam war had created almost unbearable pressures which caused him to order wiretaps and activate the plumbers in response to antiwar moves." The administration was convinced that the FBI and the CIA were not doing an adequate job of protecting the nation and the presidency from subversion. The plan was squelched when FBI director J. Edgar Hoover opposed it. All the same, Huston's analysis of the failures of existing intelligence-gathering bodies reinforced Nixon's reliance on his own operatives, including the Plumbers.

As with the period following the October 1969 Moratorium, Nixon slowly worked to regain support for his policies in Southeast Asia. Although he delivered no Silent Majority speech this time, he appeared on May 28 with his friend, the Reverend Billy Graham, at a rally in Knoxville, Tennessee. A handful of rude, chanting demonstrators in the crowd, who appeared unpatriotic and irreligious at the same time, assisted the president's cause. He also helped arrange an appearance by Bob Hope on the "Tonight" show where the popular comedian strongly defended administration policy. Finally, on July 4, Nixon sponsored an "Honor America Day" on the Mall in Washington where Hope, Red Skelton, and the Mormon Tabernacle Choir appeared before an audience of 500,000. His approval rating that summer approached 60 percent despite the weak economy and the beating he had taken over the Cambodian invasion on campuses, in Congress, and in the media.

Nixon's major political concern that summer was the 1970 congressional elections. As in all elections during this period, the Vietnam War figured prominently in the campaign. Nixon hoped to cut into Democratic majorities in both houses—he could not expect to take over either—and to punish Republican doves who had challenged his policies. His main theme would be law and order, repackaged from the 1968 campaign. It resonated even more loudly in 1970, given the increase in campus and New Left violence, as exemplified by the tumultuous response to the Cambodian invasion. While calling for an assault on the left, the president offered new peace terms to the North Vietnamese, which sounded a lot better to Americans than they really were. Nixon appeared to many as far more reasonable with his new approach than the so-called "cut-and-run" anti-war protesters. In addition, his October 12 announcement of the withdrawal of another forty thousand troops demonstrated to the electorate that he was continuing to extricate the country from the war.

The election figured as well in another of Nixon's Vietnam plans. Beginning in the summer, the Pentagon had begun preparing for a raid on the Son Tay prison camp twenty-three miles northwest of Hanoi, to rescue as many as one hundred American prisoners of war. Because Nixon feared the political repercussions of a failed raid, he moved the date for the operation from October 21 to November 18, safely after the election. The raid failed because the prisoners had been moved out in July due to flooding. In a case of the left hand not knowing what the right hand was doing, the flooding may have been caused by Operation Popeye, a secret program to seed clouds over Vietnam, producing rains that would affect transport and agricultural production. Although Nixon's poll ratings received a boost after the failed raid because Americans approved of his attempt to save the prisoners, he worried about the protesters. "Christ, they surrounded the White House, remember? This time they will probably knock down the gates and I'll have a thousand incoherent hippies urinating on the Oval Office rug."

The feared mass urination could have helped in the election. One of Nixon's speechwriters, William Safire, recalled how the anti-war movement "was useful as a villain, the object against which all our supporters could be rallied." At a meeting in late July, Nixon urged the Republicans to "tie their opponents into hippies, kids, Demos." He wanted to "Emphasize—anti-Crime, anti-Demonstrations, anti-Drug, anti-Obscenity—Get in touch with the mood of the country which is fed up with the liberals. This stuff is dynamite politically." According to one frank campaign aide, "it was a totally negative approach." Given the relative weakness of the economy and Nixon's inability to bring the war to a speedy conclusion, the negative approach was a useful diversion from more substantial issues. The president dispatched Spiro Agnew, his colorful vice president, to spread the message against the "Radiclibs." The idea was to conflate the violent, anti-American, revolutionary radicals with liberals in particular and Democrats in general. Liberals, for example, were hurt when an innocent student was killed on August 28, 1970, in the bombing by a handful of radicals of the University of Wisconsin Army Math Research Center.

When Agnew's hard-hitting speeches did not move the poll numbers much, Nixon himself took to the hustings, visiting twenty-three states during the final two weeks of the 1970 campaign. His arguments against the radicals were punctuated by a dangerous incident in San Jose, California, on October 29, where, according to Safire, Nixon was subjected to "a mob attack upon a U.S. president—unique in our history."

Nixon had been speaking in that city and, as usual wherever he appeared, anti-war and New Left young people had gathered to picket and taunt. They shouted as they marched, "One, two, three, four, we don't want your fuckin' war," a chant not designed to influence middle-class Americans. What happened next was not that spontaneous. According to Haldeman, "we wanted some confrontation" in San Jose, so we "stalled departure a little." Instead of speeding away upon leaving the auditorium, Nixon jumped onto the hood of his limousine to flash the demonstrators his famous V for victory sign. He later recalled that he "could not resist showing them how little respect [he] had for their juvenile and mindless rantings." Not surprisingly, some in the crowd allegedly began throwing objects, including a few rocks, at the president and his motorcade. He had obtained the response he wanted and milked it for all he could get.

Speaking in Anaheim the next night, he referred to the incident in San Jose and called for the mobilization of his Silent Majority. "It is time for the great silent majority of Americans to stand up and be counted. And the way you stand up and be counted is not to answer in kind. You don't have to resort to violence." All they had to do was "go to the polls and vote . . . for those men who stand with the President."

Nixon returned to this theme in a videotaped election eve speech based on a tough message he had presented on October 31 in Phoenix. The poorly prepared, grainy film, coupled with

Nixon's angry denunciation of "violent thugs," stood in stark contrast to the rejoinder presented by Maine senator Edmund Muskie. His calm and reasoned presentation and the better production values of the Democrat's program catapulted the gentle Muskie to first place among candidates for his party's 1972 presidential nomination. By the end of 1970, Muskie's poll numbers were better than Nixon's; consequently he became the main target in the White House's illegal and extralegal attempts to undermine the president's most threatening opponents before the 1972 Democratic Convention.

Until 1994 it had proven difficult for a party to present a single organizing theme for its candidates in 435 congressional elections. Such was the case in 1970, when most Americans voted on the bases of personality, local economic and social issues, and party loyalties, not because they wanted to turn out the unpatriotic and violent "Radiclibs." The Democrats lost two Senate seats but gained nine in the House and eleven governorships. The Nixon camp claimed victory in holding traditional by-election gains by the out party to a minimum. Moreover the administration was instrumental in helping defeat three dovish senators, New York Republican Charles Goodell, and Democrats Albert Gore (Sr.) of Tennessee and Joseph Tydings of Maryland. The White House was deeply involved in especially dirty politics in the Tydings campaign.

With the by-election over, Nixon could devote all his political attention to his own reelection campaign. On several occasions he privately announced his intention to pull all combat troops out of Vietnam by the summer of 1972, certainly by the time of the Democratic Convention. He believed that such a pullout in 1971 "would be a serious mistake" because he would not have much control of the situation in the South by November 1972. In March 1971 he directly warned the Democratic congressional leadership that if it interfered with his policy and timetable and forced him out of the war prematurely, he would blame them in

1972 for whatever happened to South Vietnam. As for the Democrats making an issue of his pace of withdrawal, he told his advisers that he would charge the Democrats with sabotaging his attempts to obtain a peace with honor. And he would "exploit the differences within the Democratic party" between doves like Senator Muskie and hawks like Senator Henry Jackson. Nixon was little concerned about the few critics in his own party like California congressman Pete McCloskey, who continued to talk about impeaching the president. As in the presidential elections in 1964 and 1968, the Vietnam War would be an important issue in 1972, and Nixon was prepared for it.

Whether or not the 1970 congressional elections were significantly affected by his Vietnam policy, by the end of 1970 Nixon enjoyed renewed support for his policy of Vietnamization. He had brought home close to 200,000 troops since he had taken office. U.S. battle deaths, which had reached almost 3,000 during the first six months of the year, had declined to less than 1,400 during the second six months.

Nixon felt sufficiently strong politically to approve a new escalation in February 1971, though one more modest than the Cambodian fiasco of the previous spring. On February 8 he launched Lam Son 719, a temporary invasion of Laos to interdict the Ho Chi Minh Trail system that ran from North Vietnam through Laos to South Vietnam. This time, however, the South Vietnamese would do the escalating. Because of the hostile reaction in Congress and in the nation in general to the Cambodian incursion, Nixon concluded that it would be difficult politically to send American boys into the fray. His military advisers warned him that the process of Vietnamization was not far enough along to send the ARVN into Laos alone. But pressures from the home front tied Nixon's hands. And these same pressures compelled him to order the invasion of Laos to disrupt potential North Vietnamese offensives in 1971 or 1972 that could affect his reelection.

The Laos invasion failed. Americans viewed some of that failure when their nightly television newscasts featured pictures of South Vietnamese soldiers fleeing the battle, frantically attempting to hang on to the skids of evacuation helicopters. The White House nevertheless declared another great victory, with Nixon announcing that the ARVN had "come of age." Privately Kissinger complained about the South Vietnamese: "Those sons of bitches. It's their country and we can't save it for them if they don't want to." His NSC aide, Alexander Haig, visited Vietnam in March, and later wrote that "Lam Son destroyed the cream of the South Vietnam army and was far more serious and detrimental than was believed at the time."

It was detrimental at home too. One Republican congressman noted that "Laos is one more straw—and a substantial one—on the camel's back. Most Americans—myself included—have come to feel that this war has gone on too long."

Nixon was furious at the networks that had projected images at variance with his. He charged them with having transformed a "military success" into a "public relations disaster" and a "psychological defeat." He unleashed Vice President Agnew again to "blast T.V. for distorted coverage." Nixon's renewed assault against the "biased" media helped to salvage support for his policy. At this point in his presidency, a clear majority of Americans preferred Nixon's account of the war to that of the journalists. Both Nixon and Kissinger later admitted in their memoirs that the Laos invasion had not turned out as well as they had hoped.

The same sort of sharp divide between an increasingly polarized public marked the response to Lieutenant William Calley's court martial for the My Lai massacre. On March 16, 1968, Lieutenant Calley had led his company into the South Vietnamese village of My Lai 4 in Quang Ngai province. My Lai was a suspected Viet Cong stronghold from which several lethal attacks had been launched against U.S. military personnel. But when

Calley's unit arrived in the village, it found no Viet Cong or resistance of any kind. That meant little to Calley, who proceeded to lead members of his company in a bloody massacre. It resulted in the execution-style murders of between four hundred and five hundred unarmed Vietnamese, almost all of whom were women, children, and old men.

Ronald Ridenhour was a veteran of the company involved who had heard about the massacre in 1968 while he was in Vietnam. He felt compelled to go public with what he knew in letters to more than thirty U.S. government officials. He had been waiting for a formal investigation of the incident, and when it appeared that the army was covering it up, he wrote his letter in which he remained "irrevocably persuaded that if you and I do truly believe in the principles of justice and the equality of every man, however humble, before the law, that form the backbone that this country is founded on, then we must press forward a widespread and public investigation of this matter with all our combined efforts. . . . A country without a conscience is a country without a soul, and a country without a soul is a country that cannot survive."

Ridenhour's letter accomplished what he had hoped. The army opened an official investigation that resulted in war crimes and obstruction-of-justice charges against two generals, four colonels, four lieutenant colonels, four majors, six captains, and eight lieutenants. Although the investigation was a secret affair, it leaked to the press with freelance journalist Seymour Hersh first publishing the story of My Lai on November 13, 1969, in the *New York Times*. (Nixon privately lambasted "those dirty rotten Jews from New York who are behind it.") Three weeks later *Life* published shocking pictures of the massacre that had been taken by an army photographer who had been at My Lai.

How someone like the incompetent Calley, who could not read maps and who was, according to one of his men, like "a little kid trying to play war," came to be in charge of a company is a telling characteristic of the unpopularity of the Vietnam War. In ordinary times he would have never been admitted into Officer Candidate School. But these were no ordinary times. ROTC, an important source for well-educated second lieutenants, was drying up. Either college students, protected by student deferments, were failing to join the corps or, as was becoming more common, anti-war activists had helped convince administrators to close down ROTC units on their campuses. General Westmoreland later conceded that "being an officer in the United States Army exceeded Lieutenant Calley's abilities. . . . It would have been better to have gone short of officers than to have accepted applicants whose credentials left a question as to their potential as officers."

The story of My Lai, which simmered through 1970, became a major political issue on March 29, 1971, when an army court martial sentenced Calley to life imprisonment at hard labor for the premeditated murder of twenty-two South Vietnamese civilians. As for the many other officers implicated in the cover-up, the only penalties involved the demotion of one general and a censure for his assistant.

American participation in atrocities and other crimes against civilians, such as the strategic bombing of North Vietnam, had long been a major concern of anti-war critics in the United States and Europe. All military campaigns, even those fought by the armies of democracies, produce atrocities, rapes, and other assaults against civilians. But counter-insurgency warfare is an especially messy business, primarily because it is difficult if not impossible to distinguish plainclothes guerrilla fighters from the civilians among whom they live. The French called their war in Vietnam "La Guerre Sale," the dirty war. The conservative *National Review* referred to a war full of "ambiguities." Even with this knowledge, it was and is difficult for many Americans to accept the notion that their boys could rape, pillage, and murder.

Just two months before the Calley verdict, from January 31 through February 2, the Vietnam Veterans Against the War (VVAW) held war-crimes hearings in Detroit. The so-called Winter Soldier hearings (Thomas Paine's summer soldier or "sunshine patriot" deserted in difficult times during the American Revolution) produced testimony from more than one hundred veterans who claimed they had participated in or witnessed war crimes. Hollywood stars Jane Fonda and Donald Sutherland took up residence in Detroit for several months to help organize and finance the hearings. Senator Hatfield read the sensational testimony into the *Congressional Record*, and some of the gory stories briefly made headlines. The administration counterattack, led by leaders of veterans groups who incorrectly charged that many of those who had testified had not seen combat in Vietnam, succeeded in quickly pushing the Winter Soldier hearings to the back pages.

Most Americans recoiled at the idea that their young men could have participated in such bloody assaults against civilians. Or, many contended, if civilians were killed, they were part of the collateral damage against a fiendish enemy that had never itself been concerned with fighting a clean war.

But now the U.S. military, not a bunch of ragtag anti-war veterans, had convicted one of its own for directing and participating in a well-documented massacre. The majority of Americans who flocked to Calley's side thought he was only trying to do his duty as best he could. Many who took this position came from the South and West, conservative areas that had become Nixon's core constituency. They were joined by a smaller group of liberals and anti-war critics who felt that Calley had been made the scapegoat for higher-ups who, they charged, routinely condoned and covered up such actions.

The White House received more than five thousand telegrams in the days after the Calley sentence with those supporting clemency outnumbering those opposed by 100 to 1. As usual, Nixon saw the issue in political terms. He knew that he should have let the appeals run their course, but there was in that approach "no political gain for us . . . we've got to act on the basis of what does us the most good." With most Americans opposing the sentence, Nixon wanted to "be on the side of the people for a change, instead of always doing what's cautious, proper, and efficient." He was worried "how we can hold enough support for a year and a half to maintain our conduct of the war. . . . If we don't move, the support we have for withdrawal from Vietnam etc., will evaporate or become discouraged." The year and a half would bring him to the 1972 election.

Nixon later wrote that he considered Calley's crime "inexcusable." Even so, he contended that his opponents in Congress and the media were using My Lai for political gains—"they had been noticeably uncritical of North Vietnamese atrocities." After consulting with congressional leaders who were feeling pressure from their constituents to help Calley, on April 1, 1971, Nixon ordered that the lieutenant be released from the stockade and be placed under house arrest while awaiting his appeal. When word of the president's action reached the House of Representatives, it was greeted with an enthusiastic round of applause. Nixon reported that "Reaction was particularly strong and positive in the South." In April 1974 a military court reduced Calley's term to ten years; three months later, the secretary of the army paroled him.

Calley, a Georgian, became another part of Nixon's southern strategy. The president had nominated two southern judges to the Supreme Court; when they were turned down, he had suggested that the rest of the nation was biased against that region. In Calley's case, Nixon adopted a position against his lawyer's advice to appeal to the South. In a comparable case he later supported a constitutional amendment to prohibit the use of busing to integrate schools, though he knew that such an amendment was on very shaky legal ground.

As the administration was dealing with the politics of the Calley case, the anti-war movement was preparing a wide variety of activities from April 19 through May 6, 1971, which would rock the capital. Beginning on April 19 the VVAW staged a weeklong series of events in Washington. On Saturday, April 24, 300,000 anti-war protesters attended a demonstration in Washington while another 150,000 appeared at a parallel event in San Francisco. Finally, beginning on May 3, the May Day Tribe tried to "close down" Washington through civil disobedience in an unprecedented assault on the government. Considering the number of citizens involved, few participants or observers predicted that the tumultuous spring 1971 demonstrations would be the last major offensive of the anti-war movement.

The first and the last of the activities were the most important politically for the administration and for the country. Nixon worried about the specter of several thousand veterans staging telegenic protests throughout Washington for a week. His Justice Department moved quickly to obtain a court order evicting them from the Mall, where they were encamping illegally. Chief Justice Warren Burger, among others, urged the president not to enforce the order because of the impact on many Americans of seeing veterans, some of whom were missing limbs or in wheelchairs, forcibly removed from the Mall. It conjured up images of Herbert Hoover's military attack against an unarmed contingent of World War I veterans who had gathered in Washington in 1932 to demand an advance on bonuses promised for their military service. The law-and-order Nixon administration, considering all its options, finally decided to ignore the fact that the veterans were camping without a permit.

When the polls showed a slight drop in the president's performance ratings during the week the VVAW was in town, Nixon advisers attributed it to the positive coverage of the group's activities, especially the emotional final event in which veterans individually threw their medals and ribbons over the wall at the Capitol while offering moving explanations for their unusual action. The administration's counter-attack, a "Non-Veterans Demonstration" which featured the head of the Veterans of Foreign Wars labeling many of the men on the Mall impostors, failed when the media interviewed battle-scarred veterans whose bona fides were beyond question. One veteran even proved his case by taking his glass eye out of its socket and showing it to a journalist. The White House was furious at the media who "are killing us" and who "by their own obsession created a major thing out of what should have been almost totally ignored."

On Capitol Hill, John Kerry, a young naval officer who had been wounded three times, offered eloquent testimony on behalf of the VVAW to the Senate Foreign Relations Committee. The appearance of the dignified Yale graduate concerned the White House. Charles Colson called on his colleagues to "destroy this young demagogue before he becomes another Ralph Nader."

It would not take long for the administration to regain its footing. The impressive mass demonstrations in Washington and San Francisco that followed the veterans' activities did not receive major coverage from the media, in part because they offered little that was new, even though several members of Congress spoke to the crowds. That same day, four representatives introduced a resolution in the House to approve the People's Peace Treaty, the demonstration organizers' privately negotiated treaty that "ended" the war. In addition, observers noted the large number of middle-class adults attending the rally, symbolized by a man in his fifties proclaiming, "I am a member of the Silent Majority who isn't that silent anymore." But *Time* was correct in describing the "layer of despair" that hung over the huge Washington throng. All the demonstrations since 1968 had not stopped the war or persuaded a majority of Americans that Nixon's approach to obtaining peace with honor was wrong.

More important politically was the May Day Tribe's action in the first week in May. As many as thirty thousand protesters stayed in Washington after the Saturday rally to attempt to make it impossible for the government to make war. On Monday, May 3, they planned to block bridges and major thoroughfares with their bodies and with obstructions to stop bureaucrats from getting to their offices. Like the VVAW demonstrations, here was another telegenic protest with plenty of unusual action. Unlike the earlier one, the coverage greatly assisted the administration's attempt to portray its opponents as violent radicals.

Because of useful intelligence, sometimes gathered illegally, and because agents of the government had penetrated the leadership cadre of the May Day Tribe, Nixon was ready for the civil disobedience. In dragnet sweeps the police arrested seven thousand people before noon on May 3, in actions approved by Assistant Attorney General William Rehnquist. By the third day of protests, more than ten thousand people had been arrested. The work of the government continued unhindered. That some of those arrested were young people who were in the wrong place at the wrong time, and that few were read their rights or arraigned in a timely manner, did not bother the administration or most of the public. Nixon, who labeled the civil disobedients "beasts," explained that the police "showed a good deal more concern for their [protesters'] rights than they showed for the rights of the people of Washington." Privately a Nixon speechwriter was pleased that the protesters had "played into our hands by showing . . . the vicious side" of the anti-war movement.

Most Americans, who were leery of ordinary peaceful demonstrations and rallies, strongly opposed the civil disobedience, which on their television screens looked like revolutionary violence. Seventy-six percent of those polled felt that the mass arrests were justified. In 1975 the courts, which decided that most of those arrests had been illegal, ordered the government to make monetary awards to twelve hundred demonstrators.

The administration's private response demonstrated its darker side that was later illuminated during the Watergate investigations. Charles Colson, Nixon's number one dirty trickster, sent a crate of oranges to detainees that appeared to have been a contribution from Edmund Muskie, the administration's top target among Democratic contenders. Nixon commented that Colson's "gonna get caught at some of these things. . . . But . . . he's got a lot done that he hasn't been caught at." Nixon also contemplated taking Colson up on another "trick," recruiting union "thugs" to serve as police auxiliaries. The president knew "They've got guys who'll go in and knock their heads off." Haldeman agreed: "They're gonna beat the shit out of some of these people."

The union thugs were not needed. The capital weathered the assault, as did the president. With the conventions a year away, he had apparently regained his footing on Vietnam policy. Casualties and draft calls continued to decline while anti-war opponents appeared to many Americans to have become increasingly violent and disruptive. The economy was a problem, but it could be finessed as long as the president kept voters' attention on the Radiclibs who had allegedly launched an all-out attack, by any means necessary, on the nation's political and value systems.

9

Four More Years, 1971–1972

WITH HIS SUCCESSFUL DEFENSE of the capital against the anti-war movement, President Nixon began to strengthen his position in the run-up to his reelection campaign. But he still had to confront two other perennial "enemies" who continued to make life difficult for him: the media and Congress. How he dealt with them would have reverberations in American politics far beyond the 1972 election.

On February 23, 1971, just after Americans saw on their television screens humiliating film clips of the South Vietnamese incursion into Laos, CBS television aired "The Selling of the Pentagon." Rebroadcast on March 23 with additional commentary from administration defenders, the powerful documentary revealed that the Pentagon was spending close to $200 million annually in a wide variety of public relations campaigns designed to sell its perspective on the war in Vietnam and lobby Congress to approve its weapons-procurement programs.

The documentary rekindled the administration's war against the media, with Vice President Agnew leading another vigorous attack not only against "The Selling of the Pentagon" but against several other muckraking documentaries produced at CBS. He charged that all the media "cloak themselves in a special immunity to criticism." Americans were "entitled to a fair and full accounting of the truth, and nothing but the truth, by those who

exercise great influence with their consent." Agnew was not alone in his attacks. The leadership of the Democratic-controlled House created a Special Subcommittee on Investigations of the Interstate and Foreign Commerce Committee to look into the biases projected in the CBS production and even possible crimes committed by the writers in their search for information.

At first glance it seemed surprising that the Democrats would join with the White House in aggressively going after CBS. But many Democrats recognized the popularity of attacks on the media and were concerned about the documentary's bipartisanship when it identified specific senators and representatives who enjoyed lavish Pentagon junkets. Along with the Republicans, the Democrats subpoenaed scripts, outtakes, recordings, notes, and a variety of other materials that went into the making of the documentary. CBS President Frank Stanton resisted delivering the materials on First Amendment grounds, describing the "chilling effect . . . if newsmen are told that their notes, films, and tapes will be subject to compulsory process so that the government can determine whether the news has been satisfactorily" brought to the public.

In July 1971, 181 members of the House voted to censure Stanton—an example, according to Representative Donald Riegle (R-MI), of how "their spite for the networks stops just short of hatred." The attack on CBS, and, by implication, the other networks and major media outlets, rekindled publishers' and journalists' adversarial approach that had been blunted somewhat by the administration's fall 1969 anti-media assault. As dogged reporters on several of the targeted newspapers turned up revelation after revelation about the Watergate scandals in late 1972 and early 1973, Nixon would come to rue the day he crossed swords with the emboldened media barons. Moreover "The Selling of the Pentagon" imbroglio was not the only problem posed by the media for the president in the late spring of 1971.

On June 13, 1971, the *New York Times* began publishing excerpts from "The History of U.S. Decision Making in Vietnam, 1945–1968," compiled in the Defense Department toward the end of the Johnson administration. Robert S. McNamara had commissioned the classified study, later called the "Pentagon Papers," to help future government officials understand how the United States became stuck in the quagmire of Vietnam. The three-thousand-page narrative was supported by four thousand pages of documents, most of which were not meant to see the light of day for at least thirty years. Daniel Ellsberg, one of the scholars who had worked on the in-house study and who had had access to a copy at the RAND Institute where he then was employed, secretly copied the papers and tried to make them public through leaks to friendly members of Congress and ultimately the press. He succeeded when the *Times* and then the *Washington Post* decided to publish excerpts from the study. Ellsberg, a former hawkish Marine who by the late sixties had turned against the war, thought that his leaking of the papers, filled with examples of White House and Pentagon deceit, if not lies, would arouse the public to pressure Nixon to end the war.

Ellsberg did not succeed in his primary goal, but the reaction from the White House to his purloining and peddling of the Pentagon Papers began a chain of events that led to the cover-up of the Plumbers' June 1972 break-in at Democratic Party headquarters. This led directly to the August 1974 resignation of Richard Nixon. But Ellsberg's gamble came too late. By the time Nixon quit, the United States had been out of Vietnam for a year and a half.

At first glance the publication of the study seemed to be a godsend for the Republicans because it showed how Democratic Presidents Kennedy and Johnson had misled the public and made questionable decisions about Vietnam. Haldeman noted that the administration understood that "it really blasts McNamara, Kennedy, and Johnson," while Alexander Haig recommended that the White House "keep completely clear of it because it doesn't hurt us." For a few days Haig and others referred to the documents as the "Kennedy/Johnson Papers."

Henry Kissinger was furious, though, perhaps because Ellsberg had once been his assistant whom he had recruited to help develop Vietnam policy during the early weeks of the administration. Kissinger contended that no foreign leaders would ever trust the United States again if they thought their top-secret private messages might be published only a few years later. He appealed to Nixon to take action against Ellsberg, because if he did not, "It shows you're a weakling, Mr. President." The especially insecure president never wanted to appear to be a weakling, even though he was certain that at least 95 percent of the material in the Pentagon Papers did not jeopardize national security. The second in command at the Pentagon went even further, claiming that he "couldn't find a damn thing in them on security." The president also feared that the publication of the papers might lead Congress to become more aggressive in demanding classified information from him.

Nixon was motivated too by his hostility to the press, particularly the *Times* and the *Post*. As Haldeman noted, "Nothing else that we do in this administration will give him more pleasure" than to restrain the newspapers from publishing the history. Thus Nixon ordered the Justice Department to bring suit in federal court to stop the newspapers from running the articles. After he obtained a temporary restraining order, the newspapers appealed and obtained several favorable rulings themselves. At that point, both they and the Justice Department requested that the Supreme Court make a speedy final ruling, with the head of the department's Office of Legal Counsel, William Rehnquist, advising the president that he had a strong national security case. On June 30, barely two weeks after the *Times* had begun publishing, the Court ruled by a 6 to 3 decision to permit the newspapers to continue the series. Although this was a victory for the newspapers, the justices did not dismiss the possibility of prior restraint in future cases when national security interests were clearer. Consequently, in some ways, the decision represented a blow to advocates of freedom of the press.

More important to Nixon's future were the dirty tricks he employed to "get" Ellsberg, whose "punishment" might lead future leakers to think twice about such actions. Colson felt that by destroying Ellsberg, "we can discredit the peace movement and have the Democrats on a marvelous hook because thus far most of them have defended the release of the documents."

On June 28, 1971, Ellsberg and his co-conspirator, Anthony J. Russo, were indicted for theft of government property and unauthorized possession of defense documents. That was only one of Ellsberg's punishments. Under Nixon's direction, the administration took measures to destroy the leaker's reputation by itself leaking to the media defamatory information about Ellsberg. Nixon intended to "leak stuff all over the place" and crush the miscreant in the press, just as he had used the media in the late forties to crush Alger Hiss, a government official accused of spying. "These papers are not important in themselves," Nixon asserted; "what is important is that someone stole them and that the *Times* printed them." Because he had lost confidence in the FBI, Nixon had to rely on his White House Special Investigation Unit—the Plumbers.

The president demanded, "I want him exposed . . . I don't care how you do it but get it done." One way to expose him involved the Plumbers' break-in at the Los Angeles office of Dr. Lewis Fielding, Ellsberg's psychiatrist, in hopes of discovering character-defaming tidbits in the doctor's files. Several of the people involved in that illegal operation on September 3 were the same people involved in the Watergate break-in the following June. Nixon himself later admitted that he was unsure whether he ordered or was aware of the Fielding break-in. His cover-up of the Watergate break-in, about which Nixon most likely had no foreknowledge, may have been related to his fear that his involvement in the earlier break-in would come to light.

That was not the only Plumbers operation involving the Vietnam War during the period of the Pentagon Papers imbroglio. Nixon ordered "a small team . . . to start rifling through secret documents. . . . Get some pros to handle it"—to find government files that showed how Kennedy was involved in Diem's assassination. The defamation of John F. Kennedy, he felt, could hurt the budding presidential candidacy of his brother, Senator Edward Kennedy (D-MA). To assist in the search, the president ordered the secretary of state to speed the release of diplomatic files from that era. When the smoking gun revealing President Kennedy's direct involvement in the assassination could not be found, Charles Colson instructed Howard Hunt, who had been involved in the Fielding break-in and later in the Watergate break-in, to fabricate the needed documents. Colson then took Hunt's forgeries to the press and almost convinced *Life* to run a sensational story about Kennedy and Diem. After Hunt was arrested for the Watergate break-in, John Dean broke into Hunt's White House safe to secure the forged documents and other dirty business in which Hunt had been involved. The White House counsel gave the documents to L. Patrick Gray, acting director of the FBI, for safekeeping. Gray ultimately burned them, most likely on the order of Nixon's aides. When the story came to light in 1972, Gray resigned his position.

The administration's punishment of Ellsberg continued into 1972. Hunt organized a group of thugs to beat him up when he addressed an anti-war crowd on May 3 on the Capitol steps. They were able to rough up several people in the crowd but never reached Ellsberg. As for his legal punishment for leaking the papers, things looked bright for the prosecution when Nixon inquired whether the presiding judge, W. Matthew Byrne, would be interested in the then-vacant FBI chief's job. Sensing the impropriety, in May 1973 Byrne dismissed the case against

Ellsberg because "government agencies had taken an unprecedented series of actions" which included bribery, burglary, and the withholding of information, that "the totality of the circumstances of this case . . . offend a sense of justice." Byrne's decision and his condemnatory language added to the Watergate brief of particulars against the president.

The publication of the Pentagon Papers during the early summer of 1971 was a major defeat for the administration. At the time, no one suspected that the entire affair would come to play a key role in the crisis that destroyed the Nixon presidency in 1973–1974. Despite the Supreme Court decision, the president's political position continued to strengthen during the remainder of 1971, in good measure because of the continuing return of GIs from the war and the falling number of casualties suffered by American forces. By the end of the year only 157,000 troops remained in Vietnam; in the preceding six months Americans had suffered only 276 battle deaths. Troop levels had declined below those of the end of 1965, and battle deaths had fallen to the level of the first six months of that year of great escalation. Vietnamization apparently was working as the war came full circle.

In June the House turned back the Senate's Mansfield Resolution that would have led to a total U.S. withdrawal in nine months as long as American POWs were returned. Nixon warned Mansfield that such resolutions could affect his bargaining position at the peace talks. If the talks failed, Nixon would blame the failure on Mansfield and his fellow dovish activists in Congress. He was also privately concerned that the POW/MIA families and their supporters might be attracted to such a resolution and pressure him to make damaging concessions in the negotiations. Finally, nationwide anti-war rallies on October 13 and November 6 attracted only 50,000 and 100,000 people respectively, causing one of the leaders to note mournfully, "We stand in the antechamber of a dying antiwar movement."

Even with these positive turns of events, Nixon remained insecure about the election. He hoped the war would be over before November 1972 when Americans went to the polls. In the latter part of 1971, Kissinger had begun privately to deemphasize, ignore, or otherwise obfuscate one of the key stumbling blocks to achieving a peace with Hanoi—American insistence on the withdrawal of all North Vietnamese troops from South Vietnam as a quid pro quo for the withdrawal of all American forces. He worried that time was running out since Hanoi "had every incentive to wait for the interreacting [sic] combination of unrest in South Vietnam and an American domestic squeeze" to "pave the way for their eventual control."

With the Americans beginning to yield on the issue of North Vietnamese withdrawal from the South, the last serious issue remaining involved the nature of the regime in Saigon. Until the fall of 1972, the Communists insisted that President Thieu could not be allowed to continue in power, even for a few months, after the cease-fire. For his part, Nixon did not wish to find himself in the position of the Democrats in 1963, who stood by while President Diem was assassinated.

As they had done in 1968, the North Vietnamese were again counting the months to the U.S. presidential election. They knew that Nixon hoped to strengthen his hand against any Democratic opponent trying to run on an anti-war platform. George McGovern, for example, who had been running for the nomination since January 1971, went on a fact-finding mission to Paris and Vietnam in September, declaring, "Mr. Nixon's Vietnamization policy—like its predecessor policies—is a glaring failure. . . . If American forces are not withdrawn quickly and our military operations ended, we shall see a further military, political, economic and moral debacle."

In Paris, McGovern, violating the Logan Act that prohibited private diplomacy, secretly "negotiated" his own terms for peace with North Vietnamese and Viet Cong diplomats, almost making a deal on the vexing POW issue. He held out the prospect of a congressional war-ending amendment if Hanoi would promise formally to return the POWs at war's end. Several days later, when Le Duc Tho met with Henry Kissinger, he boasted, "I really don't know why I am negotiating with you. I have just spent several hours with Senator McGovern, and your opposition will force you to give me what I want." The North Vietnamese did give McGovern something as well—they promised not to do anything during the election campaign that might help Nixon.

In late September 1971, discussing the U.S. relationship with Saigon, presidential emissary Alexander Haig told Thieu that "A further complication will be the approaching U.S. political contest which cannot but increase domestic political overtones and further complicate the issue." Haig was in Saigon to confer with Thieu about several issues, including the October South Vietnamese presidential election. A free and fair election would strengthen the administration's critics who complained that the United States was backing an undemocratic regime. Unfortunately, even with the CIA offering to bankroll Thieu's opponents to make the election look fair, Thieu won with 94 percent of the vote, a figure that caused his acerbic vice president Ky to note, "It was a ridiculous election, like a communist one." This was only one in a score of elections in client states that were held to satisfy the American need to appear to support democratic regimes. Most American observers were not fooled by the appearance of a democratic election in South Vietnam.

They would be fooled, however, by the appearance of a democratic election in the United States. In late fall 1971 the Nixon camp began its unprecedented legal, extralegal, and illegal assaults on the election process. The White House and CREEP meddled in the race for the Democratic nomination to help ensure the victory of George McGovern, the candidate who would be easiest to beat. McGovern was the most liberal of the major candidates, a group that included Hubert Humphrey and Edmund Muskie.

For a while, at the beginning of 1972, Muskie was running even with the president in the polls. Aside from Nixon's order that "we should have someone attacking Muskie as a defeatist," his campaign employed espionage, interfered with the front-runner's scheduling by canceling events, launched a Republican phone campaign allegedly in Muskie's name, published phony polls showing that McGovern was the strongest Democratic candidate, and initiated a variety of other seamy activities that resulted in a jail term, unrelated to Watergate, for the president's chief mischief-maker on the campaign trail.

Nixon helped McGovern win the nomination. With the South Dakota senator, clearly the most dovish on the war, the president could portray him as the candidate of radicals and hippies who, most Americans thought, had done so much to destroy the nation's values. In order to appear to be a responsible chief executive instead of an alleged appeaser like McGovern, Nixon had to accelerate the pace of his own honorable peacemaking in the months before the campaign.

When Muskie formally entered the race in January 1972, he called on the president to withdraw all American troops from Vietnam. His entry was followed by that of Hubert Humphrey, who also called for an immediate end to the war. Despite massive troop withdrawals up to the opening of the primary season in 1972, the Democrats meant to make the continuation of the war a key issue in the campaign. At the time, Nixon's presidential approval rating hovered around 50 percent.

The president had two aces up his sleeve to demonstrate that he was bringing the war to a speedy end—an accelerated troop-withdrawal schedule, and the announcement that Henry Kissinger, who had been meeting secretly with the North Vietnamese for almost two years, had recently offered new peace terms. Nixon and his aides planned the dramatic announcements carefully, timing them so that they would have the greatest possible impact on Democratic politics when the primary campaign heated up in New Hampshire. Haldeman boasted that the first announcement "will suck the peaceniks out and the second move will chop them all off." On January 13 Nixon announced that he was bringing home by May 1 another seventy thousand troops and that future planned withdrawals throughout 1972 would leave only twelve thousand troops in Vietnam by year's end. The North Vietnamese were pleased to hear that the United States would soon have no capacity to participate in the ground war.

On January 25 the president revealed that since 1969 Kissinger had been engaging in secret talks with the North Vietnamese and that the United States had made far more compromises than the public record at the official Paris peace talks suggested. At this point Henry Kissinger was the most popular member of the Nixon administration, the brilliant diplomat whose other secret journeys had resulted in the beginning of a Chinese-American rapprochement. His reputation among Americans in both parties was so favorable that the president frequently appeared jealous of his national security adviser.

One week later Haldeman appeared on the "Today" show, where he charged that the anti-war movement and some senators were "consciously aiding and abetting the enemy of the United States." Although he did not use the word treason, he used its official definition in his denunciation of those who were attacking the president's progress in achieving peace with honor. Haldeman's strong words, which Nixon had approved, became the lead story on all three national television newscasts. Looking back on his statement during the Watergate investigations, Haldeman insisted that the traitorous behavior of senators justified some of his extralegal activities during the 1972 campaign as well as their cover-up.

When Muskie immediately leapt to the defense of those who opposed the president's policies, Nixon called for his operatives to employ the line that the Maine senator was prolonging the war and that his behavior should be contrasted to Nixon's during

the 1968 campaign. As the Republican nominee, Nixon had refrained from criticizing Johnson's policies while delicate negotiations were taking place. The president referred to Muskie
obliquely on February 9 when he complained that some of the
responsibility for the North Vietnamese rigidity in the peace
talks had to do with those "who encourage the enemy to wait until after the election" to talk seriously about ending the war. Despite his rising poll numbers on the war issue, Nixon still worried
that the Democrats would concentrate on it if it continued
through the fall. On March 11 he warned his advisers that "a final announcement [about the end of the U.S. military commit-
ment] must be made before the Democratic Convention in July."

Although it was not directly linked to the Vietnam War, Nixon's
groundbreaking trip to China from February 21 to 27, 1972,
made the president appear to be a reasonable peacemaker who
could drink mai tais with the most bloodthirsty of Communists.
Mao Zedong himself recognized the importance of the visit for
Nixon's election prospects, noting that February 1972 was a good
time for the president to reap the political benefits of such a trip.
Although he received no concrete concessions on the war from
the Chinese, most Americans concluded that the opening of relations between Beijing and Washington would help end the Vietnam War. Certainly the North Vietnamese were unhappy that
the Chinese welcomed Nixon. They would be even more unhappy in May when Nixon journeyed to Moscow for an historic
summit conference, especially considering Nixon's escalatory actions on the eve of that summit.

    On March 30, with all but a few U.S. combat units having
been withdrawn, the North Vietnamese launched a major conventional offensive. They aimed to gain more territory in South
Vietnam and to weaken President Thieu sufficiently to prepare
the way for a coalition government in Saigon after a cease-fire. In
addition, they reasoned that a successful offensive would demon-

strate that Vietnamization had failed and would compel Congress to pressure the White House to bring all Americans home. They also assumed that potentially hostile reactions from Nixon's domestic opponents and from the Chinese and Russians would limit his retaliatory options. They were wrong.

The Communists easily cut through the ARVN, but their advances came to a halt when Nixon ordered heavy tactical bombing in the South and the use of B-52s on Hanoi and Haiphong, among other targets, in the North. The increased bombing of the North, which had little direct impact on the offensive, sparked the moribund anti-war movement to action, but it could produce a crowd of only fifty thousand on April 22 in New York. The polls narrowly backed Nixon's escalation by a 47 to 44 percent margin.

At this point Nixon claimed not to care about the polls or even the election. Not only were "the bastards . . . going to be bombed this time" like never before; he was also going to mine Hanoi and Haiphong harbors from the air in an escalation that threatened a break with the Soviet Union, North Vietnam's major maritime supplier. Even before the mining on May 8, U.S. bombs struck four Soviet vessels in Haiphong. Nixon was also angered by a report from Kissinger that at his May 2 negotiating session with Le Duc Tho, the North Vietnamese had pointed out that Senator Fulbright agreed with one of his chief arguments. In their discussions in 1972, Kissinger on several occasions warned Tho to stay out of domestic politics, especially the election.

The mining produced even more anger from congressional doves, the media, and anti-war leaders, but not much from ordinary Americans, who told pollsters they approved of the action by a 59 to 24 percent margin. The overwhelming support for the mining reflected in letters and telegrams to the White House was impressive, even factoring in the significant number generated by operatives from CREEP. Nixon was not concerned that two Democratic representatives from New York introduced an impeachment resolution during this period before the Watergate break-in, and that activists started work on a national impeachment committee. Nor was he concerned that after being arrested at a sit-in protesting the mining, the president of Amherst College commented ruefully, "I do not think words will change the minds of the men who made these decisions."

Nixon gambled here. Had the Soviets canceled the summit meeting in late May to protest the mining of their ally's harbors, the president would have suffered a severe political blow which could have been used by the Democrats during the campaign. On the other hand, had the North Vietnamese succeeded in crushing the ARVN, they might have weakened the Thieu regime so much that it could have collapsed before the election. Had that been the case, the Democrats would have had an even more potent political issue to use against the administration.

As the primary season ended in the spring, it appeared more and more likely that McGovern, Nixon's preferred opponent, would win the Democratic nomination. Republicans had labeled him the "triple A candidate"—for abortion, acid [LSD], and appeasement—with an occasional fourth A, amnesty for draft-dodgers. McGovern promised in early June that after he was elected he would go to Hanoi and end the war in ninety days. The White House rejoindered that it should take even less than ninety days for the Democratic frontrunner to surrender. Further, CREEP planned on linking McGovern to anti-war hippies such as Abbie Hoffman and Jerry Rubin, who were not especially popular on Nixon's side of the great cultural divide.

Although Rubin and Hoffman were not delegates to the Democratic Convention in July in Miami, many of those in attendance would have been refused entry in 1968 into the amphitheatre controlled by Mayor Daley. Because of Democratic Party reforms introduced as a response to the Chicago convention riots, 38 percent of the delegates who showed up in Miami were women, 15 percent were black, and 39 percent held graduate degrees. One "regular" delegate promised to work for "blood, sweat, and tears" but not for "sex, dope, and queers." As he looked over the crowd, another veteran Democratic politician commented, "I don't think that these people represent the mainstream of the party." They did, however, represent McGovern's constituency. Throughout the campaign McGovern had a good deal of difficulty attracting the support of the party faithful like George Meany of the AFL and especially Lyndon Johnson, who was not enthusiastic about the senator's anti-war position. The tables were turned from 1968 when many left and liberal Democrats, alienated by the Chicago convention and the party's failure to produce an anti-war candidate, did little to assist Hubert Humphrey in his campaign.

As for the Republican Convention in August, also in Miami, ten thousand protesters, including as many as a thousand members of the VVAW, encamped at Flamingo Park, a good distance from the well-protected auditorium. Three members of the VVAW's Last Patrol, including Ron Kovic who later wrote *Born on the Fourth of July*, penetrated the defenses and were able to shout at the delegates, "Stop the Bombing," for a brief moment before they were ejected from the hall. In the run-up to the convention, CREEP official G. Gordon Liddy volunteered his Operation Diamond to defuse the large anti-war protest expected. He proposed hiring "professional killers" to kidnap anti-war leaders and drop them off in a remote spot in Mexico until the convention ended. Although his colleagues did not approve of Operation Diamond, they did approve of an overall campaign plan, Operation Gemstone, of which the June 17 break-in at the Democratic headquarters in the Watergate apartment complex was an integral part.

At the convention, Nixon defended his Vietnam policy, pointing out that he had fulfilled his pledge to bring the war to an "honorable end." The North Vietnamese were listening carefully to what the president had to say, and, more important, as

Kissinger accurately pointed out in mid-August, they "will be watching the polls in our country." The late-summer polls showed that Nixon enjoyed a huge lead over McGovern. They reflected the Democratic candidate's clumsy handling of the problem he faced when his running mate, Senator Thomas Eagleton (D-MO), had to be dropped from the ticket because of the negative response to his post-convention revelation that he had once received electroshock therapy for mental health problems.

Eagleton's replacement, R. Sargent Shriver, caused a flurry of concern in the Nixon camp when the former ambassador to France in 1968 and 1969 brought up the 1968 Chennault affair in campaign speeches. This led Haldeman to order his minions to "destroy Shriver and his credibility." But the inflammatory charges did not attract much interest, especially when Lyndon Johnson did not step forward to affirm them. Johnson, who was less than lukewarm about the anti-war McGovern's candidacy, confided to reporters, "George McGovern couldn't carry Texas if Dick Nixon were caught fucking a sow in downtown Fort Worth."

In an important policy paper in late August, the North Vietnamese concluded that "we should not pin too much hope on McGovern." If Nixon wins the election, they feared, "The situation will be difficult for us." A reelected Nixon might be emboldened to continue the bombing and escalate further. Consequently they began to move away from their insistence that there could be no peace with Thieu in office in Saigon. But their movement through that summer was glacial. While they worried that Nixon might be tougher after the election, the administration worried that the president would confront a Democratic Congress in January that would cut funding for the war. That concerned Kissinger as he met with the North Vietnamese in August and September. In addition, the North Vietnamese were scoring points in the United States and around the world with exaggerated stories about bombing devastation, including attacks on their dike system. In the words of one of their internal memos, they were trying to exploit the "serious contradictions between the American people and Nixon, [and] between the Republican and Democratic parties concerning the Vietnam problem."

Nixon instructed his national security adviser to continue negotiating as long as it took. But he worried, as Johnson had worried four years earlier, that if a settlement were achieved too close to the election, it might appear that political factors had influenced U.S. diplomatic and military policy—which of course they did. Apparently pushed by the Russians and Chinese, as they had been in 1968, and hoping to make the best possible deal before a strengthened Nixon won the election, during September 1972 the North Vietnamese began moving toward a major concession with some alacrity. They would be willing to permit Thieu to remain as head of the Saigon government for a brief time after the cease-fire, pending arrangements for elections to replace him. Hanoi was not happy about its concession, but it recognized the short time available for negotiations before the American election. "After the election" the North Vietnamese concluded, "it will be difficult to compel the Americans to make additional concessions to those we can secure before the election." To this point, all the significant concessions had been made by Washington.

Kissinger informed Nixon on October 12 that it appeared that he and his North Vietnamese counterparts had agreed on the basics of a peace agreement. The president was sufficiently elated to break out a bottle from his private stock of Chateau Laffite Rothschild for a toast with his staff, instead of the more modest California wine he usually served them. The key problem remaining was obtaining the approval of President Thieu, who was pleased that he could stay on after the cease-fire but who adamantly objected to the earlier U.S. concession permitting North Vietnamese troops to remain in South Vietnam. He had not been involved in Kissinger's negotiations but knew about the essentials of the agreement before the American negotiator arrived in Saigon to obtain his approval. As on the eve of the election in 1968, when he had rejected Johnson's deal to begin peace talks, he now rejected Kissinger's deal, angered to the point where he admitted he wanted to punch the envoy in the nose. Unlike 1968, however, he and the Americans kept his rejections to themselves. As Kissinger pointed out, while the South Vietnamese had Nixon waiting in the wings in 1968, their alternative this time was McGovern.

Thieu's refusal caused Kissinger and Nixon to alter their timetable for the announcement of a peace agreement, explaining to the North Vietnamese that details remained for the two sides to negotiate. Suspecting that their enemy was stalling, Hanoi jumped the gun, announcing on October 25 that they and the United States had agreed on peace terms. The next day, in an October surprise that surpassed Johnson's four years earlier, Kissinger affirmed that "peace is at hand." Immediately the White House commissioned a poll to determine public reaction to the peace plan and to the related cessation of the bombing of North Vietnam.

Kissinger knew that peace was not at hand. As he wrote to the U.S. ambassador in Saigon, "Between now and November 7 [election day] we are posed with a most delicate problem. Before November 7, we cannot brutalize Thieu to the point he will kick over the traces and undertake a public confrontation and break with us. . . . After November 7 full leverage will be applied." With election virtually certain, Nixon himself began backing away from the peace. He was troubled about deserting his loyal ally in Saigon and feared criticism from hawks within his own party for his cavalier treatment of the South Vietnamese president. He may have also been distressed to see his popular national security adviser winning plaudits for the peace—"That son-of-a-bitch [wanted] me to be in his debt for winning the election." Kissinger told McGovern in 1975 that his October 26 announcement was directed to Republican hawks, not to undercut McGovern's presidential chances, slim though they were.

The announcement did undercut McGovern. It was the coup de grâce in the election campaign. All McGovern had going for him by October was his promise to end the war, and now Nixon apparently had done it. McGovern had been accused by the Nixon forces of wanting to obtain "peace by surrender," and now Nixon could claim he had achieved peace with honor. During much of October, rumors of an impending peace had produced enough interest to keep potentially damaging Watergate stories from the airwaves. As Haldeman noted, the plan "takes the corruption stuff off the front pages." The emphasis on the peace in Vietnam also fit well with Nixon's analysis on October 14 of the Republican command of issues such as "patriotism, morality, and religion" instead of the economy, where the Democrats were strong.

McGovern tried to fight back, stressing on November 5 that peace had not yet been achieved, but he was on the wrong side of America's cultural divide. He lost the popular vote in the election by 60.7 to 37.5 percent and won the electoral votes of only Massachusetts and the District of Columbia. This landslide was more a personal victory for Nixon than one for his party, which gained only twelve seats in the House while losing two in the Senate. The Democrats maintained their stranglehold on Congress. This development augured ill for Nixon's peace plan that had fallen apart because of Thieu's refusal to go along with U.S. concessions.

Considering the failure to halt publication of the Pentagon Papers, his weak showing in the polls, and the North Vietnamese offensive in the spring, the margin of Nixon's triumph in November 1972 was a tribute to the effective hardball politics played by the president and CREEP and their ability to defuse the volatile issue of the war. Unfortunately for Nixon, his landslide victory did not take the Vietnam War out of American domestic politics. Peace was not immediately at hand as the returns came in. More important, even with peace, the war played a central role in the unprecedented crises Nixon faced as his presidency began to unravel.

10

Legacies, 1973–

WITH THE ELECTION behind them, Nixon and Kissinger returned to negotiations with the North Vietnamese, armed with an historic mandate from the American people but not a mandate to continue the war. Although some in Congress knew of Thieu's rejection of the October draft treaty, most Americans assumed that the delay in completing the peace process was caused by Hanoi, not Saigon. The White House made certain that the North Vietnamese would take the fall for any rupture in the negotiations.

When the Americans returned to the peace table with Thieu's objections, the North Vietnamese, who were surprised by the length of his wish list, responded with scores of treaty alterations of their own. Soon the situation returned to that which had prevailed the previous September when peace was not at hand. After Nixon broke off negotiations, the United States responded with Linebacker II, a punitive bombing campaign against North Vietnam that lasted from December 18 to December 30. During that period, American B-52s and other planes dropped 36,000 tons of bombs on the North, more than had been dropped between 1969 and 1971. Hanoi later claimed that 2,200 civilians had been killed during the bombings.

Nixon's approval rating now plummeted 11 percent and the Dow Jones average, reflecting investor concern that the war would not be over soon, dipped lower than it had in eighteen

months. Congress was away from the capital for Christmas recess
as were college students from their campuses. From wherever
they were, congressional leaders, anti-war movement spokesper-
sons, prominent columnists, and even non-Communist foreign
leaders such as the American-educated prime minister of Swe-
den denounced Nixon's seemingly petulant resort to B-52s because he could not get his way in the peace talks. They would
have been more furious had they known that the problem was
the South Vietnamese, not the North Vietnamese.

Whatever was known about the details of the breakdown in
negotiations, congressional leaders promised a stern rebuke to
the president when they returned to Washington in January.
Nixon used the congressional threat in several communications
to President Thieu, who continued to reject the Americans' most
important concession, the retention of North Vietnamese troops
in the South. The president explained that congressional control
of the purse could leave him with no funds to support troops in
Southeast Asia or to assist the government of Saigon. On one occasion he warned a South Vietnamese diplomat that Senate
Democrats were preparing a resolution to cut off all aid to
Saigon and to demand the withdrawal of all U.S. troops in exchange for a return of the POWs. He suspected that the resolution would pass by a 2 to 1 margin. Charles Colson "took the
threats from Congress seriously," because "we knew we were
racing the clock." No doubt Nixon exaggerated the threat from
Congress to demonstrate that he was not the one selling out the
South Vietnamese. The president even helped organize the
threat by asking several senators to make public statements about
the potential resolution.

When the North Vietnamese agreed to return to the peace
table on December 30, and the bombing stopped before Congress
began its new session and before college students returned to
campus, the pressure on the president eased. Talks between
Kissinger and Le Duc Tho resumed on January 8 and by Janu-

ary 13 they agreed on a treaty that looked very much like the one negotiated in October. On January 23 they initialed the treaty that went into effect four days later. The United States promised to withdraw all troops and to dismantle all bases within sixty days of the cease-fire, the same time period allotted to the North Vietnamese to return the POWs. The political future of Vietnam was left in the hands of a yet-to-be organized Council of National Reconciliation and Concord that would arrange for elections while Thieu served in a caretaker role.

Both South Vietnamese and North Vietnamese assent to the treaty was based on promises from President Nixon that he could not hope to fulfill, even without the Watergate crisis. He threatened a still reluctant Thieu to take the treaty or leave it— the United States was going to sign it whatever he did. In addition to an increased aid package, he promised Thieu, in an exchange of letters, that if the North Vietnamese violated the treaty, the United States would "respond with full force" to smash them. Although that may have been Nixon's intention, it is hard to believe that he could have sent back the bombers, let alone ground forces, once the war was over. Opposition to a renewed war would have been so fierce in Congress and from the public that even a politically strong commander-in-chief would have had difficulty delivering on that promise.

Nixon hoped he would not have to deliver on a promise that Kissinger had made to Hanoi. To provide the sweetener to keep them from violating the treaty, Kissinger offered $3.25 billion in reconstruction aid. As with the Thieu promise, it is difficult to imagine that Congress would have granted the president's request for aid to the Communist regime in North Vietnam. While some on the left might have voted for the peace gesture, the vast majority, especially those on the right, would never have approved such largesse to the bloody Communist enemy.

Throughout the rest of his life, Nixon contended that the peace he made, including the promises to Hanoi and Saigon, was

a solid one that should have guaranteed the preservation of a
non-Communist South Vietnam. Beginning in February 1973,
however, the Watergate crises emasculated his presidency and
strengthened the hand of an allegedly irresponsible Congress
that wanted nothing more to do with American obligations in
Vietnam. In the early 1990s, he told an interviewer, "by 1975,
Congress destroyed our ability to enforce the Paris agreement."
Kissinger agreed, complaining that Watergate "sealed the fate of
South Vietnam by [its] erosion of executive authority." President
Thieu had a more realistic appraisal, contending that the peace
was doomed when the United States permitted North Viet-
namese troops to remain in South Vietnam.

The fall of South Vietnam was little more than a remote night-
mare for President Nixon as he prepared for his second inauguration on January 20, 1973. With the war over, he planned to
concentrate on domestic politics and the reshaping of the federal
government. Yet the war and its opponents would not go away,
even though peace had been achieved in Paris. On January 19 the
New York Philharmonic director Leonard Bernstein led a performance for Nixon opponents in Washington of Haydn's "Mass
in the Time of War," and at the official inaugural concert the
next day, eleven members of the Philadelphia Symphony Orchestra refused to play for the president. Nixon was pleased
when he heard that the orchestra's distinguished conductor, Eugene Ormandy, had labeled those eleven players "left-wing sons
of bitches." The president was not pleased with the fifty thousand anti-war protesters who rallied against his Vietnam policies
at the Washington Monument or by the crowds of hecklers who
lined the January 20 parade route. But they were not as numer-
ous, as disrespectful, or as potentially violent as those who had
showed up in 1969 to rain on his parade. Journalists did write
about an older man carrying a placard: "Nixon's secret plan
killed my son and 23,000 other GI's in Vietnam."

He had a point. The peace terms of 1973 that permitted the North Vietnamese to remain in the South might have been available in 1969 or 1970 had Nixon wanted to make that sort of concession years before the 1972 election. But like Kennedy and Johnson before him, he could not leave Vietnam in a way that would result in the Communists taking over the South before his reelection. He was looking for what Kissinger termed a "decent interval" between American withdrawal and the possible fall of Saigon to the Communists. His national security adviser had told him in August 1972, "we've got to find some formula that holds the thing together a year or two, after which—after a year, Mr. President, Vietnam will be a backwater. If we settle it, say, this October, by January '74 no one will give a damn" if North Vietnam gobbles up South Vietnam. Peace in 1970 might have resulted in a Communist victory before November 1972. After all, Kissinger told Ehrlichman in January 1973, "If they're lucky, they [South Vietnamese] can hold out for a year and a half."

As it turned out, the South Vietnamese held out longer than Richard Nixon, whose presidency began to self-destruct less than a month after the inauguration. On February 7 the Senate organized a Select Committee on Presidential Campaign Activities, opening the way for eighteen months of embarrassing investigations and shocking revelations. These culminated in Nixon's resignation on August 9, 1974.

Few could have expected such an outcome. Thinking he had successfully contained his problem, two days after the Senate decided to investigate, the president called on his public relations people to get out the word that while he had run a clean campaign in 1972, the McGovern campaign had been dominated by a violent peace movement bankrolled by Communists.

The Watergate crisis began officially on June 17, 1972, with the break-in of Democratic headquarters in Washington by employees of CREEP in a crime unrelated to the war. Yet much of what Senate investigators and journalists discovered in their

investigation of the original break-in and its cover-up was directly related to the war. Nixon covered up the Watergate break-
in at least in part because he most likely had foreknowledge of
the break-in, committed by some of the Watergate burglars at
Daniel Ellsberg's psychiatrist's office. Moreover, wholesale illegal
surveillance and wiretapping had begun with the president and
Kissinger's attempt to find the leaker who blew the whistle to the
New York Times about the May 1969 secret bombing of Cambodia. The secret bombing itself became one of the four formal
charges against the president in his 1974 impeachment hearings.
The president's infamous "enemies lists" also had a good deal to
do with the war, as his operatives targeted individuals and
groups that were outspoken against it. Similarly, Nixon used the
Internal Revenue Service illegally to harass anti-war opponents
and groups. On occasion White House staffers threatened to
punish television networks they viewed as offering too much
positive coverage of anti-war critics. In addition, FBI chief
L. Patrick Gray destroyed evidence of the administration forgery
relating to the 1963 assassination of Diem.

Nixon's defense, then and later, for many of his illegal and extralegal actions, concerned national security. His unprecedented
assaults against anti-war opponents in Congress, the media, and
on the streets were necessitated, he claimed, by their allegedly
dangerous appeasement policies supported by the Communist
world. One of Nixon's key aides, Jeb Stuart Magruder, "saw
continual violations of the law done by men like [anti-war
leader] William Sloane Coffin [an old friend from Yale] . . .
without any regard for any other person's pattern of behavior or
beliefs. . . . We had become inured to using some activities that
would help us in accomplishing what we thought was a cause, a
legitimate cause."

In retrospect, the longtime head of the Nixon Presidential Library considered Nixon a "war president" who had to confront
the domestic enemy that was undermining his attempts to pro-

tect the United States abroad. After all, as Nixon told David Frost in a famous series of televised interviews in 1977, when the president, whose job it is to define national security, takes actions to protect Americans, those actions are legal. Very few knowledgeable authorities, especially experts on the Constitution, agreed with him.

As the Vietnam War was intricately involved in Watergate, Watergate was intricately involved in the trajectory of the war in 1973 and 1974. President Nixon claimed that he was on the job developing and executing national security policy during the tumultuous eighteen-month roller-coaster ride of Watergate. In the late winter of 1973, though, he began to be consumed by the crisis and his many attempts to defend his administration against the investigators. An examination of Haldeman's diary entries for the period from February through April 1973—a diary replete with Vietnam War and foreign relations issues to that point—suggests that the president was spending less time on international relations and more on trying to extinguish home-front fires. Haldeman himself tied the two issues together when on August 7, 1973, facing jail time, he suggested to Nixon that he link a pardon for his aides involved in the break-in and the cover-up with a pardon for Vietnam-era draft evaders. The president rejected the proposal.

With the president weakened, the Democratic Congress began reasserting its constitutional authority, especially on foreign policy. Congressional opposition to an "imperial presidency" had been developing for close to a decade. In some cases during that time, legislators who complained about the way the Constitution had been tilted in favor of the presidency in foreign affairs were reluctant to challenge Johnson and Nixon because they feared retaliation. For example, while many in Congress knew about the main outlines of America's secret war in Laos, they preferred not to know about it.

Almost immediately after the end of U.S. military involvement in the war, the cease-fire between Saigon and Hanoi began to unravel. Both President Thieu and his Communist counterparts violated the peace treaty by trying to seize more territory. Thieu used American weapons, ammunition, and other equipment in his offensives; he would have to be resupplied if he were to hold his own against the Communists in the coming months. Congress and the American people were unaware of the secret written pledge Nixon had given to Thieu to continue support of South Vietnam militarily if Hanoi violated the treaty. It was not until April 1975 that Defense Secretary James Schlesinger, appearing on a television news program, revealed Nixon's private commitments to Thieu.

Thieu was unrealistic in expecting much more aid from Washington, let alone military assistance, whatever Nixon had promised him. It was no secret that even before Nixon's January inauguration, the House and Senate Democratic Caucuses had voted by 154–75 and 36–12 margins respectively to cut off all funds for Saigon once the U.S. withdrawal was complete and the POWs returned home.

At first the real emergency for Nixon early in 1973 involved the continued bombing in Cambodia, where the government of American ally Lon Nol confronted a revolution led by the Communist Khmer Rouge. In June, Congress passed a resolution calling for the immediate end to all military operations in Southeast Asia, with one conservative Republican commenting, "As far as I am concerned, I want to get the hell out." Nixon vetoed the resolution but was not able to quash a second, slightly reworded measure that demanded an end to all military operations by August 15. This was a momentous development. Congress had at last passed a resolution to end the war, with Kissinger commenting ruefully that "the authority of the executive has . . . been impaired."

While Congress deliberated during the summer, a case headed for the Supreme Court that appeared finally to challenge the legality of the war. Donald Dawson, a U.S. pilot, had been court-martialed because he refused to participate in the allegedly illegal bombing of Cambodia now that the Vietnam War was over. On July 15 a federal district court judge in New York agreed that the bombing was illegal and issued an injunction against its continuance. The government appealed the injunction successfully and petitioned the Supreme Court to hear its case for the bombing. The issue became moot when Congress imposed the August 15 deadline on Nixon.

Congress was not finished curtailing the president. In 1969, reacting to what it believed was his usurpation of constitutional authority, the Senate had passed a nonbinding resolution claiming that any American military commitment to a foreign power needed congressional approval. This bill had originated with Senator Fulbright, who was one of those in the forties and fifties who had called for more freedom for the president from the insular Congress. Beginning in the Johnson administration, the chair of the Foreign Relations Committee started to rethink his original support for a relatively unfettered president.

In November 1973, with Nixon politically weaker than he had been in the spring of that year, Congress passed over his veto the epochal War Powers Resolution. It called for the president to report to Congress within forty-eight hours of committing U.S. troops to a combat zone and to return to Congress for permission to retain those troops in the combat zone after the initial sixty-day period. Nixon was not the only one who considered the bill "unconstitutional and dangerous." Despite its questionable constitutionality, it is still on the books. Not only has it reluctantly been adhered to by a succession of presidents, it also has served as a restraint on contemplated military adventures. It is unlikely Congress could have overridden Nixon's veto had he been on his domestic political game during that turbulent period when his firing of the independent Watergate prosecutor was considered a "massacre."

The year 1974 was a crucial one for South Vietnam. President Thieu had used up much of his equipment in military forays in 1973, and with the departure of the United States his economy was collapsing. Confronting impeachment, an even weaker Nixon asked Congress for a $1.6 billion aid package for the fast-failing South Vietnamese. His aides pleaded with legislators, citing the nation's moral responsibility and the relationship of the fall of South Vietnam to national security. But Congress, representing a nation that was dealing with a severe economic crisis itself, exacerbated by skyrocketing oil prices, and wanting to put the Vietnam War behind it forever, limited the aid to $700 million. Considering the desperate straits in which the South Vietnamese found themselves, even the original $1.6 billion package would not have been enough to right their economy and restore their military capacity.

When Nixon resigned from office on August 9, before the full House could approve the bill of impeachment approved by the House Select Committee, the prospects for the survival of the South Vietnamese appeared bleak. They became even more grim after the congressional by-election. Not only did Democrats make impressive gains, but many of the new representatives were more liberal and anti-war than their predecessors. They were in no mood to pull Thieu's chestnuts from the fire.

In March 1975 the North Vietnamese launched another offensive, which to their surprise was so successful against the ever-weakening South Vietnamese army that on April 30 they reached Saigon. In the interim President Gerald Ford and Secretary of State Kissinger asked Congress for $722 million in emergency aid for both South Vietnam and Cambodia. They buttressed their requests once again with appeals to American morality and responsibility. Kissinger challenged Congress, saying, "The problem we face in Indochina today is an elementary question of what kind of people we are," while Ford claimed that the "tragedy" occurring in Vietnam "could have been avoided." In the preceding year the United States had provided South Vietnam with only $268 million for military supplies while the Soviet Union and China gave North Vietnam $75 million worth of supplies. Needless to say, many senators and representatives of both parties were offended by being blamed for the collapse of South Vietnam, which they in turn blamed on its leaders' corruption and incompetence. They could point to a March 1975 Gallup Poll that revealed that 78 percent of the respondents opposed further aid to South Vietnam.

Congress finally rejected a package of $177 million for humanitarian aid and $150 million for military aid. Many liberals refused to give South Vietnam further military aid, while many conservatives feared that the way things looked in April, the aid would probably end up in Communist hands. After the fall of Saigon, Congress revisited the issue and approved $507 million for refugee aid for those fleeing Communist regimes in Vietnam and Cambodia.

Despite the administration's attack on Congress for failing to support a loyal ally and even, implicitly, for contributing to the fall of South Vietnam to communism, the issue had no political resonance for Americans in 1975 or even during the 1976 presidential campaign. Most were pleased that the long and divisive war was over, and many blamed the South Vietnamese regime for its own plight. The last thing they wanted to hear was yet another debate about Vietnam policy. Although Democrats controlled Congress, many of their Republican colleagues also refused to support the South Vietnamese regime. President Ford recognized this as early as April 1975 when, ignoring Kissinger's advice, he urged an audience at Tulane University to "stop refighting the battles and recriminations of the past."

Ford himself suffered no recriminations. During the cold war and even into the new century, Republicans have been immune from attack for not being sufficiently militaristic or anti-Communist. Had Kennedy or Johnson been in the White

House when the North Vietnamese stormed into Saigon to unify the country under a Communist flag, they would have suffered political recriminations. Few Americans were interested in punishing those who "lost Vietnam." That did not mean that other divisive issues surrounding the Vietnam War would soon disappear from American politics.

A substantial minority of Americans had strongly opposed the war and supported a smaller group in its midst that actively exercised its democratic right to demonstrate against presidential policies. Yet a majority of their fellow citizens retained their anger against allegedly radical and violent anti-war protesters, especially the draft-dodgers among them, whom they perceived to be unpatriotic and who, along with the media, they held responsible for the Free World's loss of Vietnam. When members of the Vietnam generation came of age to run for political office, their opponents pored over the records of their activities in the sixties, particularly to determine how they had faced the draft.

The most famous case was that of Bill Clinton, who did everything he could to avoid the draft. More important, in a contemporary letter he described how he hated the military. Then, in 1992, he was not especially truthful about the circumstances permitting him to evade service. It made little difference that David Hackworth, the most decorated Vietnam veteran, defended Clinton's activities by announcing that had he had a son of Clinton's age in 1969, he would have done everything possible to help him avoid serving in Vietnam. To make matters worse, free of the draft as a Rhodes scholar in London, Clinton participated in anti-war demonstrations. That information resulted in the first Bush administration's controversial and ultimately fruitless search of State Department files to turn up pictures of the long-haired radical Clinton allegedly leading a protest against the United States on foreign soil.

Richard Nixon was angered by Clinton's election in 1992, because it "proves it was all right to be against the goddamned war." All during Clinton's presidency, conservatives frequently commented on his draft-dodging and hatred of the military. It did not help that the commander-in-chief always looked a bit awkward trying to salute his troops. One senator announced that the president would not be welcome on military bases in his state. Finally, in 1996, Republican presidential candidate Bob Dole's heroic service record in World War II was used by his campaigners to rekindle the 1992 charges about Clinton's draft-dodging.

Republicans as well came under scrutiny for their draft evasion. When John Engler, the conservative Republican governor of Michigan, was being promoted as a running mate for Bob Dole in 1996, intrepid journalists discovered that Engler had failed his induction physical because he had been one pound overweight. Surely a patriot like Engler, they suggested, could have found a way to lose one pound to serve his nation.

During the Democratic primary campaign in 2004, John Kerry and Wesley Clark both flaunted their Vietnam War experience to inoculate themselves against charges that their party would not be strong enough on defense and, more important, not experienced enough in understanding questions of war and peace. Kerry's prospects in the Iowa caucuses were aided by the sudden appearance on the hustings of a Vietnam veteran whose life the young lieutenant had saved. The Massachusetts senator also campaigned across the nation with wheelchair-bound Max Cleland, a former Georgia senator and severely wounded Vietnam veteran.

Kerry's emphasis on his Vietnam experience backfired. A group of navy veterans who served on Swift Boats alongside Kerry's challenged his claims to heroism under fire and the severity of his wounds. Through their television advertisements, bestselling book, and the media's coverage of their mostly unfounded charges, the anti-Kerry veterans who were linked to but not directed by the Bush administration led many potential voters to believe that Kerry was a liar. The veterans were still smarting from the role Kerry had played in the VVAW and his 1971 claims that those who served in Vietnam participated in atrocities. Kerry's Vietnam service became the biggest issue in the campaign during the summer of 2004.

The Democrats fired back with charges about President George W. Bush's National Guard service during the war, charges first aired during the 2000 campaign. Some Americans remembered that middle- and upper-class young men often chose the Guard or the reserves as a way virtually to guarantee that they would not be sent to Vietnam. Al Gore, who volunteered for service in the war where he was a combat photographer, called attention to the difference between the two kinds of military services.

This was not the first time the issue had been raised. During the 1988 campaign, George H. W. Bush's running mate, Senator Dan Quayle, came under journalistic scrutiny for his National Guard service, in good measure because he had apparently used his political connections to join, even though his unit's quota had been filled.

"What did you do in the war?" has been a question directed to political candidates by generations of Americans. Despite the unpopularity of the Vietnam War, compared to the Civil War and World War II, by the 1980s, service in Vietnam was a clear political asset, especially compared to anti-war activities during the sixties. Candidates like Kerry tried to have it both ways—being a war hero who came home to participate in the leadership of the VVAW. Pulitzer Prize–winning historian Joseph Ellis had it both ways for a while as well, fabricating for his students at Mount Holyoke College both a heroic military experience in Vietnam and a prominent role in the anti-war movement upon his return.

As for American politicians and their participation in America's several "little" wars after the Vietnam War, the end of the draft in 1973 and its replacement with the all-volunteer force has all but eliminated the "What did you do in the war?" question from domestic politics. Nixon's decision to end the draft was influenced dramatically by the Vietnam War experience. It had proven difficult if not impossible to fight a long and unpopular war with draftees. The likelihood of being drafted into that war helped to turn many apolitical young people and their parents into supporters of or activists in the anti-war movement.

The Selective Service System, on its face one of the foundations of an historically anti-militaristic democratic system proudly dependent upon its citizen army, never really was democratic. It was a *selective* institution based upon legislation that contained escape clauses for the middle and upper classes. The all-volunteer military services, still a repository for lower-class and blue-collar youth, has made it easier for presidents to send their troops into combat. During the 2003 Iraq War, when anti-war leaders complained about the waste of young men and women being sent into an unnecessary war, conservative icons such as Rush Limbaugh, whose trick knee kept him out of the armed forces during the Vietnam era, pointed out that those in the American military were professionals who understood when they enlisted that their job might entail combat action.

Many of those professionals had been previously trained by the Reserve Officers Training Corps on college campuses. Because of the draft, many young men chose to enter ROTC in order to begin their military service as officers rather than as enlisted men. ROTC guaranteed a steady stream of well-educated and well-rounded second lieutenants, often from the best universities, who had been trained not only in the military arts but in the humanities and social sciences. Even before the draft ended, the numbers of students enrolled in ROTC declined across the nation. They did not wish to end up in a shooting war in Southeast Asia, and, more important, many programs were thrown off campus because of protests led by professors and students against their universities' complicity in the war. Such protests also led at least temporarily to the end of other kinds of government and defense-related recruiting as well as the end of classified research on most college campuses.

The faculties of many of those same campuses soon became filled with former undergraduate and graduate students who had been deeply involved in the political conflicts of the sixties. More radical than their predecessors, in good measure because of their intense experiences in the anti-war movement and New Left organizations, these "tenured radicals" dominated many departments in the liberal arts and their respective professional societies. Critics complained after the collapse of the Soviet Union that the humanities departments of American colleges had become the last refuge for Marxists.

Even though presidents no longer had to confront anti-war protesters worried about the draft, the collective memory of the Vietnam War experience often caused them to think twice about foreign interventions. In 1981, when President Ronald Reagan contemplated military intervention in El Salvador, an anti-war movement quickly developed that helped convince him it could be an unpopular action. Few Americans relished getting involved in a dirty guerrilla-style war in a Third World nation that might last for months or even years. Reagan displayed his timidity again when he withdrew American forces from Lebanon after the 1983 bombing of a Marine compound in another example of what was called the "Vietnam Syndrome." His illegal secret end run around Congress to arm the Contras to attack Nicaragua's Sandinista government was again influenced by the unwillingness of most Americans to become involved in another Vietnam. Politicians and pundits alike declared it would be political suicide for a president to enmesh himself in a long, drawn-out, limited war unless the public supported such a venture, and especially unless the military had an exit strategy.

That was the judgment of George H. W. Bush and Colin Powell when they decided not to march to Baghdad in 1991 after they ejected the Iraqis from Kuwait. Their fear was that once the United States had deposed Saddam Hussein, his supporters would engage the United States in a long and messy guerrilla war in a large country with porous borders. Their judgment was correct, as demonstrated by the bloody aftermath of the 2003 war that finally removed the Iraqi dictator from power.

This was not just a Republican issue. In 1993 President Clinton beat a hasty retreat from Somalia after U.S. "peacekeeping" forces were mauled in a battle with a warlord's ragtag guerrillas in view of television cameras. Clinton's long reluctance to intervene militarily in civil wars in Bosnia and Kosovo in the mid-nineties also had much to do with the omnipresent fear of another Vietnam.

The Vietnam experience added to the popular perception that the United States backed authoritarian regimes. This contributed to President Jimmy Carter's attempt to present a new face for U.S. diplomacy in the Third World by emphasizing support for democracy and human rights. Under pressure to live up to his laudable commitment, he applied the new policy somewhat inconsistently, but he certainly made a case for it in Iran, where he strongly encouraged the shah to relax his authoritarian regime. When America's chief ally in the Persian Gulf did so, making it easier for his opponents to challenge his rule, the president pressured the shah not to use brute force to contain the budding revolution. The result was the triumph of the Islamic revolutionaries as well as the widely held belief that Carter was a weak president who had permitted American allies to fall to anti-Western and pro-Communist forces.

During Carter's presidency it appeared that dominoes began to fall in the Third World. Critics blamed this on his emasculation of America's intelligence services' capacity for launching operations abroad. This was another allegedly negative result of the politics of the Vietnam War. On the other hand, historian Robert Schulzinger has pointed out that the reform of U.S. intelligence activities was just one of several major positive reforms in American society, leading Schulzinger to conclude that the war was responsible, in part, for increasing democratization in the United States.

During the Vietnam War, Americans learned from leaks and exposés about some of their intelligence agencies' nefarious doings, especially the CIA and the FBI. The latter's wholesale violation of citizens' constitutional rights came to light when activists broke into a branch office in Media, Pennsylvania, in 1971, and sent thousands of secret documents to the newspapers. These exposés led to congressional hearings in 1975 that laid bare the excesses of both agencies. These included the attempted assassination of foreign leaders by the CIA and the harassing, illegal monitoring, and encouraging of violence by FBI agents serving as agents provocateurs in anti-war groups. Congress enacted reforms, implemented by the Carter administration, that its opponents claimed crippled the American intelligence system and permitted Communists to make gains, in the wake of those reforms, in Somalia, Nicaragua, Afghanistan, and other Third World nations. These reforms led to politically potent charges from Republicans during the 1980 campaign and through the eighties that naive liberal Democrats could not be counted upon to protect the national interest.

Anti-war activists were also in good measure responsible for passage of the Freedom of Information Act (FOIA) in 1966, which made it easier for citizens to request the declassification of documents. These were necessary, they contended, for Americans to make educated choices about their nation's foreign policies. The act is cumbersome, and the bureaucracy in charge is often slow and unresponsive. Yet it is clear that FOIA has helped make available important documents that officials routinely marked classified or top secret, even though national security was not threatened.

In addition, important civil liberties cases brought before the Supreme Court during the Vietnam era helped protect and enlarge the rights of dissenters. The Court approved the right of high school students to wear black armbands to school in a silent protest against the war, and the right of an activist to fly an American flag with a peace symbol on it; declared unconstitutional a New York state law making flag burning a crime; agreed that conscientious-objector status could rest on an individual's moral code and not necessarily membership in an organized pacifist religion; and ruled that the Georgia legislature could not bar the legally elected Julian Bond from taking his seat merely because he opposed the war. Courts also supported the First Amendment, with some qualifications, in the Pentagon Papers case. On many occasions the Supreme Court defended the rights of demonstrators against the illegal actions of the government, declaring that the Nixon administration's street-sweeping arrests of thousands of citizens in Washington without proper arraignment in early May 1971 violated their constitutional rights. Similarly, in supporting the 1971 Keith decision of a lower federal court, the Court affirmed that the government must obtain judicial permission to wiretap citizens even if they were suspected of threatening national security. Yet the Court refused on at least nineteen occasions to hear suits that tested the war's constitutionality, holding that the issue was political and therefore not justiciable.

In terms of the war's direct impact on the presidencies of Lyndon Johnson and Richard Nixon, it was the major factor in President Johnson's decision not to seek reelection on March 31, 1968, and was a central factor that led to President Nixon's resignation on August 9, 1974, before the House could formally impeach him for, among other transgressions, the actions of the Plumbers, the Pentagon Papers break-in, and illegal operations directed at the anti-war movement. No other war in U.S. history had such a negative impact on the presidents involved. Both Johnson and Nixon might have been considered among the best U.S. presidents were it not for the war. Johnson promoted and signed the Civil Rights Act and Voting Rights Act and instituted the Great

Society, the most massive reform program in American history. Nixon opened China and achieved a détente with the Soviet Union while approving a wide variety of reforms, especially in the environmental area, that made him, surprisingly, the last liberal president of the twentieth century. Over the six years of his presidency, defense spending as a percentage of the federal budget declined from 46 to 30 percent while spending for human resources rose from 33 to 50 percent.

On the other side of the White House fence, many Americans lost respect for these presidents, whom they considered congenital dissemblers, liars, heartless mad bombers, or even despotic Fascists. By 1967 anti-war passions were so strong that for the first time in modern American history, citizens in large numbers behaved so uncivilly and in such potentially violent ways that the presidents became prisoners in the White House. They were fearful to step out without a phalanx of protection or a guarantee that their meeting place or convention hall would be secured from scruffy, belligerent, disrespectful hippies or even alleged hippie-Communists.

Running a campaign to bring the turbulent nation together, Richard Nixon soon realized that the Republicans held an advantage in the polarized society. Most Americans disliked the rowdy young protesters, who looked like hippies, used dope and foul language, and seemed to disrespect authority and the flag. They appeared to be part of a movement supporting black, brown, gay, and women's power that was trying to destroy traditional American values and culture. Early on, Nixon appealed not only to Republicans but to blue-collar Democrats and conservative southerners to fashion a new coalition that would make the GOP the majority party. Certainly this was the case in his sweeping 1972 victory. He talked about consolidating his new coalition in the years to come, even toying with the idea, once broached by President Eisenhower, of establishing a new party made up of those who supported conservative values and conservative to moderate economic policies. They would dominate the liberals and radicals who had come to run the Democratic Party.

Although Watergate made it impossible for Nixon to fulfill his domestic program during his second term, he prefigured the Reagan Revolution and the transformation of the omnibus American parties into conservative and liberal parties. It became rarer and rarer in the Republican Party for someone like the anti-war Vermont senator George Aiken to coexist with his confreres in much the same way as it became more and more difficult for someone like Georgia senator Richard Russell to coexist with the majority in the Democratic Party. The clear geographical division between the "blue" and the "red" states, noted in the 2000 election, had been developing since Nixon's positive polarization in 1972 and even back to the Republicans' game plan, codified in Kevin Phillips's 1969 book *The Emerging Republican Majority*.

Many of those on the Republican side of the divide were convinced that the mainstream media in the United States were elitist, liberal, biased, and unpatriotic. That characterization of American newspapers, magazines, and television networks developed during the Vietnam War. Presidents and journalists had always been natural adversaries in American politics. But it was the war, and the media's widespread criticism and exposés of U.S. policies in Vietnam beginning in 1962, that compelled Presidents Kennedy, Johnson, and especially Nixon to add them to their "enemies lists." The assault on the media's alleged lack of objectivity resonated with many Americans. They defended the presidents' foreign policies and looked suspiciously at East Coast–based editors and publishers whom they felt did not represent Middle America.

The American political scene from 1976 through the early eighties was also affected by the impact of the Vietnam War on the U.S. economy. The unprecedented "stagflation" that the nation experienced from the Nixon administration through the early Reagan administration was partly a result of the way

Lyndon Johnson had overheated the economy. He was unwilling to call for increased taxes to finance the war, or, failing that, to cut back his beloved Great Society programs. Instead he relied on supplemental appropriations bills to finance the anticipated cost overruns when he submitted his original budgets for the war. The impact on the economy was profound, with the cost of the war rising from $5.8 billion in fiscal 1966 to more than $30 billion in fiscal 1968. No doubt internal structural and international factors accounted in good measure for the economic crisis of the seventies, but the war financing contributed to it as well. That crisis helped explain Jimmy Carter's victory over Gerald Ford in 1976 and Ronald Reagan's victory over Carter in 1980, as both challengers blamed the dismal state of the economy on the incumbents.

The economy was also affected by the peacetime costs of caring, not always very compassionately, for Vietnam veterans. No American wars have produced so proportionally large a cadre of physically and especially mentally disabled veterans. This was a result of lifesaving medical advances that permitted many horribly wounded soldiers to live, and of new diagnostic techniques that helped identify the malaise and dysfunction of as many as 300,000 veterans as post-traumatic stress disorder (PTSD). Their illnesses strained the resources of the Veterans Administration and caused so bitter a competition among veterans' lobbies that Vietnam vets felt compelled to found their own organization, the Vietnam Veterans of America. That organization also took the lead in demanding government recognition that their increased deaths from cancer and other diseases were related to exposure to carcinogens such as Agent Orange. The battle has continued into the twenty-first century.

Many vets, the families of vets, and millions of their supporters maintained that the Nixon administration had left behind several thousand POWs or MIAs in its haste to finish a peace treaty. Senator John Kerry was one of those who as late as 1992 pushed for congressional hearings that might, once and for all, resolve the emotional issue. Nixon fumed that Kerry and other old anti-war protesters were keeping the issue alive to embarrass him, even though the hearings virtually proved that in 1975 few if any American servicemen had been left behind.

While the emphasis in this book has been on the impact of the war on domestic politics, one must not ignore the impact of domestic, and especially, electoral politics on the war. Kennedy, Johnson, and Nixon all had their eyes on their reelection campaigns as they constructed military and diplomatic policies for Southeast Asia. However much Kennedy may have become disillusioned with the progress of the war, he could not withdraw until after 1964, when he would be safely reelected. Lyndon Johnson found himself in the middle between the hawks who wanted him to escalate and the doves who wanted him to withdraw. His policy of slow and careful but inevitable escalation was predicated on the idea that he could not escalate too rapidly and risk war with Russia and China, and could not withdraw and run in 1968 as the man who "lost" Vietnam.

Nixon genuinely expected he would be able to achieve a peace with honor in Vietnam during his first year in office. When the North Vietnamese were unwilling to meet his terms, he found himself in Johnson's position, hoping to defend the South Vietnamese government long enough to get reelected before disaster struck. His negotiating position was weakened significantly by Congress and the majority of Americans. They demanded periodic withdrawals of American troops and a decline in casualties in exchange for supporting Nixon's peace-with-honor policies. Thus the more troops he withdrew and the more Congress threatened to cut off funding or set an end date, the easier it was for the North Vietnamese to wait until the election and lack of American ground-combat capacity forced the United States to alter its terms.

Congress and the public also made it impossible for Nixon and Ford to do very much to support the South Vietnamese struggle from 1973 to 1975. Their opposition to further commitments in Southeast Asia sealed the fates of South Vietnam and Cambodia. It was highly unlikely, though, that the United States could have done anything to save its allies, short of returning to full-scale combat.

From the start of America's military involvement in Vietnam in 1961 to the fall of Saigon in 1975, the war in Southeast Asia played a profound role in affecting political, cultural, and economic developments in the United States. Because this divisive war was America's longest war, its often pernicious influence was felt by virtually all Americans who lived through that most turbulent era. Its effects have lingered into the twenty-first century in ways that could hardly have been imagined when President Eisenhower decided in 1954 to save South Vietnam for the Free World.

A Note on Sources

ALTHOUGH NO ONE has explicitly studied the domestic side of the Vietnam War, thousands of books and articles touch on the subject. The best place to begin is with two respected general histories of the war, George Herring's *America's Longest War: The United States and Vietnam, 1950–1975* (New York, 2002) and Robert Schulzinger's *A Time for War: The United States and Vietnam, 1941–1975* (New York, 1997). Robert Mann, in another solid general history, emphasizes the view from Capitol Hill in *A Grand Delusion: America's Descent into Vietnam* (New York, 2001). Closer to the subject at hand is Robert Buzzanco, *Vietnam and the Transformation of American Life* (Malden, Mass., 1999) and Rhodri Jeffreys-Jones's study, examining women, labor, students, and blacks, *Peace Now: American Society and the Ending of the Vietnam War* (New Haven, 1999).

For an overview of the period, John Morton Blum's *Years of Discord: American Politics and Society, 1961–1974* (New York, 1991) is still essential. Terry H. Anderson concentrates on the revolutionary developments of the period in his rollicking *The Movement and the Sixties: Protest in America from Greensboro to Wounded Knee* (New York, 1995). More sober is Maurice Isserman and Michael Kazin, *America Divided: The Civil War of the 1960s* (New York, 2000). Todd Gitlin offers a participant-observer's analysis in *The Sixties: Years of Hope, Days of Rage* (New York, 1987). Two different views of the New Left and radical students can be compared in Edward K. Spann's favorable *Democracy's Children: The Young Rebels of the 1960's and the Power of Ideals* (Wilmington, Del., 2003) and Kenneth J. Heineman's lively critique, *Put Your Bodies Upon the Wheels: Student Revolt in the 1960s* (Chicago, 2001). *The Columbia Guide to America in the Sixties* (New York, 2001), edited by David Farber and Beth Bailey, is a key reference source.

Among those who look at the history of the relationship between domestic politics and war are Melvin Small, *Democracy and Diplomacy: The Impact of Domestic Politics on U.S. Foreign Policy, 1789–1994* (Baltimore, 1996) and Michael D. Pearlman, *Warmaking and American Democracy: The Struggle Over Military Strategy, 1700 to the Present* (Lawrence, Kans., 1999). Political scientists approach the problem from a different angle in Kurt Taylor Gaubatz, *Elections and War: The Electoral Incentive in the Democratic Politics of War and Peace* (Stanford, 1999); John E. Mueller, *War, Presidents, and Public Opinion* (New York, 1973); and Andrew Z. Katz, "Public Opinion and Foreign Policy: The Nixon Administration and the Pursuit of Peace with Honor," in *Presidential Studies Quarterly* 27 (Summer 1997): 496–513. Will H. Moore and David J. Lanoue, in "Domestic Politics and U.S. Foreign Policy: A Study of Cold War Conflict Behavior," *Journal of Politics* 65 (May 2003): 376–396, contend that foreign policy has not been greatly influenced by domestic politics.

For the presidency, Louis W. Koenig offers a useful survey in "The Executive Office of the President," in George K. Osborn *et. al*, eds., *Democracy, Strategy, and Vietnam: Implications for American Policymaking* (Lexington, Mass., 1985). How the anti-war movement affected policymaking is examined in Melvin Small, *Johnson, Nixon, and the Doves* (New Brunswick, N.J., 1988) and Tom Wells, *The War Within: America's Battle Over Vietnam* (Berkeley, 1994).

David L. Anderson, ed., *Shadow on the White House: Presidents and the Vietnam War* (Lawrence, Kans., 1993) features articles on the Vietnam War presidents. How Presidents Truman and Eisenhower involved the United States in Vietnam is admirably outlined in Lloyd Gardner, *Approaching Vietnam: From World War II Through Dienbienphu* (New York, 1988). Eisenhower's political strategies are among the subjects covered in Melanie Billings-Yun's *Decision Against War: Eisenhower and Dien Bien Phu, 1954* (New York, 1988), while David L. Anderson covers his entire presidency in *Trapped by Success: The Eisenhower Administration and Vietnam, 1953–1961* (New York, 1991).

John M. Newman's provocative *JFK and Vietnam: Deception, Intrigue, and the Struggle for Power* (New York, 1992) suggests that Kennedy had made up his mind to withdraw from Vietnam after the 1964 election. William J. Rust is not as certain in *Kennedy in Vietnam: American Vietnam Policy, 1960–1963* (New York, 1985). Helpful here as well are Howard Jones, *Death of a Generation: How the Assassination of Diem and JFK Prolonged the Vietnam War* (New York, 2003) and Anne E. Blair, *Lodge in Vietnam: A Patriot Abroad* (New Haven, 1995). James N. Giglio's *The Presidency of John F. Kennedy* (Lawrence, Kans., 1991) places his Vietnam policy in perspective, along with Lawrence Freedman, *Kennedy's Wars: Berlin, Cuba, Laos, and Vietnam* (New York, 2000). That policy is lauded in David Kaiser, *American Tragedy: Kennedy, Johnson, and the Origins of the Vietnam War* (Cambridge, Mass., 2000).

The literature on Lyndon Johnson and Vietnam is vast. The best place to begin is Robert Dallek, *Flawed Giant: Lyndon Johnson and His Times* (New York, 1998), which does a fine job linking domestic and foreign policy. Lloyd C. Gardner makes that same link in his near definitive *Pay Any Price: Lyndon Johnson and the Wars for Vietnam* (Chicago, 1995). Frederik Logevall carefully describes Johnson's decision-making in *Choosing War: The Lost Chance for Peace and the Escalation of the War in Vietnam* (Berkeley, 1999), while White House operations are illuminated in David M. Barrett, *Uncertain Warriors: Lyndon Johnson and his Vietnam Advisors* (Lawrence, Kans., 1993). Doris Kearns provides juicy interviews with Johnson in retirement in *Lyndon Johnson and the American Dream* (New York, 1976). The election of 1964 is the subject of Gary Donaldson's *Liberalism's Last Hurrah: The Presidential Campaign of 1964* (Armonk, N.Y., 2003) and Theodore White's classic, *The Making of the President 1964* (New York, 1965). The last word on the controversial Gulf of Tonkin incident during that election year may be Edwin Moise, *Tonkin Gulf and the Escalation of the Viet Nam War* (Chapel Hill, 1996).

Among the many memoirs written by cabinet members, the most helpful are Robert S. McNamara with Brian VanDeMark, *In Retrospect: The Tragedy and Lessons of the Vietnam War* (New York, 1995); George Ball, *The Past Has Another Pattern* (New York, 1982); Clark Clifford with Richard Holbrooke, *Counsel to the President: A Memoir* (New York, 1989); and Joseph A. Califano, *The Triumph and Tragedy of Lyndon Johnson: The White House Years* (New York, 1991). The economy is the subject of Jeffrey W. Helsing, *Johnson's*

War/Johnson's Great Society: The Guns and Butter Trap (Westport, Conn., 2000) and is covered as well in Scott Stossel, *Sarge: The Life and Times of Sargent Shriver* (Washington, D.C., 2004).

For an overview of the Nixon presidency see Melvin Small, *The Presidency of Richard Nixon* (Lawrence, Kans., 1999). The electoral politics of the war is central to Lewis Chester, Godfrey Hodgson, and Bruce Page, *An American Melodrama: The Presidential Campaign of 1968* (New York, 1969); David Farber, *Chicago '68* (Chicago, 1988); Melvin Small, "The Election of 1968," *Diplomatic History* 28 (Summer 2004): 513–528; and especially Catherine Forslund, *Informal Diplomacy and Asian Relations* (Wilmington, Del., 2002). Jeffrey Kimball's *Nixon's Vietnam War* (Lawrence, Kans., 1998) and *The Vietnam War Files: Uncovering the Secret History of Nixon-Era Strategy* (Lawrence, Kans., 2004) are filled with new information about the politics of the final four years of the war. Useful as well is Larry Berman, *No Peace, No Honor: Nixon, Kissinger, and Betrayal in Vietnam* (New York, 2001) and, especially for the way American domestic politics affected the North Vietnamese, Pierre Asselin, *A Bitter Peace: Washington, Hanoi, and the Making of the Paris Peace Agreement* (Chapel Hill, 2002). Domestic politics irritated and constrained Henry Kissinger, as seen in Jussi Hahnhimäki, *The Flawed Architect: Henry Kissinger and American Foreign Policy* (New York, 2004).

In order to understand the role of the economy in Nixon's decision-making, Allen J. Matusow's *Nixon's Economy: Booms, Busts, Dollars, and Votes* (Lawrence, Kans., 1998) must be examined. Among the many memoirs from this administration, H. R. Haldeman's *The Haldeman Diaries: Inside the Nixon White House* (New York, 1994) is in a class by itself. Important as well are Richard Nixon, *RN: The Memoirs of Richard Nixon* (New York, 1978); Henry Kissinger, *The White House Years* (Boston, 1979); Alexander M. Haig, Jr., with Charles McCarry, *Inner Circles: How America Changed the World* (New York, 1982); and Leonard Garment, *Crazy Rhythm: My Journey from Brooklyn, Jazz, and Wall Street to Nixon's White House, Watergate, and Beyond . . .* (New York, 1997). Nixon's musings in the 1990s are recorded in Monica Crowley, *Nixon in Winter* (New York, 1998).

The classic Watergate monograph is Stanley I. Kutler, *The Wars of Watergate: The Last Crisis of Richard Nixon* (New York, 1992). See also Fred Emery, *Watergate: The Corruption of American Politics and the Fall of Richard Nixon* (New York, 1994) and the up-to-date Keith W. Olson, *Watergate: The Presidential Scandal That Shook America* (Lawrence, Kans., 2003). For the end of the war see John Robert Greene, *The Presidency of Gerald R. Ford* (Lawrence, Kans., 1995) and T. Christopher Jesperson, "The Bitter End and Lost Chance in Vietnam: Congress, the Ford Administration, and the Battle Over Vietnam," *Diplomatic History* 24 (Spring 2000): 265–296.

Robert R. Tomes dissects the views and activities of the influential American literary and intellectual community in *Apocalypse Then: American Intellectuals and the Vietnam War* (New York, 1998). David Levy, *The Debate Over Vietnam* (Baltimore, 1995) is also useful on the subject. Most of America's intellectual elite participated in the anti-war movement, which is analyzed in Charles DeBenedetti with Charles Chatfield, *An American Ordeal: The Antiwar Movement of the Vietnam Era* (Syracuse, 1990). Melvin Small, *Antiwarriors: The Vietnam War and the Battle for America's Hearts and Minds* (Wilmington, Del., 2002) is a brief history of the movement. Joseph G. Morgan chronicles another group of interest in *The Vietnam Lobby: The American Friends of Vietnam* (Chapel Hill, 1997).

In *War in the Media Age* (Creeskill, N.J., 2000), A. Trevor Thrall contends that the Vietnam War was not alone responsible for changes in the relationship between the media and the government. James Keogh in *President Nixon and the Press* (New York, 1972) does not agree with Marilyn Lashner's perspective in *The Chilling Effect in TV News: Intimidation by the Nixon White House* (New York, 1984). William M. Hammond presents a well-researched and balanced perspective in *Reporting Vietnam: Media and Military at War* (Lawrence, Kans., 1998). The media were not as favorable to the anti-war movement as Nixon contended, as can be seen in Melvin Small, *Covering Dissent: The Media and the Anti-Vietnam War Movement* (New Brunswick, N.J., 1994). They did, of course, publish the Pentagon Papers, described in David Rudenstine, *The Day the Presses Stopped: A History of the Pentagon Papers Case* (Berkeley, 1996). The fascinating central figure in the story, Daniel Ellsberg, has written

Secrets: A Memoir of Vietnam and the Pentagon Papers (New York, 2002), which should be balanced with Tom Wells, *Wild Man of the Left: The Life and Times of Daniel Ellsberg* (New York, 2001).

The most exhaustive study of Congress and the presidents during the war is William Conrad Gibbons, *The U.S. Government and the Vietnam War*, 4 vols. (Princeton, 1986–). See also William Earl Walker's "Domesticating Foreign Policy: Congress and the Vietnam War," in Osborn *et al.*, eds., *Democracy, Strategy, and Vietnam*. Focusing on narrower topics on Capitol Hill are Terry Dietz, *Republicans and Vietnam, 1961–1968* (Westport, Conn., 1986); Ezra Y. Siff, *Why the Senate Slept: The Gulf of Tonkin and the Beginning of America's Vietnam War* (Westport, Conn., 1999); and P. Edward Haley, *Congress and the Fall of South Vietnam and Cambodia* (Rutherford, N.J., 1982). See also Carole F. Ziemke, "From the Tonkin Gulf to the Persian Gulf: The Devolution of the Senate's Role in Warmaking," in William Head and Lawrence E. Grinter, eds., *Looking Back on the Vietnam War: A 1990s Perspective on the Decisions, Combat, and Legacies* (Westport, Conn., 1993). John Hart Ely concentrates on the warmaking power in *War and Responsibility: Constitutional Lessons of Vietnam and Its Aftermath* (Princeton, 1993).

As for individual senators, the best place to begin is Randall B. Woods, ed., *Vietnam and the American Political Tradition: The Politics of Dissent* (New York, 2003), whose fine group of authors offers biographical sketches of prominent dissenters. Full biographies and autobiographies of senators that merit attention are Woods's magisterial *Fulbright: A Biography* (New York, 1995); William C. Berman, *William Fulbright and the Vietnam War: The Dissent of a Realist* (Kent, Ohio, 1988); Dominic Sandbrook, *Eugene McCarthy: The Rise and Fall of Postwar Liberalism* (New York, 2004); Francis R. Valeo, *Mike Mansfield: Majority Leader: A Different Kind of Senate, 1961–1976* (Armonk, N.Y., 1999); Don Oberdorfer, *Senator Mansfield* (Washington, D.C., 2003); Ronald Steel, *In Love with Night: The American Romance with Robert Kennedy* (New York, 2000); Joseph A. Palermo, *In His Own Right: The Political Odyssey of Robert F. Kennedy* (New York, 2001); James C. Olson, *Stuart Symington: A Life* (Columbia, Mo., 2003); Barry M. Goldwater, *With No Apologies: The Personal and Political Memoirs of United States Senator Barry M.*

Goldwater (New York, 1979); and Robert Alan Goldberg, *Barry Goldwater* (New Haven, 1995). For House members, Tip O'Neill with William Novak, *Man of the House* (New York, 1987) and Don Riegle, *O Congress: A Diary of the Years 1971–1972* (New York, 1972) contain material on the war.

Complicated economic issues are clarified in Anthony Campagna, *The Economic Consequences of the Vietnam War* (New York, 1991) and Robert Warren Stevens, *Vain Hopes, Grim Realities: The Economic Consequences of the Vietnam War* (New York, 1976). Peter B. Levy, *The New Left and Labor in the 1960's* (Urbana, 1994) and Frank Koscielski, *Divided Loyalties: American Unions and the Vietnam War* (New York, 1999) offer valuable insights into the role of organized labor during the war. Judith Klinghoffer addresses another important political issue in *Vietnam, Jews, and the Middle East: Unintended Consequences* (New York, 1999).

On the draft, Lawrence M. Baskir and William A. Strauss, *Chance and Circumstance: The Draft, the War, and the Vietnam Generation* (New York, 1978) provides valuable data while George Q. Flynn, *The Draft, 1940–1973* (Lawrence, Kans., 1993) is the best general history of the subject. Problems of insubordination in the military during the Vietnam era are explored in David Cortright, *Soldiers in Revolt: The American Military Today* (Garden City, N.Y., 1975) and Shelby L. Stanton, *The Rise and Fall of an American Army: U.S. Ground Forces in Vietnam* (New York, 1985). Bruce Franklin, in *M.I.A. or Mythmaking in America* (New Brunswick, N.J., 1992), offers a scathing attack on how the issue was used for political purposes. Mark Sauter and Jim Saunders maintain it was not a myth in *The Men We Left Behind: Henry Kissinger, the Politics of Deceit, and the Tragic Fate of the POWs after the Vietnam War* (Washington, D.C., 1993).

For the aftermath of the war in American culture and politics, John Hellman, *American Myth and the Legacy of Vietnam* (New York, 1986) is a good place to begin, along with Tom Engelhardt, *The End of Victory Culture: Cold War America and the Disillusioning of a Generation* (New York, 1995) and Jerry Lembcke, *The Spitting Image: Myth, Memory, and the Legacy of Vietnam* (New York, 1998). Anthony Lake edited an early but still perceptive series of articles assessing *The Vietnam Legacy* (New York, 1976). Veterans' conditions and attitudes are surveyed in Ellen Frey-Wouters and Robert S. Laufer, *Legacy of a War: The American Soldier in Vietnam* (Armonk, N.Y., 1986) while Gerald Nicosia's *Home to War: The Vietnam Veterans' Movement* (New York, 2001) covers their politics.

The war affected the U.S. educational system in a variety of ways, as can be seen in Willis Rudy's Vietnam chapter in *The Campus and a Nation in Crisis: From the American Revolution to Vietnam* (Cranbury, N.J., 1996) and Vincent Davis, "The Vietnam War and Higher Education," in Osborn *et al.*, eds., *Democracy, Policy, and Vietnam*. W. J. Rorabaugh and Tom Bates analyze the era on two turbulent campuses in *Berkeley at War: The 1960's* (New York, 1989) and *RADS: The Bombing of the Army Research Center at the University of Wisconsin and Its Aftermath* (New York, 1992) respectively. David Maraniss brilliantly portrays a few days in Vietnam and at Wisconsin and also follows up on the lives of his protagonists in *They Marched into Sunlight: War and Peace: Vietnam and America, October 1967* (New York, 2003). Public schools are the focus of John W. Johnson, *The Struggle for Student Rights: Tinker v. Des Moines and the 1960's* (Lawrence, Kans., 1997).

Index

Civil liberties: anti-war demonstrations
  effect on, 210–211; First
  Amendment rights, 174, 211. *See also*
  Civil rights movement.
Civil Rights Bill, 25, 30
Civil rights movement, 39–40; anti-war
  movement and, 54, 85–88; Black
  Panthers, 86, 87; Black Power
  movement, 85–86; Johnson
  administration, 25, 30, 211–212;
  Nixon administration, 132, 168;
  urban riots, 40, 61–62, 98. *See also*
  Black power movement; Civil
  liberties.
Clark, Joseph, 45, 47, 67
Clark, Ramsey, 95
Clark, Wesley, 205
Class differences: anti-war blurring of,
  72; college-educated vs. labor, 88,
  107; draft and, 52–53, 107, 206,
  207–208; Kennedy Democrats vs.
  Johnson, 69; war's emphasis of, 87;
  Weatherman take on, 126. *See also*
  Anti-poverty programs;
  Conservatives; Economy (U.S.);
  Labor; Liberals; Polarization.
Cleaver, Eldridge, 86
Cleland, Max, 205
Clifford, Clark, 102–104, 106, 117, 121,
  122, 123, 135–136
Clinton, William, 204–205, 209
Coffin, William Sloane, 47, 198
Colgrove, Albert M., 9–10
Colleges: draftee reserves, 52–53;
  intelligence investigations of, 134,
  198; protests, 41–42, 58, 60–62, 107,
  207–208; violence, 159. *See also*
  Draft; Students.
Colson, Charles, 143, 150, 155, 170, 172,
  177, 194
Committee for a Sane Nuclear Policy
  (SANE) Washington rally, 58
Committee to Reelect the President
  (CREEP), 126, 181–182, 186, 187
Communism and U.S. foreign policy:
  China, 9, 11, 25–26, 36; Cuba, 13;
  Democratic Party, 7, 9, 13, 203–204;
  labor views, 88–89, 156; Laos, 12–13;
  media coverage of, 76–77; media
  outlets, 87, 133; party politics and, 9,

11, 13, 21, 25–26, 71, 75, 126–127,
203–204, 210; Persian Gulf, 209;
protest movement allied with,
80–81; radical U.S. groups and, 60,
208; railroading domestic enemies
using, 68; reconstruction aid, 195;
Republican Party, 13, 21, 25–26, 45,
75, 203–204, 210; USSR, 12, 13;
Vietnam, 9–11, 13, 21, 36, 39, 45, 126,
197. *See also* North Vietnam; South
Vietnam; Withdrawal.
Congress: anti-war sentiment affected
by, 47, 71–72; Civil Rights Bill, 25,
30; Cooper-Church amendment,
154; Democratic role in, 36, 74, 131,
138, 152–154, 162, 191, 202;
Dominican Republic intervention
funding, 49–51; foreign policy role,
199–200; Freedom of Information
Act, 210; Gulf of Tonkin Resolution,
30–33, 47, 85, 90, 153; "imperial
presidency" and, 30–31, 199, 201;
Johnson support poll, 91; Korean
War resolutions, 30; McGovern-
Hatfield amendment, 153–154;
Mansfield Resolution, 179;
negotiation attempts by members,
82–83, 90, 170, 194; Newspaper
Preservation Act, 146; polarization
within, 45–47, 49–50, 51–52, 59,
63–81, 82, 89–90, 140–141, 155;
public opinion gauged by, 71–72;
Republican role in, 40, 74, 89, 155,
162, 191; restrictive Vietnam War
bills, 153–154; Select Committee on
Presidential Campaign Activities,
197–199; Senate Preparedness
Subcommittee of the Armed
Services Committee hearings, 90–91;
Special Subcommittee on
Investigations of the Interstate and
Foreign Commerce Committee, 174;
support of Vietnam War by
members, 45, 47, 51–52, 64, 81,
140–141; Symington subcommittee
on foreign commitments, 139;
television bias investigation, 174;
Vietnam bombing views, 44–48,
82–83; Vietnam policy criticism by,
24, 106, 139–140; Vietnam

Communism and U.S. foreign policy
(*continued*)
  resolutions, 25, 28, 30–33, 47,
  139–140; Vietnam War funding by,
  14–15, 20, 46–47, 53–54, 55–56,
  84–85, 96–97, 139–140, 153–154, 194,
  200, 203; Vietnam War opposition by
  members, 32–33, 45–47, 49–50, 59,
  63–81, 82, 89–90, 140–141, 152–155,
  162, 164, 167, 170, 179, 194, 199–204;
  War Powers Resolution, 90, 201;
  withdrawal policies, 139, 200–204
Congress on Racial Equality (CORE),
  87
Connally, John, 155
Conservatives: Johnson's concerns and,
  39, 40; media criticized by, 16–17, 27,
  77–79; polarization from liberals, 80,
  89–90, 104–105, 115–116, 117–118,
  125–126, 148–149, 155, 160–161, 204,
  212–213; war for furthering agenda
  by, 23. *See also* Communism and
  U.S. foreign policy.
Constitution: bending of, 199, 201, 211.
  See also Civil liberties; Civil rights
  movement.
Contributors to presidential
  campaigns, 118, 120
Cooper, John Sherman, 32, 45, 89, 140
CORE (Congress on Racial Equality),
  87
Counter-insurgency warfare, 66
Country Joe and the Fish, 130
CREEP (Committee to Reelect the
  President), 126, 181–182, 186, 187
Crosby, Stills, Nash, and Young, 130
Cuba, Bay of Pigs, 13, 128–129
Cultural effects of Vietnam War:
  family splits, 60, 61, 91, 106; labor
  issues, 72, 88–89, 138, 148–149,
  155–157; length of war and, 3–5,
  216; music, 130–131; opposition to
  anti-war protesters, 80, 115, 117–118,
  125–126, 148–149, 155–156, 160, 171,
  204, 212–213. *See also* Conservatives;
  Liberals; Media; Polarization.
Czechoslovakia, invasion of, 113

Daily Worker, 133
Daley, Richard, 105, 113–115

Dawson, Donald, 201
Dean, John, 134, 178
Dearborn anti-war referendum, 72
Death of a President (Manchester), 83–84
De-escalation of Vietnam War:
  Johnson administration, 103–104,
  106–107, 112–113; Nixon campaign
  speeches, 116–117. *See also*
  Withdrawal.
Defense Department: funding of
  Vietnam War by base closures,
  33–34; Nixon's secrecy and, 133;
  Senate Preparedness Subcommittee
  of the Armed Services Committee
  hearings, 90–91; subterfuge on
  bombing, 75–76
Deficit spending on Vietnam War, 96,
  97
Democratic Conventions: 1964, 39–40;
  1968, 113–116; 1972, 186–187
Democratic party: civil rights
  movement and, 39–40; Communism
  as an election issue, 11, 71;
  Communism policies, 9, 74;
  Communism policies as viewed by
  Republicans, 13, 203–204, 210;
  Congressional role, 36, 74, 131, 138,
  152–154, 162; Conventions, 39–40,
  113–116, 186–187; dovish aspects, 40,
  46–47, 54, 59, 63–81, 89, 91–92,
  112–113, 138–139; Johnson's
  popularity with, 59–60, 64–65,
  68–69, 89, 91–92; Kennedy
  Democrats, 68–69, 83–84, 93; liberal
  alliances, 155; McCarthy support by,
  104; Nixon's influence on, 148–149;
  Nixon's manipulation of, 181–182,
  184, 186, 187; Nixon's tactics, 135,
  163–164; splits within, 40, 59–60,
  68–70, 75, 83–84, 89, 91–92, 93–94,
  109, 110, 112, 114–116, 186–187, 213;
  television bias investigation headed
  by, 174; USSR support of, 120;
  Vietnam War role, 175–176. *See also*
  Congress; Election platforms.
Demonstrations. *See* Anti-war
  demonstrations; Pro-war activities;
  Protests.
Department of Justice. *See* Supreme
  Court.

Escalation (*continued*)
106, 175–179; Kennedy
administration, 13–14, 175–176;
McCarthy followers favoring,
104–105; mining, 185; napalm, 87;
Nixon administration, 116–117,
140–142, 149–155, 159–160, 163–164,
188–189, 193; nuclear weapons, 6,
27–28, 34, 38, 118, 140; public
support for, 54, 185; reserve military
call-up, 51–52. *See also* De-
escalation.
Esquire Vietnam War coverage, 42

Family life: alienation due to Vietnam
War, 60, 61, 91, 106; POW/MIA
organizations, 137–138, 179, 214–215
FBI (Federal Bureau of Investigation):
anti-war Congress member
investigations, 68; anti-war protester
investigations, 80–81, 98, 158;
Chennault investigation, 122–123,
188; evidence destroyed by, 198;
journalist investigations, 133–134;
NSC investigations, 133–134; public
image, 210; student organization
investigations, 134–135
FCC (Federal Communications
Commission), Nixon's uses of,
129–130, 143, 144
Festival of the Arts, boycotting by
liberals, 59–60
Fielding break-in, 177–178
First Amendment, journalistic rights,
174, 211
Fishel, Wesley, 8
FOIA (Freedom of Information Act),
210
Fonda, Jane, 167
Ford, Gerald R., 45, 202–204, 214
Forrestal, James, 91
Forrestal, Michael, 25
Fowler, Henry, 96, 108
France: handover of Vietnam to U.S.,
8; Vietnamese war for independence
from, 5–7
Frankel, Max, 42
Freedom of Information Act (FOIA),
210
Frost, David, 199

Fulbright, J. William, 4, 14, 32;
Johnson and, 45, 46, 49–51, 54,
64–68, 70, 90; Nixon and, 140;
presidential powers bill, 201; Senate
Foreign Relations Committee
Vietnam War policy hearings,
65–68; Symington subcommittee on
foreign commitments, 139; Vietnam
War national debate, 42; withdrawal
support, 32–33, 45, 46, 50–51, 185
Funding of Vietnam War: base
closures by Defense Department,
33–34; Congressional, 14–15, 20,
46–47, 55–56, 84–85, 96–97, 139–140,
153–154, 194, 200, 203

Galbraith, John Kenneth, 68, 93
Gans, Curtis, 71, 92–94
Gardner, John, 102
Gavin, James M., 67, 93
Geneva Accords, 7, 9
Germany, erection of Berlin Wall, 13
Gilpatrick, Roswell, 53
Gold crisis, 102, 107–108
Goldwater, Barry: election platform,
26–35; public image, 27–28, 33, 38;
Vietnam War policies, 24, 26–27,
29–30, 32, 45
Goodell, Charles, 89, 156, 162
Goodwin, Richard, 68, 111
Gore, Albert Sr., 33, 162
Gore, Albert Jr., 206
Government. *See* Congress; U.S.
government; *presidents by name.*
Graham, Billy, 159
Gray, L. Patrick, 178, 198
Great Society, 23, 35–36, 37–38, 51,
56–57, 74, 81, 87, 97, 101–102, 131,
211–212; extension to South
Vietnam, 37
Ground warfare, 51–53, 54–55,
149–151, 157–158
Gruening, Ernest, 46–47
Gulf of Tonkin incident, 28–33, 47;
governmental subterfuge suspicions,
31–32. *See also* Gulf of Tonkin
Resolution.
Gulf of Tonkin Resolution, 30–33, 47,
85, 90, 153

A NOTE ON THE AUTHOR

Melvin Small is Distinguished Professor of History at Wayne State University. Born in New York City, he studied at Dartmouth College and the University of Michigan, where he received a Ph.D. A prizewinning author of a number of books in American history, his writings include *Antiwarriors*, *The Presidency of Richard Nixon*, *Diplomacy and Democracy*, and *Covering Dissent*. He is married with two children and lives in Royal Oak, Michigan.